Blacks in the White Establishment?

To Jeff,
With hopes that the
good times keep on rolling,
and best wishes,

Bill
March 21, 1999

Blacks
in the White
Establishment?

A Study of Race and
Class in America

Richard L. Zweigenhaft and
G. William Domhoff

Yale University Press   New Haven and London

Designed by Richard Hendel.
Set in Stempel Garamond type by
G & S Typesetters, Austin, Texas.
Printed in the United States of America by
Edwards Brothers, Ann Arbor, Michigan.

Library of Congress Cataloging-in-Publication Data
Zweigenhaft, Richard L.
Blacks in the white establishment? : a study of race
and class in America / Richard L. Zweigenhaft and
G. William Domhoff.
p. cm.
Includes bibliographical references and index.
ISBN 0-300-04788-6 (cloth)
0-300-05433-5 (pbk.)
1. Social mobility—United States—Case studies. 2. Afro-
American college graduates—Case studies. 3. Private
schools—United States—Case studies. I. Domhoff,
G. William. II. Title.
HN90.S65Z94 1991
370.19'34—dc20 90-38640
CIP

A catalogue record for this book is available
from the British Library.

The paper in this book meets the guidelines for permanence
and durability of the Committee on Production Guidelines for
Book Longevity of the Council on Library Resources.

10 9 8 7 6 5 4 3

Contents

Preface

Many people provided us with advice that made the completion of this project possible. We are grateful to social psychologist Thomas Pettigrew of the University of California, Santa Cruz, for helping us develop an overall framework for our findings as well as for suggesting specific studies for us to read. At a critical juncture in our writing, sociologist Joe Feagin of the University of Texas opened up new possibilities for us during two lengthy telephone conversations. We also benefited greatly from his fine textbook, *Race and Ethnic Relations,* and from the first fruits of his new interview work with successful black entrepreneurs in Texas.[1]

Sociologist Garry Rolison of the University of California, Santa Barbara, stimulated our thinking in helpful directions and suggested many valuable references. Sociologist Sharon Collins of the University of Illinois at Chicago Circle shared her ideas drawn from extensive interviews with black corporate executives and gave us her perspective on several general issues as well. Gini Matute-Bianchi of the Board of Studies in Education at the University of California, Santa Cruz, shared her creative research on the education of Mexican American high school students, providing us with ideas that could be transferred to our study. She also directed us to an exciting literature on minority education that has been created by cultural anthropologists. Sociologist David Wellman of the University of California, Santa Cruz, provided us with incisive critical comments on several theoretical perspectives, based in good part on his own excellent research on racism in the United States.[2] Management con-

1. Joe R. Feagin, *Race and Ethnic Relations,* 3d ed. (Englewood Cliffs, N.J.: Prentice-Hall, 1989), "The Continuing Significance of Race: Discrimination in Contemporary America" (Paper presented at the Association of Black Sociologists Meeting, San Francisco, August 1989), and "Barriers to Black Students in Higher Education: Learning from Qualitative Research" (Position paper for the Center for Research on Minority Education, University of Oklahoma, September 1989). See also Joe R. Feagin and Leslie Inniss, "The Mythology of the Black 'Underclass' in U.S. Race Relations Theory" (Manuscript, Department of Sociology, University of Texas at Austin, 1989).
2. David Wellman, *Portraits in White Racism* (New York: Cambridge University Press, 1979).

sultants Edward Jones and James Lowry, of South Orange, New Jersey, and Chicago, respectively, helped us to understand the experiences of our interviewees in the business world based on their own extensive involvement with black business executives.

Pettigrew, Feagin, Rolison, Collins, Wellman, Jones, and Lowry gave us helpful comments on all or parts of a first, very different, version of this manuscript, as did writer and editor Tom Engelhardt and three anonymous reviewers. In addition, psychologist Jackie Ludel of Guilford College provided an exceptionally careful and useful editorial critique of that early draft of our manuscript, thereby improving the readability of the final manuscript dramatically.

Anthropologist John Ogbu of the University of California, Berkeley, gave us supportive comments on our first draft. Sociologists Peter Cookson and Caroline Persell, the authors of *Preparing for Power*, a sociological study of American prep schools, read an early version of one chapter, and their comments and encouragement are much appreciated.[3] George Perry, a lawyer in Boston and the author of a 1973 study of the early graduates of the "A Better Chance" (ABC) program, provided us with valuable feedback, as did William Berkeley, the president of ABC from 1966 to 1974. We would also like to thank O. Chance Brown, a recent graduate of the University of California, Santa Cruz, for his thoughtful comments. We are deeply indebted to our editor at Yale University Press, Gladys Topkis. Both her excellent organizational ideas and specific editorial suggestions greatly improved the quality of the manuscript. Additionally, we appreciate the careful editing by Laura Jones Dooley and Jane T. Hedges.

None of these people should be taxed with responsibility for any mistakes or insensitivities that might remain in our writing. Nor are they necessarily in agreement with us. What we have learned from interacting with them is how extraordinarily difficult and perplexing the issues are in the field of race relations.

This book would not have been possible without ongoing and substantial support from Guilford College. We would like to express our special appreciation to Sam Schuman, vice-president for academic affairs. In addition to his personal interest in and support for this project, over a period of years he has provided the first author with a series of small grants (ranging from $150 to $600) from the Dean's Research Fund. The college

---

3. Peter W. Cookson, Jr., and Caroline Hodges Persell, *Preparing for Power: America's Elite Boarding Schools* (New York: Basic Books, 1985).

also granted the first author a sabbatical leave in the fall of 1988 to work on this book. Wesleyan University was kind enough to welcome him as a visiting scholar that fall, which also facilitated the work on this book.

Anita Atwood, Cynthia Daniello, Libby Happel, Mildred Redmond, and Dot Warren, all employees of Guilford College, and Sara DeHart and Catharine Justice, students at the college, provided invaluable assistance by typing lengthy transcripts of the many hours of taped interviews. Their genuine interest in the stories our interviewees had to tell fueled the first author's own enthusiasm. In addition, Robey Callahan, a work-study student, was consistently good-natured and efficient in providing research assistance to the first author.

Many others have assisted in the work that went into the writing of this book. We wish to express our gratitude to those graduates of A Better Chance who so willingly shared their time and their accounts of their experiences. We also wish to thank those who have worked for or with A Better Chance who were kind enough to assist us in this project.

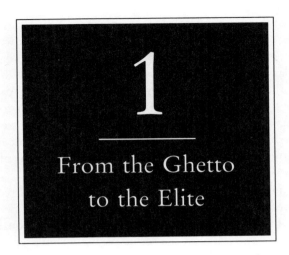

1

From the Ghetto to the Elite

On a September day in 1966, Sylvester Monroe, a black fifteen-year-old known as Vest to his friends, left the decaying tenement in the poorest neighborhood in Chicago, where he lived with his mother, his younger brother, and his five younger sisters. His destination was St. George's School in Rhode Island, one of the most exclusive prep schools in America. Now, almost twenty-five years later, interviewed in the downtown Washington office where he works as a writer for *Newsweek*, he vividly remembers that trip and the greeting he received upon his arrival.

He had been provided with a detailed itinerary that included a bus to the airport in Chicago, a plane to Providence, and then another bus to Newport. Never having left Chicago before, he was struck most powerfully by how dark it was on the night ride from Providence to Newport; he was used to a place where "the lights come on at night." Such small differences, and a number of larger ones, were to surprise Sylvester and others like him over the next few years.

In his initial moments at St. George's, Vest Monroe received the first of many lessons about what was and was not acceptable in the elite world he was about to enter. Smiling at the recollection, he recalls the greeting he received: "My adviser, a biology teacher named Gilbert Burnett, meets me on the steps and looks at me. I had been a member—not a very active member, but a member, out of necessity more than anything else—of a street gang. It was a well-known gang called the Blackstone Rangers, and, as a member of this gang, I dressed in a certain way. When I arrived at St. George's, I had on a pair of black-and-white Stacy Adams wing-tipped shoes, a pair of high-waisted reversible pleated pants, a long-collared shirt, dark glasses, and a big hat. Mr. Burnett said to me, 'Do you have any other clothes?' And I said, 'Yeah, just like this. Why?' And he said, 'Because that'll never do, particularly the shoes won't do for Sunday chapel.' So the next day, he put me in this Land Rover, and we drove off to the Anderson Knitting Mill in Fall River and he bought me a blue blazer, two pairs of gray flannel slacks, two suits, and a pair of black tie shoes to wear to Sunday chapel."[1]

Attire was just one of the many issues Sylvester Monroe confronted when he moved from the Robert Taylor Homes, a row of twenty-eight sixteen-story buildings that stretches for two miles and houses twenty thousand people,[2] to St. George's, a scenic New England prep school that caters primarily to the children of the American upper class. Indeed, St. George's is singled out by sociologist E. Digby Baltzell as among the sixteen most exclusive of the many boarding schools that "serve the sociological function of differentiating the upper classes from the rest of the population."[3]

Monroe was one of 430 students between the ages of thirteen and sixteen who had been selected to participate in the "A Better Chance" program in 1966. The ABC program was founded in 1963 by sixteen inde-

1. These events and the quotations used are drawn from our interview with Sylvester Monroe in Washington, D.C., on March 14, 1986. Monroe went on to write a moving account of his return to the projects in which he grew up ("The Brothers," *Newsweek*, March 23, 1987). A longer version subsequently appeared in book form; see Sylvester Monroe and Peter Goldman with Vern E. Smith, Terry E. Johnson, Monroe Anderson, and Jacques Chenet, *Brothers: Black and Poor—A True Story of Courage and Survival* (New York: William Morrow, 1988). Unless otherwise attributed, all quotations throughout the text are from interviews conducted by the first author between 1986 and 1988.

2. See Nicholas Lemann, "The Origins of the Underclass," *Atlantic Monthly*, June 1986, 32. Lemann claims that the "four-block stretch of the Robert Taylor Homes between Forty-seventh and Fifty-first Streets has the distinction of being the poorest neighborhood in the United States." According to sociologist William Julius Wilson, writing in *The Truly Disadvantaged: The Inner City, the Underclass, and Public Policy* (Chicago: University of Chicago Press, 1987), "Although in 1980 only a little more than 0.5 percent of Chicago's more than 3 million people lived in the Robert Taylor Homes, 11 percent of the city's murders, 9 percent of its rapes, and 10 percent of its aggravated assaults were committed in the project" (25).

3. E. Digby Baltzell, *Philadelphia Gentlemen: The Making of a National Upper Class* (Glencoe, Ill.: Free Press, 1958), 293.

pendent secondary schools, with assistance from Dartmouth College, the Merrill Foundation, and the Rockefeller Foundation. The program was rather clearly a response to the ferment of the civil rights movement. As one of the private school headmasters who created the program later commented, "The revolutionary implications hit even us, we the headmasters. I mean, we knew history was moving fast."

About 70 percent of the 430 students who joined the program in 1966 were black; the other 30 percent included students of Hispanic, Oriental, native American, and Eskimo backgrounds. Other programs developed for minority students, such as Upward Bound, typically consisted of after-school, weekend, or summer tutoring aimed at improving the students' performance in their own schools. In effect, they prepared the students for possible entry into the middle class. But the ABC program took students away from their homes, their neighborhoods, and their local high schools to attend the finest secondary schools in the country. These students were being brought into contact with the top one-half of 1 percent of the social structure, the rich and the super-rich.

The small ABC staff traveled to low-income junior high schools throughout the East, Midwest, and South to introduce the new program to faculty, counselors, and the teenagers themselves. They also relied heavily on community resource people, including church leaders and community leaders, to help them identify promising prospects. Potential students were asked to take the standardized test used for admission to private schools and to fill out a written application. Students were accepted on the basis of their grades, their test scores, and the recommendations of teachers and counselors. If accepted, they were then "matched" with participating prep schools. The prep schools made the final decision whether to accept the students ABC recommended.

Before they headed off to prep school, the students attended an eight-week summer orientation program. The first year this program was held at Dartmouth; in subsequent summers there were also orientation programs at Mt. Holyoke, Duke, Carleton, and Williams. The summer program was designed to help correct what were thought to be social, as well as academic, "deficiencies." As one of the headmasters of a participating school condescendingly put it, revealing the attitude many of the black students would encounter, "They couldn't come to Andover or Northfield from Harlem in September and fit, because many of them didn't know a knife from a fork."

Sylvester Monroe was not the only ABC student who found the world of elite prep schools to be full of surprises. Back in 1966, Cheryline Lewis was in her first year as an ABC student at the Abbott School. Cheryline, known as Cher, was baffled when one of her classmates told her that another classmate was Jewish. "What does that mean?" she asked. Though her hometown of Richmond, Virginia, has one of the oldest Jewish communities in the country, she had grown up in a black neighborhood and had attended all-black schools. The distinction between Jew and Gentile was not one that meant anything to her. "In Richmond," she said, "I knew white people and I knew black people." Now she knows Jewish people; in 1981 she married one.

After graduating from Abbott, and then from New York University, Cher worked for a few years in New York and then received an M.B.A. from the Columbia Business School. By the time she finished business school, she was living with Josh Feigenbaum. They had met seven years earlier, while she was at NYU and he was studying sociology at Rutgers. They became friends and a few years later began dating seriously. By that time, Josh was working for the magazine *Transaction* (now called *Society*). After living together for a few years, Cher and Feigenbaum married. She was then one of the highest ranking black employees at Citibank, and he was an independent producer of radio shows. A few years later, they had twin daughters, Emma and Zooey.

At the time of our interview, twenty years after entering the ABC program as a girl from Richmond who didn't know what a Jew was, Cher Lewis found herself married to a successful Jewish businessman and living in an elegant Fifth Avenue apartment. With the help of a Haitian governess (their third governess—the previous two were English and Norwegian), she was busy raising her two daughters. She had quit her job at the bank and was not sure what she was going to do next, though she doubted that she would work for a bank again. She was thinking of returning to her early love, writing.

In the heyday of the ABC program, from 1964 to 1975, more than one hundred schools across the country were participating. Most called themselves "independent private schools," but a few public schools had been added to the program by the late 1960s. The first spurt of growth was made possible by public funds totaling $4,759,548 over the five-year period 1965–1969, most of which came from the Office of Economic Opportunity. This allowed ABC to provide substantial support for each student: $2,500 for tuition, room, and board, plus $250 for pocket money, travel costs, and medical expenses. To make the money go even further, ABC worked out an arrangement whereby it would pay a greater portion of the student's tuition and other expenses to those schools that accepted two or more ABC students.

The next dramatic increase in funds came from private donors, especially corporations and foundations. Before 1968, the most the ABC program had received from private sources was slightly more than $500,000. From 1969 through 1974, ABC raised more than $900,000 a year from private sources, and for five of those six years the amount exceeded $1 million. The program also found other sources of public funding after the big federal grant from the Office of Economic Opportunity was cut back unexpectedly in 1967, owing to the escalation of the Vietnam War.

By 1983, when ABC celebrated its twentieth anniversary, more than five thousand students had completed the program. The inner-city schools they would have attended and the elite schools they did attend differed in many ways. There were, of course, fewer blacks at the elite schools, and the schools (and their settings) were far more luxurious than their ghetto counterparts. The teachers and administrators at the elite schools were more likely to have come from upper-class backgrounds, to have graduate degrees, and to have attended prestigious colleges. The classes were smaller, more homework was assigned, and there was a wider variety of well-organized extracurricular activities.

But perhaps the clearest difference between the two educational environments is that the student who graduated from an elite prep school was much more likely to go to college, especially to a high-status college. In the late 1960s, only about 40 percent of the black students who completed high school went on to attend college.[4] In contrast, 99 percent of the graduates of the ABC program attended college, and many attended the best-known colleges and universities in the country.[5] Participation in the ABC program put students onto a different educational track, one that was

4. Alexander W. Astin, *Minorities in American Higher Education* (San Francisco: Jossey-Bass, 1982), 35. Also see Peter Cookson, Jr., and Caroline H. Persell, "English and American Residential Secondary Schools: A Comparative Study of the Reproduction of Social Elites," *Comparative Education Review*, 1985, 29 (3), 296. On the basis of 1982 census data, Cookson and Persell report that only 33 percent of "all high school graduates" attend college after secondary school graduation.

5. The 99-percent figure is drawn from George Perry's study of ABC students from 1964–1972 ("A Better Chance: Evaluation of Student Attitudes and Academic Performance, 1964–1972" [Study funded by the Alfred P. Sloan Foundation, the Henry Luce Foundation, and the New York Community Trust, March 1973, ERIC Document 075556], 100). Cookson and Persell, "English and American Schools," report that "more than 95 percent of American boarding school graduates attend college after sec-

much more likely to lead to the best colleges, to graduate or professional schools, and to a life of economic comfort and security.

Jesse Spikes, whose story will be told in more detail in a later chapter, was one of the ABC students propelled onto an educational fast track that led to economic security. Jesse was the eleventh and youngest child of a Georgia sharecropper and his wife. Neither of his parents had more than a sixth-grade education, and none of Jesse's siblings graduated from high school. After completing the ABC program, he was accepted at Dartmouth on a full scholarship. He spent his sophomore year in France and part of his senior year in Nairobi. Upon graduation from Dartmouth, he spent two years at Oxford as a Rhodes Scholar, then returned to the United States to attend Harvard Law School.

After working for a few years as a lawyer in Atlanta, Spikes was offered the chance to go to the Middle East as legal adviser for the Al Bahrain Arab African Bank. He spent four and a half years working for the bank as legal adviser and special assistant to the chairman and managing director. Most of his time was spent on the road—and in this case "on the road" meant traveling from the Middle East to Europe or the United States. "I was just tired most of the time," he recalls, "and working seven days a week." In December 1985, he returned to Atlanta, where he now works in a large law firm.

Much of the attention the ABC program has received in the mass media has resulted from a few tragic stories concerning its graduates. The most widely publicized has been the case of Edmund Perry, a 1985 honors graduate of Exeter. Ten days after graduation, Perry was killed in Harlem by an off-duty policeman. The story made headlines, not only in such New York publications as the *New York Times*, the *Daily News, New York* magazine, and the *Village Voice* but in national periodicals like *Newsweek* and *Time*. All the stories noted that Perry had been a student at Exeter, that he had been accepted at Stanford . . . and that he had come to Exeter through A Better Chance.

In 1987, two years after Perry's death, his story had a second round in the media when journalist Robert Sam Anson's book *Best Intentions: The Education and Killing of Edmund Perry* was published.[6] The book was reviewed widely and elicited yet another wave of columns and editorials

---

ondary school graduation . . . and two-thirds attend the most highly selective colleges in the country" (296).

6. Robert Sam Anson, *Best Intentions: The Education and Killing of Edmund Perry* (New York: Random House, 1987).

about what had gone wrong. In a painstaking piece of investigative reporting, spurred on in part (and aided) by the fact that Anson's own son had been at Exeter with Perry, Anson discovered a side of Perry that had not been uncovered in the earlier round, a side that included extensive drug dealing on Perry's part.

The implicit message underlying much of the coverage of ABC graduates who did not make good runs like this: even with the opportunities provided by elite prep schools like Choate and Exeter, black kids from the ghetto are still, well, black kids from the ghetto. In our view this is an unfortunate and inaccurate message, for the *real* story of A Better Chance has not been the few tragedies but the many successes. Although there *have* been tragedies, and there have been those for whom the program did not work, the large majority of students who went through the program in its early years were well served and emerged not only well educated but psychologically intact.

More typical of the program is Eric Coleman, whose run-in with the law was for very different reasons than Perry. Coleman grew up in downtown New Haven, where he lived with his mother, his two brothers, and his sister. When the opportunity arose to attend the Pomfret School as an ABC student, he took it. After Pomfret he attended Columbia, and, after Columbia, the University of Connecticut Law School. Since January 1983, much of his time has been spent as a member of the Connecticut House of Representatives, where he tries to represent the interests of "women, minorities, small business owners, children, workers." He was arrested for his support of a striking union at Colt Firearms Company. Along with forty-four other protesters ("the Colt 45"), he was cheered by about four hundred members of Local 376 of the United Auto Workers as he was escorted by police to a patrol wagon.[7]

Like many other advocacy organizations launched in the civil rights era, the ABC program has met with hard times, particularly due to the loss of all types of government funding. Foundation funding also declined from $800,000 in 1978 to $610,000 in 1985, but corporations picked up some of the slack by increasing their donations from $387,000 to $603,000. The guest of honor at the twenty-fifth anniversary dinner in 1988 was John F. Akers, chairman of the board of directors of IBM and a director or trustee of the *New York Times*, the Business Roundtable, and the Metropolitan Museum of Art. The chairman of the committee overseeing the ABC din-

7. Susan Howard, "3 Legislators among 45 Arrested in Colt Protest," *Hartford Courant*, May 14, 1986, A1.

ner, Lewis T. Preston, was chairman of the board of Morgan Guaranty Trust and a director or trustee of General Electric, New York University, the Business Council, the Council on Foreign Relations, and the Sloan Foundation. With such support, ABC is likely to be around for the foreseeable future.

Still, ABC has had to curtail its scholarships and its recruitment of low-income minorities. In 1984, ABC's board of directors decided to end all support payments to participating schools. With this decision, the program lost much of its remaining clout with the schools and turned inexorably in the direction of recruiting middle-class black students. Thus, ABC is becoming more like a referral service for the placement of black students. Black middle-class parents are coming to ABC for help in finding private schools rather than, as in the past, ABC going to the public schools to find low-income students for the prep schools.

The changing role of ABC and the increasing entry of middle-class blacks into private schools are reflected in the one survey we know of that provides a comprehensive look at the racial composition of elite prep schools in the 1980s. It indicates that the number of black students has leveled off and that more of them are from the middle class. In their study of 2,475 freshmen and senior students at twenty prep schools, Peter Cookson and Caroline Persell found that 106 were black (4 percent). Notably, the fathers of seventy percent of their black sample were professionals: 17 percent were doctors, 14 percent were lawyers, 6 percent were bankers, 8 percent were college teachers, and 25 percent were secondary school teachers. One-third of the black respondents indicated that their families earned more than $75,000 per year, and almost half (44 percent) reported having traveled outside the United States.[8]

Social Structure and Identity

In 1982 we published a book exploring the relationship between the upper class and wealthy Jews in America. We believe the title captures the key

8. Peter W. Cookson, Jr., and Caroline Hodges Persell, "Integration and Isolation: The Black Experience at Elite Boarding Schools" (Paper presented at the annual meeting of the American Sociological Association, Atlanta, Ga., August 24, 1988). Additional evidence indicates that the number of black students has leveled off or decreased at some private schools. Eric Coleman, who is on the board of his alma mater, Pomfret, told us that there were more black students at the school when he was a student there than at the time of our interview. Similarly, Sara Lawrence Lightfoot reports

issues of the book—the assimilation of those of a different religion into the institutions of an overwhelmingly Protestant upper class and the effects of that process on the social identities of those being assimilated.[9] In the present book we ask a similar but slightly different question: Are there blacks in the white establishment?

In writing our earlier book we had a dual purpose. On the one hand, we wanted to see whether upper-class leaders had developed both attitudes and institutions capable of ensuring the perpetuation of their dominant class position while incorporating people of new wealth and power, even though the newcomers were of a different (and often despised) religion. This was a sociological question concerning social structure and power. On the other hand, we wanted to examine the effects of incorporation on the social identity of the Jews themselves. This question of identity falls within the realm of social psychology.

Our findings revealed that the Protestant Establishment was flexible enough to incorporate successful Jews into its prep schools, private universities, cultural organizations, and corporate boards, and to some extent into its social clubs. But the acceptance was not complete by any means. As for the effect on the Jews themselves, they came to be less Jewish in a traditional sense, or at least they reciprocated by developing an upper-class style, fashioning a new Jewish identity that fit comfortably with an upper-class orientation. For example, we found that Jews in the corporate elite were less likely than other Jews to mention membership in Jewish organizations in their *Who's Who in America* biographies, less likely to marry Jews, and less likely to be concerned with Israel or to say that their Jewishness was important to them. Furthermore, whether a family was of German or Eastern European origins, the longer it had been wealthy, the greater the changes in the members' Jewish identities. Social class, we concluded, is more important than religion at the top of the American social structure.

This book has the same dual purpose. By studying the life histories of atypical newcomers, we still want to examine how social structure and social psychology interact at the top of the class system. We recognize, however, that questions of assimilation and identity are far more complicated and emotionally charged when they involve the incorporation of

---

in her book, *The Good School* (New York: Basic Books, 1983), that there were forty-five black students at St. Paul's in 1969, but only twenty-three in 1980 (243).

9. Richard L. Zweigenhaft and G. William Domhoff, *Jews in the Protestant Establishment* (New York: Praeger, 1982).

blacks into a completely white establishment. Now it is not religion that is competing with the forces of class assimilation but a highly visible racial identification that has been burdened with the unique confluence of slavery, segregation, and negative racial stereotyping, making the situation of blacks qualitatively different from that of any other ethnic, religious, or racial group in America.[10] In this study we examine an extraordinary program: young blacks from economically impoverished backgrounds entered the elite world of the upper-class prep schools, a world permeated by overt and covert, blatant and subtle forms of discrimination. Yet in spite of their families' poverty, in spite of the discrimination they faced, they competed successfully with the scions of the most privileged families in America. These black youngsters not only endured a very difficult experience, they flourished.

In this book, then, we are dealing not with the assimilation of a few wealthy black families but with the creation of new elite individuals through a special educational program. And as a result of their education, these individuals may move from the lower-class black ghetto to the upper-class elite in just a very few years, possibly leaving behind friends and families, perhaps even the black subculture as a whole. Thus this unusual program provides a rare opportunity to investigate how quickly and thoroughly an upper-class style and identity can be acquired.

Our interest in the interplay between class structure and social identity led us to pose two basic questions for the present study. First, how did the program affect the people who participated in it, and how have they fared as adults in the larger society? Most important for our purposes, are these people rising to positions of power in corporations and in government? We shall answer these questions in chapters 2 through 6, primarily on the basis of interviews with thirty-eight men and women like Vest Monroe, Cher Lewis, Jesse Spikes, and Eric Coleman, most of them successful, some not, but almost all of them from low-income families to begin with. We shall also draw on earlier research on ABC students and recent research on blacks in large corporations to fill out the picture.

Second, and more generally, what do our findings contribute to the ongoing controversy over the relative importance of race and class in the United States? Are these well-educated blacks with tastes and cultural

10. Stanley Lieberson, *A Piece of the Pie: Black and White Immigrants since 1880* (Berkeley: University of California Press, 1980), and Thomas F. Pettigrew, "Integration and Pluralism," in *Modern Racism: Profiles in Controversy,* ed. Phyliss A. Katz and Dalmas A. Taylor (New York: Plenum Press, 1988), 19–30.

styles similar to those of high-status whites assimilated into the upper class or the top echelons of the corporate community? Do the graduates become less race conscious and more class conscious, as a class-oriented theory might expect? Or do they become more race conscious, as a theory stressing the predominance of race over class would predict? Or do they perhaps become both more race conscious and more class conscious as a result of the emergence of a new situation for black Americans?[11] We address these questions in our final chapter.

Just as the theoretical issues are more difficult in this study than in our earlier one, so too were the problems of gathering empirical information. At the outset, our efforts to gain access to information on the ABC program met with resistance. The leaders of the program would not provide us with the names of early graduates to interview; the president of the program did not respond to our letters or phone calls. More than a year after our initial request, through the private cooperation of an ABC employee, we received a partial list of program graduates that allowed us to begin our interviewing.

Because of these difficulties, we worked very hard to ensure that our sample was representative of all those who participated in the program during its early years. We searched carefully for individuals who might be considered "failures" or "dropouts," for we know that the successful are more likely to respond to an interview request. Then, too, we developed a "snowball" or chain referral sample using some of the tactics recommended to improve the quality of such samples with difficult-to-locate populations.[12] For a detailed account of the sampling and methods used, see appendix A.

Once we had located our first group of interview subjects, the study went more smoothly. All those interviewed were gracious and, with a few exceptions, quite forthcoming. Significantly, all but one agreed to have the interview taped. They did not seem at all hesitant to speak frankly, but we were careful to look for signs of tension or holding back. Never-

11. See William Julius Wilson, *The Declining Significance of Race: Blacks and Changing American Institutions* (Chicago: University of Chicago Press, 1978); Sharon M. Collins, "The making of the Black Middle Class," *Social Problems*, 1983, *30* (4), 369–382, and "The Marginalization of Black Executives," *Social Problems*, 1989, *36* (4), 317–331; and Thomas F. Pettigrew, "Race and Class in the 1980s: An Interactive View," *Daedalus*, 1981, *110* (2), 233–255.

12. Patrick Biernacki and Dan Waldorf, "Snowball Sampling: Problems and Techniques of Chain Referral Sampling," *Sociological Methods and Research*, 1981, *10* (2), 141–163.

theless, despite our confidence in what we were told, the fact is that the interviews were conducted by a white male, the first author of this book. We are aware that a white interviewer might not be able to elicit the full depth of concerns, fears, and problems facing these highly educated blacks in the corporate offices and government corridors of the white establishment. Such a possibility would be supported by earlier studies showing that black subjects are more forthcoming with black interviewers in survey studies. [13]

Still, the differences between findings with black and white interviewers in survey studies are a matter of degree, not of kind. And evidence from a study done in New Orleans in the 1950s indicates that blacks may be no less open with white interviewers. [14] Nevertheless, we paid very close attention to even mildly negative comments, just in case our interviewees were holding back, which we doubt. Equally if not more important, we also compared one part of the interview with other parts to discern whether differences existed from topic to topic. When our subjects spoke positively of their long-standing personal friendships with their white prep school and Ivy League classmates, and then voiced despair at the callous, insensitive, and often unfair attitudes and practices thwarting them in the corporate world, we believe we were hearing both the good and the bad as we tried to probe sensitively along the racial divide that has always run through American society. Then, too, we were careful to compare our findings with those of black interviewers who have interviewed black corporate leaders; the similarity of our findings to theirs greatly reinforces our belief that our respondents were candid. [15] Fi-

13. See Thomas F. Pettigrew, *Profile of the Negro American* (New York: Van Nostrand, 1964), 50, for summaries of such studies. Joe R. Feagin has pointed out the usefulness of black interviewers in his work on rising middle-class blacks. See Joe R. Feagin, "The Continuing Significance of Race: Discrimination in Contemporary America" (Paper presented at the Association of Black Sociologists Meeting, San Francisco, August 1989) and "Barriers to Black Students in Higher Education: Learning from Qualitative Research" (Position paper for the Center for Research on Minority Education, University of Oklahoma, September 1989), and Joe R. Feagin and Leslie Inniss, "The Mythology of the Black 'Underclass' in U.S. Race Relations Theory" (Manuscript, Department of Sociology, University of Texas at Austin, 1989).

14. John H. Rohrer and Munro S. Edmonson, *The Eighth Generation* (New York: Harper and Brothers, 1960), 4–7.

15. See, for example, John P. Fernandez, *Racism and Sexism in Corporate Life: Changing Values in American Business* (Lexington, Mass.: Lexington, 1981); Edward W. Jones, Jr., "Black Managers: The Dream Deferred," *Harvard Business Review*, 1986, *86* (3), 84–93; Collins, "Marginalization of Black Executives."

nally, our confidence in the openness of our interviewees is supported by studies showing that blacks who have been educated in majority white schools have more white friends and are more likely to live and work in integrated settings.[16]

We did not begin our study with a specific set of hypotheses to be tested. But we realized that leaders within the upper class have used co-optive strategies in the past when faced with insurgent groups, and we suspected that this program might involve a similar strategy since it was initiated in the early 1960s. Until we discovered some little-known evaluations that were carried out in 1969 and 1973, we also did not have much idea how the graduates of the program had fared. Indeed, we knew more about the program's failures than its successes, for, as we have noted, it is the failures that have been highlighted by the media.

For these reasons, our study draws in part on the open-ended qualitative research tradition within sociology and social psychology called "grounded theory," which is more inductive in approach than traditional social science while being no less concerned with developing and testing new explanatory concepts.[17] Thus, we found some of our ideas as we conducted our interviews, and we assessed the interest of our findings partly on the basis of the surprise they caused us. We also interviewed at length on a given question only until we were satisfied that we were learning nothing new, and from that point on we stressed questions that had not been fully answered in early interviews or had been rendered problematic or more interesting by earlier interviews. For example, our early interviews convinced us that we understood how the graduates felt about the program, so we spent more time in later interviews trying to understand their adult personal lives and the possible effects of racism on their careers.

Only after we had a sense of how the program operated and how its graduates were doing did we begin to look for ideas within the race rela-

16. J. H. Braddock, "School Desegregation and Black Assimilation," *Journal of Social Issues*, 1985, 4 (3), 9–22; J. H. Braddock, R. L. Crain, and J. M. McPartland, "A Long-term View of School Desegregation: Some Recent Studies of Graduates as Adults," *Phi Delta Kappan*, 1984, 66, 259–264; Joe R. Feagin, *Race and Ethnic Relations*, 3d ed. (Englewood Cliffs, N.J.: Prentice-Hall, 1989), 242.

17. Barney G. Glaser and Anselm L. Strauss, *The Discovery of Grounded Theory: Strategies for Qualitative Research* (Chicago: Aldine, 1967); Susan A. Ostrander, "Upper-Class Women: Class Consciousness as Conduct and Meaning," in *Power Structure Research*, ed. G. William Domhoff (Beverly Hills, Calif.: Sage, 1980), 74–76; Anselm L. Strauss, *Qualitative Analysis for Social Scientists* (New York: Cambridge University Press, 1987).

tions literature to help us understand our findings. After considering a wide variety of options brought to our attention by the social scientists we acknowledged in our preface, we adopted the general framework on race and class in America developed over the past ten years by Thomas Pettigrew. His work has the virtue of being equally attentive to social structure and social psychology. Although he is well aware of the contributions a comparative approach can make to understanding race relations, his concepts have the advantage of being tailored to the historical uniqueness of the American situation. He has also argued convincingly that concepts developed to explain the experiences of immigrant groups do not help much in comprehending the problems facing black Americans. Moreover, our findings have convinced us that Pettigrew is right in claiming that race remains of paramount importance even though the importance of class is also increasing.[18]

Although we interpret our findings in the final chapter within the general framework provided by Pettigrew's work, we also make use of the concept of "oppositional identity" developed by cultural anthropologists and others who study the situation of minorities within the American educational system. They argue that many blacks fight back against the degrading racism and poverty they face by developing a collective social and cultural identity that is not merely different from the stance of the white majority that subordinates them but in opposition to it. This oppositional identity now includes a rejection of the white emphasis on the importance of schooling, in good part because the job ceiling placed on blacks historically has meant that education for blacks has not had the payoffs it is supposed to have. Through a complex process, many black teenagers come to define success in school as both "acting white" and leaving behind a black social identity. Thus, there are often severe peer-group sanctions against doing well in school, including rejection and physical abuse. We have found these ideas useful in understanding why some black students begin to perform poorly in school in their teenage years; this includes middle-class black teenagers who do not do as well in school as middle-class whites and other minorities from similar educational and income backgrounds.[19]

18. Pettigrew, "Race and Class in the 1980s," see also Pettigrew, "Integration and Pluralism."

19. John U. Ogbu, *Minority Education and Caste: The American System in Cross-cultural Perspective* (New York: Academic Press, 1978); John U. Ogbu and Maria Eugenia Matute-Bianchi, "Understanding Sociocultural Factors: Knowledge, Identity, and School Adjustment," in *Beyond Language: Social and Cultural Factors in School-*

Further, we use the findings on oppositional identity to develop our own ideas about why most of the people in our study were able to avoid or overcome any tendencies to reject education as "acting white." We argue that the program we studied served the function of an "initiation" from a degraded to a valued status. Its demanding and controlling atmosphere was in effect a "total institution" in the sociological sense of the term. Thus, these youngsters were "destigmatized" and taught a new social identity that would reward them handsomely if they were willing to pay the price. Just what those rewards are and what the price has been are the major topics of the ensuing chapters.

Researching and writing this book has made us in some ways hopeful yet in other ways pessimistic. Our findings show that the "best and the brightest" from the ghetto competed successfully with their white counterparts from the country clubs. In that sense, our book celebrates many success stories of triumph over very tough odds.

Our research, however, has not made us optimistic about the American class and power structures. An innovative program has had to struggle to stay alive and has been forced to shift toward a middle-class constituency to do so. At the same time, the "modern," more subtle racism prevalent at higher levels of elite bureaucracies is now beginning to discourage the graduates we interviewed, as well as black executives studied by other investigators.[20] These young men and women have gone more than halfway to meet the demands of white culture, changing in ways that the white power structure in effect demanded of them. But the power structure has changed little to meet them, and it continues to exclude them. It remains a structure that institutionalizes the values and practices of upper-class white males. The setbacks for most blacks in life expectancy, education, and employment during the Reagan years are only the most glaring evidence for the resistance of the white power structure to black equality.

The result is that relatively few blacks—or other people of color, or women of any color—are likely to make it into positions of status and

ing Language Minority Students (Los Angeles: Evaluation Dissemination and Assessment Center, 1986), 90–91; Maria Eugenia Matute-Bianchi, "Ethnic Identities and Patterns of School Success and Failure among Mexican-descent and Japanese-American Students in a California High School: An Ethnographic Analysis," American Journal of Education, 1986, 95 (1), 233–255.

20. For a discussion of "modern, subtle racism," see Thomas F. Pettigrew and Joanne Martin, "Shaping the Organizational Context for Black American Inclusion," Journal of Social Issues, 1987, 43 (1), 41–78; for other investigations of black executives, see sources cited in note 15 above.

power. We have to conclude that institutional racism—that is, values, practices, and ways of thinking that work against minorities whether they are meant to do so or not—joins with persisting sex discrimination and class bias in creating a power elite of privileged white males from the upper class and corporations who monopolize positions of decision and influence in each generation.[21] The few people at or near the top who are not white males are truly the exceptions that prove the rule—daughters or wives of wealthy founders, tokens, celebrities, and concessions to affirmative action laws and community pressures.

As we contemplated the barriers faced by blacks in America in the light of our own research and other evidence, we were impressed once again by the uniqueness of the ABC program. It would be extremely expensive and difficult to develop and sustain such a program on a large enough scale to begin to make a real difference in the lives of most black people, who continue to live in segregated neighborhoods, attend segregated schools, and face constant white insinuations about their abilities. The results of the program give reason to hope, for they demonstrate what is possible when black people are given an honest chance. However, such programs must be seen for the most part as token gestures that are temporary responses to black protests, at least until such time as the commitment toward equal opportunity is expanded to the point where it can address the full nature of the problem that was created by slavery and segregation and is now perpetuated by a more subtle white racism.

---

21. Institutional racism as a concept was first introduced by Stokely Carmichael and Charles Hamilton in 1967 in *Black Power* (New York: Random House), and since that time, this term has become widely accepted by social scientists. Institutional racism refers to the practices and norms of an organization or institution that are based on white assumptions and attitudes and that systematically exclude or victimize blacks even if they are not intended to. Thus, screening out blacks by the use of tests based on experiences typical to the white middle class is a form of institutional racism. So is using textbooks that ignore black contributions, or providing reading lists for literature courses that include no black authors. Not serving foods favored by blacks in the cafeteria and not hanging pictures of blacks in the classrooms and hallways are other forms of institutional racism. See Herbert L. Foster, *Ribbin', Jivin', and Playin' the Dozens* (Cambridge, Mass.: Ballinger, 1974), 2.

The term *power elite* is defined in chap. 6. For an earlier discussion of our use of the term, see G. William Domhoff, *Who Rules America?* (Englewood Cliffs, N.J.: Prentice-Hall, 1967), 8–11.

2

The Summer Program

"This Is Your Spring Training, and That's Where Pennants and World Championships Are Won"

Bobette Reed Kahn, who graduated from the MacDuffie School, Williams College, and the Harvard Divinity School and at the time of our interview was a fund raiser for the University of Connecticut Law School, remembers quite well her eight weeks at the 1966 summer transitional program at Mount Holyoke.

When I hit Mount Holyoke, they provided little packages for us— toothbrush, toothpaste, a hardbound *Webster's* dictionary, which I still have. They gave us all different kinds of things they thought were important to females, and not in a condescending way. They gave us all kinds of sanitary devices, and we appreciated that. Our resident person, our tutor, was in charge of making sure that each one of us was being educated in the proper way, but never in a group, never in a way that would really embarrass any one person. . . .

They took us to Tanglewood, and what an incredible experience! Most of the girls had not been exposed to classical music so that was just a wonderful experience to have. . . .

They did all kinds of things. Had I ever heard of field hockey? No.

We all had to learn how to swim, we took ballet, they took us out to dinner and we had to order for ourselves. Most of us had never been to a restaurant, let alone order. We had one meal a week with dress-up, and afterwards we had demitasse—I'd never had coffee, let alone had demitasse—and we'd learn how to hold the cup.

When we interviewed graduates of the ABC program more than twenty years after they had entered the program, they had vivid memories of their summers at Dartmouth, Mount Holyoke, Williams, Duke, or Carleton. Many referred to the summer program as being like "summer camp." Cher Lewis had attended traditional summer camps and had hated them all—she even came home early from one. However, she loved her summer at Mount Holyoke so much that she said it was "like a magic summer camp." When asked if they remembered enjoying the summer, almost all of those interviewed said without hesitation that they had, though many were quick to point out that they worked quite hard. Most smiled as they recalled specific aspects of the summer that had enchanted them. Some mentioned the thrill of seeing ballet for the first time. Others mentioned how much they enjoyed canoeing or being in the woods.

Beyond the niceties and small touches, the "primary mission and consuming concern," as it was phrased in a report written about the first summer program, was "to improve each student's chances for survival" at prep school. On the assumption that academic survival would depend especially on verbal and mathematical skills, the decision was made to focus intensively on English and math. Though adjustments were made for individual students as needed, the basic weekly class schedule included nine hours of English literature and composition, six hours of reading instruction, and nine hours of math.

The intensive academic work was supplemented by social and cultural activities, athletics, and weekend trips. One of the most important social activities was eating dinner with other students, faculty and their families, and invited guests. For these meals the male students were expected to wear jackets and ties, the females dresses. In addition, they were expected to follow the examples set by their faculty and resident advisers, which included such behaviors as using the proper silverware at the proper time and politely asking for things to be passed rather than reaching across the table. The decorum expected at the evening meal and the manner by which it was taught are reflected in the following account of an event that occurred during the 1966 summer program at Dartmouth: "Once, on the next to the last evening, the boys were surprised to find the tutors acting as waiters and responding with mock gravity to requests of every kind; there was, understandably, a little less decorum than at other evening meals, when tutors and faculty taught, by example mainly, the etiquette to be expected at their schools."[1]

The students were encouraged to engage in conversation with those around them. At times, the seating of students and their guests was based on mutual interests: "A scientist might sit with students interested in nuclear physics; a reporter with students active on school newspapers; a professional actor with those rehearsing for the ABC play; or a visiting headmaster with the students accepted by his school."[2]

Frequently, there were after-dinner talks by faculty or guests. One of the highlights that first summer at Dartmouth, 1964, when all fifty-five of the participants were male, was a dinner visit by Jackie Robinson, who told the students: "This is your spring training, and that's where pennants and world championships are won."[3]

During the 1964 summer program, the students attended Sunday evening concerts by the Community Symphony, and they saw performances of *As You Like It* and *Rhinoceros* by the Dartmouth Repertory Theater. For much of the summer, the staff resisted pressure from the students to have a dance (on the grounds that they wanted the students to "learn to endure"); finally, ten days before the end of the program, the staff gave in. The dance, however, was not simply an occasion for a group of teenage boys to invite a group of teenage girls to dance to their favorite music in a gymnasium. It, too, became a lesson designed to prepare ABC students for the kinds of social events they would encounter as prep school students. As the summer report explains: "In capitulating, we gave the students both the privilege and responsibility for issuing invitations, meeting their guests, escorting them to dinner, the dance, Sunday breakfast and church. They were superb—as were their young ladies."[4]

Almost every weekend, the resident tutors took groups of six or seven students on outings. Some of these trips were to explore local mountains and lakes, some were to visit New England prep schools, and some were to work on a nearby farm. Typically, on one of the eight weekends, Saturday classes were cancelled to allow for longer trips to Quebec and Boston.

Athletics formed another important component of the summer pro-

1. Summer report, Dartmouth, 1966, 38.
2. Summer report, Dartmouth, 1964, 25.
3. Ibid.
4. Ibid., 25–26.

gram, but not the sports the students were used to playing. The staff purposely chose activities that were common to prep schools but that the ABC students were unlikely to have encountered. Every student received swimming instruction almost daily, and soccer, volleyball, canoeing, and rock climbing were among the other athletic activities. "Perhaps of all the summer activities," the 1964 final report states, "the rock climbing was most symbolic of ABC spirit and goals. The apprehension, the ascent, the longing but not quite daring to turn back; and finally, the confidence and joy that [come] with doing a difficult task well."[5]

All these academic, social, cultural, and athletic events were part of a rigorous daily schedule modeled on the schedules the students would encounter at their prep schools. The day began early, and from the time the students awoke until the time they went to bed, they were kept busy with scheduled activities. The daily schedule shown in table 1 reveals all the features of what sociologists call a "total institution," one that controls every aspect of a person's life. One characteristic of a total institution is that "life is tightly scheduled."[6] In their detailed study of private schools conducted in the early 1980s, Peter Cookson and Caroline Persell present a typical schedule for private independent schools, also included in table 1, which is remarkably similar to that used by the ABC summer transitional program twenty years earlier.[7]

One of the ABC graduates interviewed for this study, Kenneth Pettis, at the time of our interview a vice-president of Bankers Trust in New York, believes that the structure of the summer transitional program was much more important than its content. In his view, the purpose of the summer program was "more to get us used to being away from home than anything else, and being supervised by people other than our parents." Comments such as this made us realize that these students were being initiated into a new "culture," a point we will elaborate on in the final chapter.

---

5. Ibid., 27.
6. G. William Domhoff, *Who Rules America Now?* (Englewood Cliffs, N.J.: Prentice-Hall, 1983), 26, characterizes boarding schools as "total institutions." For the classic work on total institutions, see Erving Goffman, "On the Characteristics of Total Institutions," in his *Asylums: Essays on the Social Situation of Mental Patients and Other Inmates* (Garden City, N.Y.: Anchor Books, 1961), 1–124.
7. Peter W. Cookson, Jr., and Caroline Hodges Persell, *Preparing for Power: America's Elite Boarding Schools* (New York: Basic Books, 1985), 35–36. Their analysis, like Domhoff's in 1983, portrays prep schools as total institutions.

TABLE I
Daily Schedules, Dartmouth 1964 and Prep Schools 1980s

Daily Schedule Dartmouth, Summer 1964		Typical Schedule Prep Schools, 1980s	
Day began	6:50 A.M.	Rising bell	7:00 A.M.
Breakfast	7:15	Breakfast	7:15
Class	8:00–8:50	Work period	7:55–8:10
Class	8:55–9:45	Class periods	8:20–9:55
Break	9:45–10:05	Chapel	10:00–10:10
Class	10:05–10:55	Recess	10:15–10:40
Class	11:00–11:50	Class periods	10:45–12:20
Lunch	11:55	Lunch	12:30 P.M.
Faculty appts	1:00–2:00 P.M.	Class periods	1:20–3:15
Athletics	2:30–4:30	Athletics	3:15–5:20
Free time	4:30–5:30		
Dinner	6:15	Dinner	5:55
Study period	7:15–10:30	Study	7:00–10:00
Lights out	10:00–12:00	Day ended	10:00

The rigorous academic program, numerous cultural activities, and carefully planned schedule all contributed to an emphasis on the participants' worth. Cher Lewis, for example, mentioned how "special" she was made to feel by the attentiveness of the sophisticated and worldly college women who were tutoring the ABC girls the summer she spent at Mount Holyoke. In addition, knowledgeable, cultured, even famous guests came to dinner, and they were interested not only in telling the students about themselves but also in hearing what the students had to say. Even the *New York Times* considered their activities fit to print. When the ABC boys from Dartmouth and the ABC girls from Holyoke got together for their one social encounter at the end of the 1965 summer program, the *Times* covered it as if it were a significant society event:

> Dartmouth was the host this week-end to a delegation from Mount Holyoke at a college house party for teen-agers.
> For a 24-hour period beginning noon yesterday, the group, mostly eighth and ninth graders, enjoyed a respite from an eight-week

course of concentrated study. The course was to acclimate them for the academic and social life at some of the most prestigious preparatory schools in the nation.

The group dined in Thayer Hall and strolled around the picturesque campus with its hourly chimes from the tower of Baker Library.

Last night the teen-agers danced until midnight to recorded music. This morning, before their final campus meal at noon, they worshipped in the Bema, a wooded glade nestled in a hollow between glacial boulders at the northeast edge of the campus. . . .

A choir of ABC project girls softly practiced a hymn on the platform made of indigenous rock as birds twittered in the sheltering elm, hemlock, and birch trees. . . .

In the choir, wearing black robes and white surplices, were girls from a dozen states. The girls included Gloria Shigg and Sarah Palmer of Darien, Ga.; Marian Hayes of Atlanta; Jacqueline Brownley of St. Louis and Maria Viera and Judy Kreijanovsky of New York.[8]

There was another side, to the summer program, however. Many of those we interviewed stressed some of the difficult aspects, two in particular: first, the academic work was more rigorous and the expectations were higher than most of them had previously encountered; and, second, many, away from home for the first time, were homesick.

All these students had done quite well in their own schools, and some had done so without having to work especially hard. Suddenly they were surrounded by other students who had also excelled in their schools. Francisco Borges, at the time of our interview the treasurer of the state of Connecticut, has distinct memories of the academic demands at Dartmouth in the summer of 1966: "The intensity of the competition was extraordinary. I have been in very competitive environments—prep school, obviously, college, law school. None of them was as intense as the competitiveness that was there that summer for eight weeks. There were some of the brightest, sharpest, most capable students I'd ever been across. Having come out of a place where all of us were star students in our class, and all of a sudden you're sitting there in a room where everybody was a star, and, let me tell you, it was a struggle to keep up."

Not only were the students bright, but the staff was both capable and demanding. Borges recalls that small groups of students were assigned to

8. John H. Fenton, "Dartmouth Greets 140 Studying in Talent Project," *New York Times*, August 16, 1965, 27.

counselors who gave them additional tutoring in the evening. His counselor was Robert Reich, at the time a graduate student and now a Harvard faculty member and author of numerous books on neoliberalism. Reich, he recalls, "was a real tough son of a bitch . . . I was a royal pain in his ass."

In addition to being asked to work very hard, many ABC students were told they needed to do some remedial work to be able to compete successfully at the prep schools they were to attend. Harold Cushenberry, now a judge in Washington, D.C., recalls how his "ego was bruised" during the summer of 1965: "I assume all of us who came were the cream of the crop from the environments that we came from, myself included from my segregated environment. I didn't realize how deficient my writing skills were, and that's what really plagued me early on. I never got any practice writing. We didn't do a lot of writing. I was used to going home and going through the encyclopedia and basically parroting what came out of the encyclopedia, as opposed to being given a short story to read and then composing something fairly quickly in a quiz. That was very difficult for me. My ego was bruised a great deal when I didn't do as well as I thought I would on the written material."

Harold Cushenberry remembers struggling with his writing skills while others recollect their struggles with math; Bobette Reed Kahn, the fund raiser quoted at the beginning of this chapter, recalls, "I was horrendously deficient in math. I was a wonderful straight A student who was really not a straight A student." Yet even if the students had not caught up (and most had not) by the time they started prep school, they knew what their academic deficiencies were, and they knew what they needed to work on. They were not overwhelmed by these realizations on top of all the other adjustments they had to make as one of the few minority students in a predominantly WASP school.

The second difficult aspect of the summer program was not unique to these students. As in any summer camp that includes some youngsters who have never been away from home before, many of the ABC students very much missed their parents, their siblings, and their friends. Jesse Spikes missed his rural Georgia family so badly during the summer of 1965 that his best friend nicknamed him "Homesick." And unlike many children who go to summer camp, many of the ABC students had never before been outside the city limits of their hometowns. Calvin Dorsey, who now lives in Atlanta and works with Cox Communications, recalls that when he left Clarksdale, Mississippi, for New York City on his way to attend the summer program at Williams College, he had never before spent a single night away from home. When he had to spend his first night away from home at a YMCA in New York City, he was "very, very afraid . . . because I had heard all these stories about New York." Bobette Reed Kahn told us: "One of the biggest things about going to that summer program was that they sent you a plane ticket in the mail. And I said, 'I have to fly? Please, put me on a bus, put me on a train—I will not fly.' Thirteen years old and never been out of the city, and then all of a sudden you're put on a plane. I was scared, but my parents said, 'On the plane you go.'" She was "dreadfully homesick," but so was everyone else, she recalls, and they comforted one another.

Some students faced another problem, one that foreshadowed a difficulty many more would encounter after they had been at prep school for a while: explaining their new lives to their old friends at home. The negotiation of two very different identities is a potentially difficult problem that will recur as a topic throughout the rest of the book. One ABC graduate interviewed by Robert Sam Anson, while thinking back to his summer experience at Dartmouth in 1965, recalled worrying about what his friends in Harlem would think when his picture appeared in a photograph that accompanied a *New York Times* article:

> I always wondered, knowing there were so many other people around me who were so much more talented than I was in so many ways, Why me? Why was I taken? You feel happy to get out, but guilty, too. You feel you don't deserve it. . . .
>
> When I was selected, they sent all of us up to Dartmouth that summer to prepare us for life in prep school. There were fifty of us altogether and the *New York Times Magazine* did an article about us. The article had a picture. I kept wondering whether my friends at home would see it. I kept wondering what they would think.[9]

Many of those we interviewed indicated that one reason they enjoyed the summer transitional program, despite the academic pressure or homesickness or worries about what their friends back home would think, was that they made new friends. Many stayed in touch with summer ABC friends who later attended nearby prep schools. In fact, having ABC friends at other prep schools was, for many students, of considerable importance. Though unable to see each other often, knowing other students, like themselves, who were struggling with the adjustment to aca-

9. Robert Sam Anson, *Best Intentions: The Education and Killing of Edmund Perry* (New York: Random House, 1987), 41.

demic and social life at prep school was comforting. In addition to exchanging letters, they periodically had occasion to see one another at athletic events, glee club concerts, or mixers. As Bobette Reed Kahn recalls: "There were two other [summer] programs in New England—one at Williams, one at Dartmouth. Dartmouth came down—all the boys came down—and spent a weekend with us, and we went up to Williams and spent a weekend up there. . . . When it came to the god-awful mixers that we all had to go to for three years, we had friends. There was a whole network of ABC kids, at least on the East Coast."

The network formed among ABC students was strengthened when ABC scheduled special events for all the ABC students in New England, as was occasionally done in the early years. Bobette Reed Kahn recalls that "ABC did something wonderful" in her second year at the MacDuffie School: "They invited us all to go to Dartmouth and spend Thanksgiving at Dartmouth. So there were tons of us from the East Coast, and we all got together at Dartmouth. They planned a program for us, an awful lot of it was entertainment, but we got to see each other. We got to form more friendships, and to continue friendships."

Many consider the summer program to have been the linchpin of the ABC program: after the students had been recruited and selected but before they went off to prep school, the summer program provided a transitional experience that was crucial to the success of the program. There was, therefore, much discouragement when, over the years, the summer program had to be whittled down from eight weeks to six weeks, from six weeks to two weeks, and, then from two weeks to one day because of financial pressures. In the view of one ABC graduate, with six or eight carefully planned weeks, you could have a genuine "transitional program." With one or two days, you could have an "orientation program." The difference, he said, was that in the latter, "You just talk about it, you don't learn it." Finally the one-day orientation program was also eliminated.

At the time of our interview, Janice Peters, an ABC graduate of Milton Academy, was working for Prep for Prep, an after-school tutorial program in New York that prepares students for prep schools. She was quick to say that despite her work for what could be considered a competing program, she remains loyal to ABC and continues to support it in any way she can. Because of her work in the schools, she has frequent contact with ABC students and their parents. When she hears them voice concerns about the ABC program, she shares them with the ABC staff, with whom she is in fairly frequent communication. One of the issues she feels most strongly about is the elimination of the summer transitional program: "I have said to ABC that I thought that the summer preparatory program was crucial, was important. The fact that it no longer exists is a mistake because I think that not only did it serve to help students with transitioning, but it really did serve to solidify the group. I think it created more of an allegiance to the program because people did feel that solidarity. And so I did make that suggestion because I thought that was an important part of it for me, as well as for other students who were participants at the time."

In fact, ABC cut back on the summer program only with great reluctance. Yet, despite the lack of a summer program, ABC organizers believed that the growing numbers of black students at the various prep schools, along with ABC's new emphasis on recruiting more intensely in a few large urban areas, would provide adequate support networks.

Still, sociological theory supports Janice Peters's observation. The sense that their experience was to be a group one, not an individual one, was essential not only in staving off homesickness but also in relieving any feelings of guilt over leaving their peers behind. If other blacks were involved, and if they could feel that they were proving a point for blacks as a group, they would be less likely to feel they were breaking their collective identity with other blacks. They were less likely to suffer conflict over allegedly "acting white" by taking school seriously.

Then too, the summer program provided the beginnings of the same kinds of social networks that each new generation of upper-class people builds on the basis of its experiences in elite institutions, from the church preschool to the corporate boardroom. Thus, this seemingly "special" program really gave its participants only what the wealthy students at the prep schools already had and took for granted. Eliminating the program placed the ABC students at a bigger disadvantage than may be realized at first glance. It is the gradual accumulation of advantages at the top and disadvantages at the bottom of the social structure that is overlooked by those commentators who praise the "initiative" and "efforts" of our rich leaders and then blame the poor for their alleged personal failures.

But the elimination of the summer program came later. Those we interviewed had still been able to take part in it. These individuals enjoyed later success in school and developed a strong sense of self-worth, and we believe the intense summer program, combining intellectual work with social solidarity, played a large role in their success.

3

The Prep School Years

Into the Crucible

As ABC's black teenagers left their homes in New York, Philadelphia, Richmond, Atlanta, Chicago, and other American cities to live and learn among the children of the nation's wealthiest families, they faced a paradoxical situation. On the one hand, they encountered physical and economic comfort the likes of which they had never seen before. On the other hand, they were placed in an environment in which it was often difficult to feel comfortable.

The spaciousness, the elegance, and, in some cases, the grandeur of America's prep schools confirmed the assumption held by many ABC students that by choosing to attend prep school they had chosen to enter another world. With the exception of the specific geographic location, the following description of the Lawrenceville School could apply to many American boarding schools: "The school is located on 330 magnificently landscaped acres of New Jersey countryside just five miles south of Princeton. Its physical plant—including a nine-hole golf course, mammoth field house and covered hockey rink, library of some 23,000 volumes, science building, arts center with 900-seat auditorium and professionally equipped stage—would be the envy of most colleges."[1]

1. R. Gaines. *The Finest Education Money Can Buy* (New York: Simon and Schuster, 1972), 10. Lawrenceville is not exceptional—at least, not in the exceptional world of the elite prep school. For similar descriptions of Deerfield and Exeter, see John

Most colleges would be pleased to have Lawrenceville's endowment as well. In 1983, Lawrenceville and the other fifteen prep schools that make up Baltzell's select sixteen had a combined endowment of $381 million, and their physical plants were valued at about the same amount. These schools continue to draw on gifts from alumni and other supporters to add new gyms, libraries, art buildings, planetariums, and dorms, and they often use internationally renowned architects to plan these buildings. "In effect," Cookson and Persell claim, "the combined real estate holdings of American boarding schools represent a 'Prep National Park,' a preserve free from state and local taxes, where boarding school students are allowed to explore, backpack, horseback ride, rock climb, play, and temporarily escape from the pressures of adolescence and the total institution."[2]

Though most of the students are economically privileged, and attendance at these costly and often luxurious schools is part of the system that allows them to maintain (or enhance) their economic advantages, life in the prep school is not without its harsher side. Cookson and Persell assert that these institutions place "relentless" pressure on students. For most prep school students, this pressure begins early in life, but it intensifies upon their arrival at boarding school. "From the cradle," Cookson and Persell write, "most prep school students are told 'to be somebody.' . . . From the moment they jump (or stumble through) the hurdles of admission to an elite school, they must prove their worth by mastering the curriculum, the student culture, and their own vulnerability. . . . We began to see boarding schools as crucibles, from which some students emerged as tempered steel and others were simply burnt to a crisp."[3]

McPhee, *The Headmaster: Frank L. Boyden, of Deerfield* (New York: Farrar, Straus and Giroux, 1966), 9, and Robert Sam Anson, *Best Intentions: The Education and Killing of Edmund Perry* (New York: Random House, 1987), 103.

2. Peter W. Cookson, Jr., and Caroline Hodges Persell, *Preparing for Power: America's Elite Boarding Schools* (New York: Basic Books, 1985), 46–47. Sometimes just one wealthy alumnus can have an enormous impact on the physical plant of a school. According to John Cooney, author of *The Annenbergs: The Salvaging of a Tainted Dynasty* (New York: Simon and Schuster, 1982), 381, Walter Annenberg "almost rebuilt the campus" of his alma mater, the Peddie School in Hightstown, New Jersey. Cooney writes that Annenberg contributed millions of dollars to the school (though still far less than the $250 million he put into the Annenberg School of Communications at the University of Pennsylvania). This, of course, can have some undesirable side effects; according to Cooney, Annenberg's "philanthropy" led him "to consider Peddie as much his as were his publishing properties."

3. Cookson and Persell, *Preparing for Power,* 20.

These schools have become crucibles, Cookson and Persell argue, in order to serve an important function: to transform highly privileged individuals into "soldiers for their class." The schools are central to the socialization process that passes on the values of the upper class to the children of the upper class. As the students learn that they are part of a larger privileged class, their individualism is melted down into "the solid metal of elite collectivism." The schools encourage not only the development of a collective identity but also the adoption of values that serve to legitimate privilege. Not everyone succeeds under such pressures; some students, according to Cookson and Persell, become "prisoners of their class," trapped in a system they don't accept but can't escape; and some are destroyed by the prep school environment.[4]

Ronald Raymond, a psychologist who has studied the psychological effects of relocation, provides some empirical evidence that the transition from living at home to living in a prep school is quite stressful for some students. Unlike Cookson and Persell, he does not examine the demanding nature of the prep school environment per se; rather, his point is that relocation as a process, whether to a prep school, a college, or a new city because of a corporate transfer, creates a "tremendous amount of stress." Drawing on the research and consulting he has done over fifteen years, he estimates that 25 percent of the students who attend prep school have a "significant problem" adjusting to their new environment.[5]

Raymond's focus on the general stress of relocation and Cookson and Persell's portrayal of the prep school crucible indicate that even for many white Anglo-Saxon Protestant students, the transition to prep school is not easy. There can be no doubt that this transition was even more difficult for ABC students in the 1960s and early 1970s.

Not surprisingly, there is considerable evidence that prep school administrators and students have demonstrated many of the same prejudices found in the larger society over the years. The experiences of Jews and blacks at Andover are instructive because that school has long prided itself on educating "youth from every quarter," and it was one of the first boarding schools to accept black students. Frederick Allis's history of Andover, *Youth from Every Quarter*, is unlike many of the histories written about prep schools for it does not gloss over embarrassing or distasteful moments. Allis provides ample evidence that, for Jews and blacks at An-

---

4. Ibid., chap. 7, "The Prep Crucible," esp. 124.
5. "On Becoming Uprooted: The Beinecke Symposium," *Wooster News*, Spring 1985, 20–21. See also Ronald Raymond, *Grow Your Roots Anywhere, Anytime* (Ridgefield, Conn.: Wyden, 1980).

dover, anti-Semitism and racism were likely to be part of their prep school experience. In the 1930s, when about 3 percent of the student body was Jewish, the headmaster wrote to a colleague: "We shall never have a larger percentage, and I am trying to reduce it just a little. On the other hand some of them make first class students and real leaders, although very few of them are permitted to hold important social positions." Some Jewish students were given the "silent treatment" by the other students in their dormitory. And though Andover accepted black students relatively early, it did not accept very many, and they were not especially welcomed by the community. Prior to the 1950s, Allis writes, "the School had done little if anything for blacks." For example, in 1944, in response to a request from an alumnus that Andover accept more black students, the headmaster responded that there were currently two black students at the school, and that accepting more might "cause trouble."[6]

Evidence of anti-Semitism and racism at other prep schools where Jews and blacks were accepted much later than at Andover also abounds. Charles Dey told us that early in his tenure as headmaster at Choate, he received a note from a man in Texas whose son had been turned down by Choate in the 1930s. The son had gone on to be quite successful and had just received an award of some sort. The father enclosed a photocopy of the original rejection letter from Choate. The letter stated that the school's "Jewish quota" had already been filled. "The only redeeming feature," commented Dey, "is the fact that it [the letter] was honest."

Choate was even more overt in its intolerance of blacks. A graduate of Choate writes the following of his alma mater: "At Choate, during the Eisenhower years, racist remarks were as much a part of our daily lives as the chapel services which we were required to attend each night. In fact, at the first Sunday service I attended there, Seymour St. John, the school's headmaster and also its chaplain, began his sermon with a joke about 'Old Darky Joe' and his friend 'Moe.' The humor that the sons of America's (mostly Republican) elite shared with one another was considerably blunter."[7]

Julian Bond, the Georgia legislator and son of an eminent black academician, attended the George School in the mid-1950s. He recalls that his

6. Frederick S. Allis, Jr., *Youth from Every Quarter: A Bicentennial History of Phillips Academy, Andover* (Hanover, N.H.: Phillips Academy, Andover, 1979), 616, 626.
7. Paul Cowan, *The Making of an Un-American* (New York: Viking, 1967), 4.

fellow students were not very concerned about hiding their prejudices. "You'd be sitting around a room and some kid gets a package from home and there'd be some cakes in it," Bond recalls, "and he'd pass it around and miss somebody and the kid would say: 'What am I—a *nigger* or something'—Then he'd say,' Oops! Bond's here!'"[8]

Bond was more upset by something an administrator said to him. He was dating a white girl, and, like other George School couples, they used to walk to Newtown, the town near the school. Bond recalls with some bitterness that the school dean asked him not to wear his much-loved George School jacket when he was walking into town with his girlfriend. Bond concluded that the George School in the 1950s was a "hotbed of racism."[9]

This, then, was the world ABC students entered in the mid- to late 1960s: comfortable, often luxurious physical environments that did not necessarily make students, especially black students, comfortable, and psychological environments that could be overtly bigoted.

Getting There

How were ABC students placed in the particular schools they attended? William Berkeley, president of the ABC program from 1966 to 1974, describes the program as a "huge mail order operation." As he recalls, "We would read the files—it would be like an admissions office—we'd have a team of people read the files. Each person had to put down some schools they thought the kid would work in best, and then somebody was assigned to sort of be the shepherd for that kid. Using the notes in the file, we would make mailings out to the schools, and the understanding was that the schools could turn down any kid that they didn't want and send him back and we would send them more, which was fine with us. We really wanted the schools not to feel they were being assigned kids." Each school was aware that it was the only school to receive a particular ABC

8. John Neary, *Julian Bond: Black Rebel* (New York: William Morrow, 1971), 43.
9. Ibid., 44–45. Neary reports that after this story appeared in a magazine article about Bond people at the George School claimed it was false. The Reverend James H. Robinson, the founder of Operation Crossroads Africa, wrote in his autobiography, *Road without Turning: The Story of Rev. James H. Robinson* (New York: Farrar, Straus, 1950) that in the early 1940s he was invited by the graduating class of the George School to be their commencement speaker, but "the board of directors forced the president to withdraw the invitation" (253–254).

applicant's file and that it had a brief period to decide whether or not to take the student. If the school chose not to accept a student, his or her file was then sent to another school. Once accepted, most students attended the prep schools for three years, though some graduated after only two years; most, upon entering, did not need to repeat a year, though some did.

Even before they arrived at their prep schools, many ABC students had to deal with the kinds of problems that would soon set them apart from their more affluent white peers. First of all, many had to convince their parents to let them leave home to attend a school the parents had never heard of. Some of those we spoke with said that their parents thought they were too young to leave home and that they had to get uncles, aunts, grandparents, or favorite teachers to help persuade their parents to let them go. One ABC graduate told us that her mother didn't want her to attend a girls' school because she feared that the girl would become a lesbian. Within a few years after the program began, the ABC staff realized that in addition to providing an in-depth eight-week orientation for the young ABC students who were about to attend prep school, they needed to address the parents' concerns in a more structured and consistent fashion.

There were other problems as well. Jennifer Casey Pierre (who holds an M.B.A. from Columbia and is now an executive at R. J. Reynolds) recalls that the seemingly simple task of getting from her home in Baltimore to the Baldwin School outside Philadelphia was "a struggle." Her father had died when she was four, her mother had never obtained a driver's license, and none of her close relatives had a car. Her mother solved this problem by putting aside some money to pay "a guy who said he would be willing to drive us, and all my belongings, to the school."

Other ABC students encountered similar "struggles" that ABC and the prep schools didn't foresee. In the summer of 1969, Gordon Right, a thirteen-year-old who had won a scholarship to Groton through the ABC program, faced what appeared to him to be an insurmountable obstacle when he received a notice from Groton instructing him to bring various items with him when he arrived at school. The lengthy list included blankets, sports jackets (three of them), slacks, luggage, and towels. Gordon, who lived in Harlem with his blind mother, four younger brothers, and a sister, owned a pair of sneakers, a pair of dungarees, two shirts, two sets of underwear, and not much else. The state legislature had recently eliminated special grants that would have allowed families on welfare, like Gordon's family, some money to pay for unusual back-to-school costs. As a result, Gordon feared that he would not be able to attend

Groton. "I never heard of Groton," he said late in the summer of 1969, "until a few months ago, then I was spending days preparing for the tests, then I won it, and then comes the clothes list. I figured I'd lose it all." But Gordon Right overcame this hurdle with the help of a group of sympathetic social workers who voted to provide $300 from their "brotherhood committee." He headed off to Groton with blankets, sports jackets, slacks, and even the required seven dozen name tags, ready to confront new challenges.[10]

Even after he had managed to acquire everything on Groton's list, Gordon Right may have felt quite intimidated when he saw what other students brought to school. Peter Prescott provides the following description of students arriving at Choate in the late 1960s: "The cars are pulling up to Hillhouse. Most are station wagons, some with zippy names like 'Et Cetera Too' stenciled on the driver's door, but there is a sprinkling of Cadillacs and Mustangs as well. From the cars the trunks and suitcases tumble, and the tennis rackets, the sports jackets temporarily suspended from wire hangers, bookcases, barbells, and chest-pulls, chairs too big to squeeze through dormitory doors, guitars and radios, phonographs and rifles, fans, tape recorders, and mothers in tailored suits."[11]

Many of the ABC graduates we interviewed were appropriately impressed when they first saw the schools they were to attend, though their reaction was not always unequivocal. *Newsweek*'s Sylvester Monroe recalls that when he got his first glimpse of St. George's School in Newport, Rhode Island—the school was founded in 1896 on a scenic promontory overlooking the Atlantic Ocean—he was struck not only by the beauty of the place but by the looming presence of "this gothic chapel that to me looked like some medieval castle with dungeons." Monroe's ominous impression of his new school underscores how unfamiliar and threatening the boarding school could be for nervous young blacks from the inner cities.

By way of contrast, arriving at prep school was like "coming home" for many white students, especially those "legacy" students whose parents and grandparents had attended the same school. Compare the following recollection by a 1972 graduate of Groton with Monroe's image of a castle with dungeons: "When I first arrived at the school in the fall of 1967 and

10. Francis X. Clines, "Caseworkers Pool Funds to Aid Groton-Bound Harlem Student, *New York Times*, August 2, 1969, 17.
11. Peter S. Prescott, *A World of Our Own: Notes on Life and Learning in a Boys' Preparatory School* (New York: Coward-McCann, 1970), 40.

discovered the Georgian brick buildings arrayed around the lawn called the Circle, and the high-towered Gothic chapel, I felt oddly that I was coming home. I recognized the buildings—Hundred House, School House, Brooks House—from our family's dinner plates, and I knew the chapel from a watercolor that my father had painted as a boy in the class of '17 and later hung in my bedroom."[12]

Being There

EARLY MEMORIES

As a therapeutic technique, the psychoanalyst Alfred Adler used to ask his patients to recall their first memories. He used a patient's earliest memory as the starting point for analysis and considered it a key to understanding that person. The fact that a person remembered one early event rather than the many others that could have been recalled was, in Adler's view, psychologically significant. Even if the recalled early memory could be shown to be the result of fantasy and distortion, it still was of psychological value because it revealed the world as that person remembered it.[13] As Freud wrote in his oft-cited discussion of memories of childhood seduction, such early memories revealed "psychical reality" if not "material reality."[14] Other psychologists have since used Adler's method of eliciting an individual's earliest memories as a type of projective technique.[15]

In our interviews with ABC graduates, we did not ask for their first memories of prep school. However, in response to our more general question about how they liked being at Hotchkiss, or Milton, or Loomis, many responded by describing events that took place on the very first day they arrived—and in some cases, during the very first minutes after they arrived. These early memories may or may not reflect material reality; they certainly reflect psychic reality.

Some of these memories concerned clothes. Typically they revealed the newly arriving students' realization that their wardrobes did not measure up to their classmates'. As we described earlier, Sylvester Monroe, then a

12. John Sedgwick, "World without End," *New England Monthly*, 1988, 5 (9), 54.
13. Alfred Adler, *Problems of Neurosis: A Book of Case Histories* (New York: Harper and Row, 1964), 121–128.
14. Sigmund Freud, *An Autobiographical Study* (New York: Norton, 1952), 64.
15. H. H. Mosak, "Early Recollections as a Projective Technique," *Journal of Projective Techniques*, 1958, 22, 302–311.

fifteen-year-old member of a Chicago gang, remembers that the very first moment he set foot on the campus at St. George's School, his adviser informed him that they would have to go shopping the next day to buy him some suitable clothes. Bobette Reed Kahn recalls that one of the first things she noticed was that "all the girls were wearing these wonderful clothes, and I wasn't." And Calvin Dorsey remembers, with both pain and amusement, that the airline had lost his luggage, and he therefore had to wear the same suit for three days: "Can you imagine? Unsure, trying to make a good impression, with no clothes and no money!"

Others remember that the issue of race came up immediately. Bobette Reed Kahn, who like her father is very light-skinned, recalls that the day before she left for prep school, her father warned her that people were going to ask her: "What are you?" It did not take long for a prep school classmate to prove him right: "I got to MacDuffie early for some reason. I was the first one there. There were no other students there, and I kind of puttered around. It's scary anyway, but then when there's no one there and you're feeling lost in this place. . . . Finally, two other girls came and they were introduced to me, and we went down for lunch. And do you know the first thing they said to me? 'What are you?' I couldn't believe it. And then the next thing the girl said was, 'I've never been near anyone black except for my maid.' And, I thought, I'm going to have problems here. I'm going to have real problems here."

Bobette Reed Kahn's experience of being informed, not very subtly, that she was different in terms of both race and class was not typical, but neither was it unique. The girl who told Bobette that the only black she knew was a maid was both thoughtless and cruel, though it is possible that she did not intend to offend Bobette as much as she did.[16] Other students' memories leave no doubt about intent. One particularly ugly encounter also took place at a student's first meal at prep school:

> I remember the first night I went to dinner at school. To my right was an heiress to a cosmetics fortune. To my left was an heiress to a

---

16. Gail Lumet Buckley, Lena Horne's daughter, in her book about the Horne family (*The Hornes: An American Family* [New York: Knopf, 1986], tells the following story about her mother visiting a Hollywood set in the early 1940s: "Tallulah Bankhead, the star of the picture, greeted Lena with open arms—and with the words 'My daddy had a beautiful little pickaninny just like you.' Lena was so bowled over by the sheer audacity of Tallulah, who had been one of the great theatrical stars of the 1920s (as well as a famous 'free spirit'), that all she could do was laugh. And she laughed the rest of the afternoon. Tallulah was no bigot—she was, in fact, one of show biz's great liberals" (184–185).

department-store fortune. Across the table from me was an heiress to an oil fortune. And they were all talking about the places they had been, the things they had bought, the vacations they were going to take, as if I wasn't even there. Finally, one of the girls—it was the department-store heiress—tapped me on the elbow and said, "You better be nice to me, because I'm paying for half your scholarship." I almost got sick to my stomach. I didn't say anything, I just got up from the table and walked out. It was two weeks before I could bring myself to go back into the dining hall.[17]

Another frequently occurring early memory involved the difficulties of the person's initial living situation. Many prep schools had never had black students before, and those in charge of assigning roommates often did not know where to put them. The schools differed in the policies they employed. Some schools assigned ABC students to room with other ABC students, while others would not allow ABC students to room together. Some placed ABC students with white students but sent letters to the white students beforehand alerting them to the fact that their roommate would be black, while other schools simply let the roommates discover this when the students met. Some schools simply placed the ABC students using the seemingly random assignment systems they had always used.

Some of the schools apparently tried to sidestep the question of roommates by giving the first black students single rooms. For some students, like Ken Pettis, this worked out fine: "My first year at Taft I lived in a single—a single for a freshman was very unusual. Not only that, but I was in a single on a floor that didn't have that many students on it. As a matter of fact, there were three of us on the floor (I had a single and they had a double right next door to me), and the three of us that were on the floor are all still in touch. One of them was just in my wedding. He has become a lifelong, very, very good friend of mine."

But for some, their earliest prep school memories of being isolated, different, and alone were exacerbated by physical isolation. For example, Cecily Robbins, now an executive with the Big Sisters Program in Washington, D.C., recalls her first semester at Walnut Hill: "My room happened to be sort of at one end of the hall. My next-door neighbor on one side was the infirmary and then there was the stairwell on the other side

17. Anson, *Best Intentions*, 91.

and the rest of the hall. Nobody had to walk by my room unless you were going into the infirmary. And I sort of would go upstairs and isolate myself."

One former ABC student recalls that her school told her there was no room for her to live on campus. Instead, arrangements had been made for her to live with a faculty member and his family. This did not work out well: "It was an incredibly regimented family, and I hated it. I used to try and get away from that family to have dinner on the campus which was only two blocks away and this caused some upsets. Actually, I preferred being on the campus and eating that grade C food to sitting and eating this wonderful food with this family that I hated." After complaining to the director of admissions, she was able to move onto campus the second semester, and "everything smoothed right out."

As these poignant examples clearly show, the initial days and weeks were trying times for most ABC students, reminding them they were black in a white world. Many also said that they were terribly homesick. Of course, many had been homesick during the summer transitional program, but in the summer they had been surrounded by others who were also homesick (and also black); furthermore, they knew the summer program would be over in a matter of weeks. At prep school the ABC student was often the only black or one of a few blacks, and he or she knew the semester would not end for months. Gail Warren, now back in her hometown of Atlanta where she works for an advertising agency, remembers that she phoned her mother so often during her first semester at Andover that her mother finally said, "Look, what do you think if I fly you home for a weekend? I think that would be less expensive than the phone bills we're getting."

Some students developed strategies for going home. While participating in the first summer program at Dartmouth, a homesick Jesse Spikes heard an ABC staff person tell a group of students that the program was still very much in the experimental stage, and that he wasn't even sure how the Southerners would adjust to the amount of snow they would encounter in New England. Jesse recalls saying to himself, "Aha. That's my answer. I'll just wait until the first big snow and I'll just freak out. And, at that, I'm relieved of the responsibility—it's not my fault, I just couldn't handle the weather. And I'll go home." But when the first big snow came, Jesse Spikes—by then playing halfback on the football team, doing well academically, and having made friends—had abandoned his plan. Sylvester Monroe had a different plan:

I got there, I didn't want to be there. I had discussed this with my mother—my mother was a very wise lady, though not well-educated. She said to me: "Look. I think you ought to try it. You ought not to turn down this opportunity. If you see it and you don't like it, then come home."

So I went with the intention of staying a couple of weeks and then coming home. I got out there, I had been there about two or three weeks, when I got sick. I had eaten something, got a stomach bug. I went into the infirmary because I couldn't keep anything down. I remember thinking, "This is it. This is terrific."

So I called my mother and I said, "Hey, Mom, this place is terrible. It's made me sick. I can't keep anything down." She said, "What's the matter with you?" I had asked the doctor what was wrong with me. My vocabulary was not so extensive. The doctor said, "I think you've got a bad case of nostalgia." So, when I called my mother up and she said, "What's the matter with you?" I said, "Well, doc says I've got a real bad case of nostalgia. Can I come home?"

Luckily, "nostalgia" *was* in my mother's vocabulary. She said, "Yeah, under one condition." I said, "What's that?" She said, "If it's in a box." So I was crushed. I expected her to say, "Poor baby, come on home." So, I figured that nobody wanted me at home. I might as well stay and make the most out of it.

ACADEMICS

Academic pressures contributed to the difficulty many students had adjusting to life at their prep schools. Many had been warned during the summer transitional programs that they might not yet be ready to compete successfully at the prep schools they would attend. And for many, this turned out to be true. Cecily Robbins remembers her shock and disappointment when she received her first grades in Latin: "I had gone to parochial schools and I had gone to a school where Latin was taught. We had numerical grades and none of my grades in Latin were lower than 90. Usually I got 90, 95, right? My first grade in Latin at Walnut Hill was an F. My first F in my life, my first failure, and it was horrible." Harold Cushenberry recalls that he was "almost crushed that first semester" when he got his grades: "I mean, I didn't come anywhere near flunking. Doing poorly to me was C's. I got C's on my compositions and I had always had 100's basically, or 99.9, and to have someone say this is worth a C was crushing to me, and not to be able to confide that sense of personal failure to anyone, not to have any support, was doubly difficult."

Some discovered rather quickly that they could handle the academic work. When, for example, LaPearl Winfrey, now a Chicago psychologist, was the only person on her dormitory floor at the Masters School to make the honor roll, she was able to relax. "I didn't go to Switzerland for Christmas," she recalls, but "I had a good sense of myself."

For others, it took a year or two to catch up. Ken Pettis's experience at the Taft School was not unusual: "On the academic side, I faltered a bit at first. . . . The level of the academics started higher than I was used to and moved a lot faster than I was used to. Once I got used to the pace, I did better. I was not a star. I was never honor roll the entire time I was there. I was an average student in that environment. . . . And it really didn't bother me, not being at the top, because there were some very smart people there. Some very, very smart people—people who had been exposed to a lot more than I had during their early years."

Some of those we spoke with were at or near the top of their classes by the time they graduated. As we shall see in the next chapter, many ABC graduates (including Ken Pettis, with his average grades at Taft) were strong enough students to be accepted by the most selective colleges in the country. In addition to the substantial evidence we gathered in our interviews concerning academic success, George Perry's study of the first eight years of the ABC program demonstrates that by the time they graduated, ABC students had caught up with their classmates. Perry's study examined the performance of all ABC students from 1964 through 1972. Using their twelfth-grade rank in class as a measure of academic performance, he found that the ABC students were nearly evenly distributed in class rank, with a median rank just below the middle (at the 47th percentile). Thus, he concludes, their standing was "approximately the same as that of their non-ABC classmates." [18]

To our surprise, and thus of great interest to us, the primary memory some ABC graduates have of academic life at prep school is what might be called "academic liberation." Some of these students came from tough inner city schools where they felt strong pressures *not* to do or be inter-

---

18. George Perry, "A Better Chance: Evaluation of Student Attitudes and Academic Performance, 1964–1972" (Study funded by the Alfred P. Sloan Foundation, the Henry Luce Foundation, and the New York Community Trust, March 1973, ERIC Document 075556), 38 and 42.

ested in academic work. Monique Burns, who left Brooklyn to attend the Concord Academy, expressed such feelings: "I had an image of being such an academic person at my other school, and I was sort of an out-cast. . . . This was part of the reason why Concord was such a good experience for me. For once I wasn't just the smartest kid. I was always threatened with physical violence and all for being so smart. So when I went to Concord, here were some people who were more like me. In terms of intellectual interests and ideals, they were very much like me."

Bobette Reed Kahn has similarly harsh memories of her high school back in Cleveland. In junior high school, she had been fortunate to have a wonderful English teacher, and she had developed a close relationship with the assistant principal. But her high school—the John F. Kennedy High School—was a different story: "There were very few days I could go through the hall and not be felt up or in other ways molested. And there were always codeine bottles in the bathroom, people shooting up, gunshot fights in the halls and things like that. The only reason why I didn't come out, I guess, scared more than I was was because my sister, my older sister, was hot stuff. And her friends, her street friends, pro-tected me, and literally, at times, beat people up for messing with me. And I was just having problems coping in this school socially. I was very quiet, very shy, and it was not a good thing to be smart." Thus, for some students, like Bobette Reed Kahn and Monique Burns, a central compo-nent of their academic experience in prep school was the freedom to de-velop academically to their fullest potential, and this helped to balance their negative experiences there.

Bobette Reed Kahn's and Monique Burns's experiences are not at all atypical in predominantly black high schools around the country. As we noted in the first chapter, many academically talented black students are jeered or attacked by their peers for "acting white," and several studies have suggested that this peer pressure has an adverse effect on school per-formance by setting up a conflict between the values students internalize about achieving in school and their desire to be part of the in-group. Some black students develop coping strategies, such as excelling in sports or playing the role of clown or publicly defying teachers, so that they can continue to achieve and still be accepted by their friends. The pervasive-ness of the problem can be seen by the fact that even the great basketball star Kareem Abdul Jabbar encountered this attitude in Philadelphia at the same time Bobette Reed Kahn and Monique Burns were under siege in Cleveland and Brooklyn. He writes in his autobiography:

I got there [Holy Providence School in Cornwall Heights, right outside of Philadelphia] and immediately found I could read better than anyone in the school. My father's example and my mother's training had made that come easy; I could pick up a book, read it out loud, pronounce the words with proper inflections and actually know what they meant. When the nuns found this out they paid me a lot of attention, once even asking me, a fourth grader, to read to the seventh grade. When the kids found this out I became a target. . . .

It was my first time away from home, my first experience in an all-black situation, and I found myself being punished for doing everything I'd ever been taught was right. I got all A's and was hated for it; I spoke correctly and was called a punk. I had to learn a new language simply to be able to deal with the threats. I had good manners and was a good little boy and paid for it with my hide.[19]

Given this tension between an oppositional black subculture and school achievement, it is understandable that many ABC students would like prep school, contrary to our initial expectations.

FRIENDSHIPS BETWEEN BLACKS AND WHITES

Though most of those interviewed could recall racist comments or racist incidents while they were in prep school, almost all claimed that these were rare and that without too much difficulty they were able to avoid those students who were prejudiced. Moreover, almost all of those interviewed indicated that they had become close friends with white students, and for many those friendships have persisted to the present. This too seemed surprising to us at first, almost a wish more than a fact, but we came to believe that such friendships could be genuine even though racist remarks by some white students at the same time heightened the racial awareness of the black students.

Cher Lewis recalls encountering people with racist views for the first time. Prior to attending the Abbott Academy, she had lived in a black community in Richmond, and she had never before met people who seemed to hate her only because of the color of her skin. Still, she learned

19. Kareem Abdul-Jabbar and Peter Knobler, *Giant Steps: The Autobiography of Kareem Abdul-Jabbar* (New York: Bantam Books, 1983), 16. Cited in Signithia Fordham and John U. Ogbu, "Black Students' School Success: Coping with the 'Burden of "Acting White,"'" *Urban Review*, 1986, *18* (3), 177.

to deal with these people, and she became close friends with some white students at Abbott. She remains in regular communication with her four closest Abbott friends, all of whom are white.

Harold Cushenberry experienced no overt discrimination as a student at the Taft School. "I was more of a curiosity than anything else," he recalls. He does remember feeling animosity from some of the southern students: "I sensed a hostility there, but likewise, I don't recall anything said to me directly. I think maybe my second or third year there may have been some off-color comments every once in a while, but certainly nothing that was so troubling that they got me all bent out of shape. Confederate flags, things like that, but those were the southerners who were at the school."

A few recall more overt racial incidents, but often these memories are vague, unlike many of the other memories people have of life at prep school. For example, Greg Googer, a graduate of Andover and Vanderbilt, now living and working in his hometown of Atlanta, responded to a question asking if he recalled any racial incidents while he was at Andover in the following way:

> The only racial incident that springs to mind is the night—I don't know exactly what happened, and I've always wondered, and I always wondered if I dreamed this or if the person who told me this dreamed this. There was one friend of mine, he mentioned once walking across campus late one Saturday night. He mentioned there were some guys who were walking around in sheets. I said "No, you gotta be kidding," but he insisted that they were, and that he knew who they were. But nothing ever came of it. Nothing ever came of it one way or another. Those guys who supposedly were wearing sheets, and like I said I'm not sure if the guy who told me this was dreaming or if I was dreaming, they never did anything to instigate anything, and no one ever delved any deeper to find out whether anything was actually happening. That was the only truly racial incident that I remember ever coming across while I was at Andover.

Many students clearly recall being offended by the naiveté of questions they were asked, and some of the women recall being offended by white students who wanted to touch their hair. Jennifer Casey Pierre responded to a question about whether she had made friends with white students when she was at the Baldwin School by saying: "Yes, I did. Over time. The major problem I had was because of the advent of the Afro a lot of my Caucasian counterparts wanted to touch my hair but what they didn't realize is that I had a lot of hair and that if they did this they messed it up, and that it was part of my pride, my symbol, and so I resented that. . . . But over time I did develop some very good friendships and things worked out well."

In 1983, Greg Pennington received a grant from the Whitney Young Foundation to do a study for ABC. His final report, "The Minority Student Experience in Predominantly White High Schools," noted that there were "remarkable similarities" between what he had experienced as an ABC student in the late 1960s and what he heard from black ABC prep school students he interviewed in the early 1980s. Some of the ABC students he spoke with in the early 1980s experienced racism while at school, and some depicted ugly incidents. Still, he concluded: "The instances of actual physical assault or abuse of a racial nature are few and far between. Ignorance is far more frequent, though experienced just as painfully."[20]

As the schools increased the number of black students enrolled, and as race relations in the country changed in the late 1960s, some black ABC students experienced pressure from other black students *not* to be friends with whites. Thus, *when* an ABC graduate attended prep school affected the extent to which he or she was likely to become close friends with white students. The experiences of Harold Cushenberry and Eric Coleman (the state legislator in Connecticut) underscore the changing situation.

After participating in the first summer program at Dartmouth in 1965, Cushenberry attended the Taft School. When he arrived there were five other blacks at Taft, but the closest friendships he made were with white students. "It's really strange," he muses, "the other black students I'm not in touch with, but I'm in touch with a lot of the white students I went to school with." Upon graduating from Taft in 1968, Cushenberry went to Harvard, where, as he recalls, "I had no white friends at all." Martin Luther King, Jr. had been assassinated, there had been serious racial unrest in many cities, and like many blacks at Harvard, Cushenberry chose to interact primarily with other blacks.[21] Despite his experience at Harvard, some of which he regrets ("I think I missed a great deal of what Harvard had to offer"), Cushenberry remained true to his prep school

20. Gregory Pennington, "The Minority Student Experience in Predominantly White High Schools" (Report for the Whitney M. Young Foundation and A Better Chance, December 1983), 1 and 15.
21. ABC graduate Sylvester Monroe, who was attending Harvard at this time, wrote an article that appeared in the *Saturday Review of Education* ("Guest in a Strange House: A Black at Harvard," February 1973, 45–48) in which he criticized himself, and fellow blacks, for this stance. See chap. 4.

friends, many of whom he still sees regularly. "We were all kids together," he says, "and no matter how old you get you always see each other, not as a successful whomever, but as a skinny twelve- or thirteen-year-old, so that common bond keeps those friendships intact a lot more than later in college or law school."

Cushenberry's insights are consonant with well-known social psychology principles about the way in which common adversity, particularly in initiatory situations, creates close social bonds.[22] His comments also demonstrate how much progress can be made toward racial integration, even starting as late as ages twelve to fifteen, given the right kind of setting.

Eric Coleman, a few years younger than Cushenberry, had a different experience at Pomfret, another Connecticut prep school. Coleman was at Pomfret when Cushenberry was at Harvard, and though he was friendly with some white students, he mostly hung out with his black friends. By that time there were about twenty black students at Pomfret, and most of them, like Eric, were good athletes. "We were either in classes or at basketball or football practice or track or we were in the bus going somewhere to compete at sports. After meals we would end up together."

George Perry's study of ABC students includes some data that support the idea that blacks were more likely to become close friends with whites during the early years of the program than during the late 1960s and early 1970s. In the spring of 1970 and again the fall of 1971, a 127-item attitude questionnaire was administered to 125 black ABC seniors and 134 entering black ABC tenth-graders. One of the questions asked: "Thinking of your five best friends, how many of them are white?" Most respondents included at least one white among their best friends, but there was a revealing difference between the responses of the seniors and those of the sophomores. Only slightly more than half (54 percent) of the sophomores stated that at least one white was among their five best friends, but nearly two-thirds (66 percent) of the seniors' responses revealed at least one white best friend. This difference may indicate that the longer blacks were in prep school, the more likely they were to become friends with whites. It may, however, reflect the development of black pride and

22. The classic research on this topic is summarized in Muzafer Sherif, "Experiments in Group Conflict," *Scientific American*, 1956, *195* (5), 54–58; for a summary of the extensive literature on this topic since that time, see K. L. Dion, "Intergroup Conflict and Intragroup Cohesiveness," in *The Social Psychology of Intergroup Relations*, ed. W. G. Austin and S. Worchel (Monterey, Calif.: Brooks/Cole, 1979) and D. A. Wilder and P. N. Shapiro, "Role of Out-group Cues in Determining Social Identity," *Journal of Personality and Social Psychology*, 1984, *47*, 342–348.

separatism occurring at that time. Most of the seniors tested had entered prep school in 1967 (and some in 1966); the sophomores tested had entered in the fall of 1971. Thus, the differences between these two groups may reflect the changing times more than the impact of the schools between a student's sophomore and senior year.[23]

For the most part, however, Perry's study shows that during the early 1970s, the interracial experiences at the prep schools were perceived by black tenth- and twelfth-graders, and by a "control" group of white prep school students, in more positive than negative terms. Of the eleven items dealing with racial relationships, the following three were most frequently chosen by both the black ABC students and comparison groups of white prep school students as characterizing race relations at their schools: "They learn from each other" (80 percent of the black students agreed, and 72 percent of the whites); "They tolerate each other" (80 percent and 79 percent); and "They treat each other fairly" (64 percent and 82 percent). In contrast, the following three items were the ones least likely to be chosen by both black and white students as characterizing race relations: "They try to put each other down" (20 percent of the black students, 7 percent of the white students); "They avoid each other" (16 percent and 15 percent); and "They fight each other" (9 percent and 2 percent).[24]

Those ABC graduates who recalled feeling pressure from other black students not to be friendly with white students indicated that, for the most part, this bothered them but they did not reject their white friends. Ken Pettis remembers that most of his friends at the Taft School were white, and he "picked up a lot of grief for that from the other black students." Monique Burns recalls that she was the only black freshman when she started at the Concord Academy, and though she was friendly with some of the other black students who were older than she, most of her friends were other freshmen and therefore they were white. "It was very important to me not to be exclusive," she recalls. "I didn't believe in that. I still don't as a human being. I never did. Part of it had to do with me genetically and the fact that I was so fair, that I always felt I had one foot in one race and one foot in the other. I actually had some amateur histo-

23. Perry, "A Better Chance," 23. Perry was not unaware of the difficulties inherent in interpreting these findings. He wrote: "It might have been better to test the same group of students twice. At this point, however, it is necessary to base tentative conclusions on the comparison between sophomores and seniors, acknowledging that there are several problems with this methodology."

24. Ibid., 152–153.

rians in my family—I knew what my family tree was." Monique Burns entered Concord Academy in 1969. Though her views did not change, the amount of pressure she felt as a student at Harvard four years later did. Thus, though this was not a serious issue for her at Concord, it became one when she was in college.

The issue persisted for blacks at prep schools at least into the mid-1970s. In "A Journey from Anacostia to the Elite White World," Gregory Witcher, a black student at Exeter in the mid-1970s, described the following event: "One of my first friends at Exeter was another sophomore named Sterling. He was white. After a Sunday brunch at the Elm Street dining hall, we were walking back to my room in Soule. We were planning a hike along the river through nearby woods to admire the parade of autumn colors. Walking toward us in the opposite direction was a group of black male students. When I waved and said hello I heard one of the fellows say loudly, 'Hey, man, what the hell are you doing with that white boy?'"[25]

Black ABC students who became friends with white prep school classmates were stepping across not only racial boundaries but in almost every case class boundaries as well. Most of the white students were from upper-middle- or upper-class families, and some were from the wealthiest and best-known families in America. Many of those we interviewed had specific memories of their interactions with these especially wealthy students. As we've already seen, one ABC student remembered a "department-store heiress" telling her that her family was paying for half the ABC student's scholarship. The following four recollections indicate that interactions with the extremely rich led to a variety of responses.

After noting that most of his best friends at Hotchkiss were "middle-class whites," Alan Glenn (at the time of our interview a banker with Manufacturers Hanover Trust) described his friendship with a student who was, as he put it, from the "upper crust": "One of my best friends at Hotchkiss was William Clay Ford III, of the Ford family, and in spite of all his money and his background, he treated me as well as anyone at Hotchkiss. We were friends. I can't say that I went out to his house in Michigan or this or that or the next thing. Because of the geographics of it that never happened, but we started out in the ninth grade in the same Latin class and we used to goof around because we had this really old

25. Gregory B. Witcher, "A Journey from Anacostia to the Elite White World," *Washington Post*, January 13, 1980. The article was reprinted in the May 1980 issue of *Independent School*, 31–33.

teacher and she just had some strange nuances about her. She got really upset if you said 'shut up' in class, stuff like that. She would send you up to the dean's office for saying 'shut up' and, you know, a ninth-grader is definitely going to make fun of stuff like that. And then we would always pull pranks that would get her somewhat upset, all because we wanted to disrupt class because we didn't want to be studying Latin."

Sylvester Monroe remembers being confused by what seemed to be contradictory behavior on the part of his wealthy classmates at St. George's. He remembers a particular encounter with a grandson of Averell Harriman: "He was not a good friend of mine, but I knew him. Coming from the South Side [of Chicago] I was into dressing in a certain way and I get there with all these kids with money who didn't give a shit what they look like. One of the things that threw me, I had never ever liked penny loafers. Something that I just never liked. David and these guys would wear them and the soles would wear out and they would put tape on them. I went to David once and I remember saying, 'David, why won't you buy a pair of shoes?' and he said, 'I don't need a pair of shoes.' Very hard for me to understand things like that. The same guy was bragging at that time about having bought a $600 stereo." (Some were less confused by, and more directly critical of, their wealthier classmates' spending habits. As one woman scornfully recalls, "I watched kids spend as much money in a week on junk food as my mother would spend to feed six people.")

Ken Pettis, who, like Sylvester Monroe, was from Chicago, had become a hall monitor by his senior year at Taft, and one of his younger charges was a grandson of Chicago department store magnate Marshall Field. "He was a freshman and the other kids used to really take advantage of this guy. I mean, they would borrow things and never return them, and they would give him endless shit. I didn't like seeing this, and I was just being nice to him. He invited me down to their plantation down in North Carolina. They apparently own a lot of land in North Carolina. . . . I didn't go because I thought I'd feel uncomfortable, even though I'd kind of taken care of him throughout the year."

And in some cases, ABC students established lifelong friendships with wealthy white friends from prominent families. When Michael Shivers, a graduate of St. Paul's and the University of Pennsylvania who was living and working in Winston-Salem at the time of our interview, was asked if he had stayed in touch with his St. Paul friends, he responded: "I just talked on Sunday to Blair Scribner [of the Scribner publishing family]. Blair and I went to St. Paul's together, and we ended up going to Penn together and living across from each other our freshman year, so we've known each other now for twenty years. We keep in touch. We visit one another, we call one another."

Our findings on friendship point up the complexity of race relations in America. Many genuine friendships developed that have persisted through the years. Yet the extent of these friendships depended on the number of black students at the school and the temper of the times. When there were more than a few blacks, there were fewer black-white friendships. Some of this may have been due to a tendency for the black students to stick together because of shared interests and a common avoidance of racism. But there was probably hesitation on the part of whites to encounter more than just a few blacks, a phenomenon analogous to the "tipping" phenomenon in neighborhoods.

SPORTS

In his classic book, *The Nature of Prejudice*, Gordon Allport asserted that prejudice could be reduced when there was "equal status contact between majority and minority groups in the pursuit of common goals." [26] For many newly arriving ABC students, self-conscious about their clothes and unsure about their academic preparation, the nature of much of their early contact with the "majority group" was not "equal status." Furthermore, the intensely demanding and competitive atmosphere at many prep schools made the cooperative "pursuit of common goals" unlikely (in John Knowles's *A Separate Peace*, set at a fictional boarding school called Devon but clearly based on Knowles's alma mater, Exeter, the narrator asserts, "There were few relationships among us at Devon not based on rivalry"). [27]

For many of the male ABC students, participation in athletics became the great leveler. How much money your parents had meant nothing when you stepped into the batter's box or took a jump shot from the key. Not surprisingly, therefore, many of the men recall that they first began to feel they belonged at their schools as a result of their participation in athletics and that ultimately through this participation they developed important friendships.

As those who planned the summer transitional program realized, ABC

26. Gordon W. Allport, *The Nature of Prejudice* (Garden City, N.J.: Doubleday, 1958), 254.
27. John Knowles, *A Separate Peace* (New York: Macmillan, 1959), 36.

students encountered sports in prep school they had never played or even heard of before. For some, especially those who were good athletes, this allowed them the enjoyable opportunity to learn new sports. Bill Lewis, at the time of our interview a vice-president at Morgan Stanley, became so adept at lacrosse at Andover that by his senior year he was captain of the varsity team; he went on to play lacrosse at Harvard for four years (his lacrosse stick leans against a wall in his twentieth-floor midtown Manhattan office, near a large photograph of his Harvard lacrosse team). Ed McPherson, a track star at Andover and at the time of our interview a New York banker with Swissbank Corporation, recalls that a friend of his from Maine had taught him to play hockey, and he, in turn, taught his friend to shoot pool.

Some ABC students were exceptional athletes who would have participated in varsity sports at any secondary school in the country. Many, like lacrosse player Bill Lewis, track star Ed McPherson, or Rhodes Scholar Jesse Spikes, went on to participate in varsity sports at the college level. Others acknowledged that because the competition was not as stiff as it would have been at their public high schools and because their prep schools had teams below the varsity level, they were given an otherwise unavailable chance to participate. Harold Cushenberry's comments are instructive:

> Sports was the way for me to initially show . . . that I belonged. I wasn't and would not have been a great athlete in other places, but I was pretty good at Taft. . . . In the fall I played football and that's when I first began to demonstrate some of my athletic ability. I was pretty good in football. Because of that, it helped break down the social barriers, and I began to be buddies with some of the folks and became co-captain of the lower-mid team and eventually went up to varsity as captain of the varsity football team. And, likewise, in the wintertime, I played basketball and eventually became captain of the basketball team. And I played baseball—I disappointed so many of the people there who [assumed] that because I was black I'd be a great baseball player. And I was not. I was a horrible baseball player. I could never hit a curve ball. But I found another sport which I ended up being fairly good at, which was lacrosse. I ended up playing lacrosse after failing in baseball miserably as a lower-mid. So I played lacrosse the rest of the time.

Black historian C. L. R. James writes in *Beyond a Boundary* that playing cricket at prep school during the First World War—and coming to understand what "wasn't cricket"—taught him what "fairness" was about. He did not, he asserts, learn moral discipline from the Oxford and Cambridge masters at the secondary school he attended in his native Trinidad, Queens Royal College. "Inside the classrooms," he admits, "we lied and cheated without any sense of shame." But on the playing fields things were different. There he learned basic concepts of fairness, of sportsmanship, of generosity, and of subordinating one's personal inclinations for the good of the team. "This code," he claims, "became the moral framework of my existence." [28]

Though their participation in sports may not have provided the ABC students with the moral framework of their existence, it did provide valuable information about their fellow students. Did they play fair? Were they willing to subordinate their inclinations for the good of the team? Were they gracious in defeat? Did they earn respect—as opponents and as teammates? Those who participate in sports, whether at the professional, the varsity, or the "lower-mid" level, often assess such qualities in those with whom they participate. So, in the equal-status context of athletics, black ABC students had the opportunity to gain some particularly valuable insight into their classmates. Some they liked and admired, some they didn't. Some they became friends with, some they did not.

Fred Williams, a 1969 graduate of the Berkshire School, now a law professor at North Carolina Central University, recalls how a shared interest in athletics led to a lifelong friendship with a white classmate from a wealthy Connecticut family: "[I am in touch with] Bill Keeney, who happens to be a carbon copy of me in terms of our interest in sports. He was the other end on the football team. He was the other forward on the basketball team. He was my high jump partner. He was my pole vault partner. He was my friend. He was the only person that I pretty much did everything with, and we had similar interests. We were devilish in the same ways. We had the same kind of let's-get-back-at-the-establishment kind of ideas. I was always invited home with somebody over long weekends, and I started wondering whether anybody would ever come to my home in Durham. . . . He came to stay with me during spring break . . . and he got to feeling comfortable around my friends at my old high school. I see him to this day."

For the women, athletics was less central to their prep school experience, and they were less likely to refer to participation in sports as important to becoming accepted by their peers. They were more likely to ex-

28. C. L. R. James, *Beyond a Boundary* (1963; reprint New York: Pantheon, 1983), 35.

press surprise and satisfaction that they had become proficient in sports they had never heard of before enrolling in prep school. The following comment by Monique Burns was not atypical: "I had not even, until Mt. Holyoke and Concord, really done any sports. I found actually that I was talented and I did very well. I learned to play all these preppy sports, like lacrosse. By the time I was a senior I was captain of that team. Soccer, basketball and all, I was pretty good at that stuff."

POPULARITY AND STUDENT POLITICS

Perry's study found that ABC students felt themselves to be popular. In fact, in response to an item asking, "How popular do you think you are in school this year in comparison with *all* the other students in your grade," black ABC students indicated they felt more popular than did a control group of white students at their schools. (More than one-third of the black respondents felt themselves to be among "the most popular," and less than one-tenth thought themselves to be among "the least popular.")[29]

Not only were black ABC students popular, they were also valued as leaders in dealing with teachers and administrators. In the charged atmosphere of the late 1960s, with its demands for all kinds of freedoms, they could become the central figures in negotiations with a frequently divided faculty and a seemingly intransigent administration. Just such a situation arose at Andover, where an intriguing series of events revealed how black ABC students could be both popular among their peers *and* useful in bringing about institutional change. Ironically, the person they had to confront and defeat was headmaster John Kemper, one of the founders of the ABC program.

As was true at many schools in the late 1960s, the Andover student body challenged the administration to abolish various long-standing rules concerning such things as compulsory chapel and the wearing of coats and ties to dinner. Simultaneously, some faculty were increasingly upset by the length of some students' hair and began calling for restrictions on hair length. According to Andover historian Allis, hair length was a "highly emotional issue that exercised the School community . . . and polarized the Phillips Academy Faculty." After one particularly heated faculty debate on the topic of hair length, headmaster John Kemper declared that he would be "czar" on this matter. Under his policy, if a fac-

29. Perry, "A Better Chance," 133.

ulty member thought a student's hair or sideburns were too long, he would send the student to Kemper, who would make the final decision to trim or not to trim.[30]

Allis presents this episode in a jocular tone, as if to recall how silly things got in the late 1960s. He points out, for example, that one boy with an "impeccable" "page boy hair-cut" was forced to cut his hair and "emerged looking much worse than before."[31] But in actuality, the disputes over hair length, the dress code, and required attendance at chapel reflected a serious challenge to institutional authority. These conflicts revealed a breakdown in confidence and communication between Andover students and Kemper, who had provided leadership at the school for more than two decades. As Allis acknowledges elsewhere in his history of Andover:

> In the 1950's without question the great majority of Andover undergraduates respected John Kemper, even if they did not feel close to him. In the 1960's this relationship began to deteriorate, even before the crises evolving out of student protest late in the decade. . . . He had developed a nervous habit of clearing his throat frequently during his speeches, and the undergraduates, annoyed by this habit, used to clear theirs at the same time. When, after the Surgeon General's report, the School banned smoking completely, he continued to smoke, which angered some students. Most important, he was by training and principle completely opposed to the student life style of the 1960's—the drugs, the long hair, the general sloppiness, the mocking of old institutions and practices.[32]

It was in this atmosphere that the student body of 840 students (40 of whom were black) surprised many people (including the faculty, the administration, the *New York Times,* and, most likely, themselves) by electing blacks as presidents of the sophomore, junior, and senior classes for the 1969–70 academic year. As the *New York Times* breathlessly and historically informed its readers, Andover, "the alma mater of the Lees and Washingtons of Virginia and the Quincys and Lowells of New England, has elected three Negro students from the ghettos of Chicago and Oakland as class presidents for 1969–70."[33]

30. Allis, *Youth from Every Quarter,* 655.
31. Ibid.
32. Ibid., 581.
33. John Leo, "Negroes Elected President of Three Classes at Andover," *New York Times,* June 11, 1969, p. 33.

By electing blacks as class presidents, Andover students had managed to make things much more difficult for the Andover administrators, who were forced to move cautiously to insure that student-administration differences didn't take on racial overtones. Newly elected senior-class president Freddie McClendon preferred wearing a dashiki to a coat and tie, but could wear it only to those classes whose teachers had given special permission. When he asserted that "the administration doesn't understand the white social values imposed by the coat-and-tie regulation," Andover's administration suddenly had a tougher issue on its hands (the accusation of institutional racism) than a simple challenge to the dress code. One student, referred to in the *Times* as an "upper middler" (an eleventh-grader), provided the following political analysis after the election: "There's no doubt in my mind that they elected guys who were going to be militant and get something done about the rules." Another referred to Freddie McClendon (who had a beard) as "the only guy on this campus strong enough to stand up to Kemper." More sardonically, one of the black students commented, "It's ironic that a rich little white boys' school elects three blacks to defend them from a white administration."[34]

Ed McPherson was one of the three Andover students elected class president in 1969. He thinks the *New York Times* account overemphasized the differences between the students and the administration in order to highlight what he called "the us-them conflict" in the country at the time. Each of the three class presidents, he believes, won for different reasons. Still, he acknowledges the element of truth in the claim that students had chosen leadership capable of confronting John Kemper. McPherson remembers the campaign in sharp detail:

> There may have been some cynical students who were voting for Freddie McClendon out of a sense of what Freddie was saying as being anti-administration, and I think, yes, Freddie articulated a point of view that was very true for his class. . . . Freddie was a true radical. . . . The seniors had a real intense us-them attitude, and Freddie's hard-line stance was what the seniors were voting for. . . . Freddie was a musician, straddled five or six different constituencies if you will. The other people who ran against him only had one con-

34. Ibid. Kemper was not happy with this analysis. In a letter to the editor ("Events at Andover," *New York Times,* July 3, 1969, 30) in response to the article, he wrote: "It was no kindness to the three newly elected presidents to put them on the spot of attempting to measure up to the statement that 'some observers think they will speak of demands and confrontations . . . when their numbers are large enough.'"

stituency. It was no surprise he won; he voiced their concerns best.

Tim Black was the eleventh-grade class president. Tim was a musician, a singer; he's a professional musician in California today, very soft-spoken. . . . Freddie and Tim are complete opposites, so certainly the eleventh-grade students weren't voting for Timmie for the same reasons the twelfth-graders were voting for Freddie.

And there I was, also very different from both of them. . . . I didn't even campaign. My class presidency was really a popularity contest, with a lot of guys wanting to show up [my opponent] because [he] was an honor roll student and a very bright guy and a very serious guy. By contrast, I was a much more relaxed guy.

Whether they were voting for McClendon's "hard-line stance," Tim Black's "soft-spoken" qualities, or McPherson's "relaxed" personality, in that spring election of 1969 the Andover students revealed their admiration for and confidence in their black classmates, and, in doing so, they helped bring about some changes that were already in motion. Although Kemper "had always insisted that compulsory chapel would never be abolished while he was Headmaster,"[35] within a year of the election, compulsory chapel had been eliminated; so had rules on hair length, facial hair, and the wearing of jackets and ties to class.

THE IMPORTANCE OF THE HEADMASTER

"As the high priest of the status seminary," write Cookson and Persell, "the head presides over the prep rite of passage, ensuring that the school's program and personnel are committed to the goal of producing an elite cadre of patricians and parvenus."[36] More specific to the focus here, the interviews with ABC graduates demonstrated that who the headmaster or headmistress was, and what kind of leadership he or she provided, could make a major difference in the experience of a young black student trying to survive the prep rite of passage. Francisco Borges provided perhaps the most graphic evidence of the importance of the head. Borges, described by one journalist as "a nattily tailored corporate lawyer who often employs a street fighter's jive-talking demeanor,"[37] has very vivid memories of two different headmasters when he was a student at the Millbrook School. The first he does not recall fondly:

35. Allis, *Youth from Every Quarter*, 660.
36. Cookson and Persell, *Preparing for Power*, 123.
37. Daniel J. Shea, "The Rebuilding of Frank Borges," *Bond-Buyer*, June 1, 1987, 1.

One day the son of a bitch was standing in front of a tree, and he pulled me over and he said, "You know, Frank, you'll never make it in this place." I was, like, maybe I'd just turned fifteen. I was a kid. And this grown man—I was struggling, let me tell you, I was struggling academically. And I was scared shitless because I knew my father. If I flunked out—other kids, if they flunked out, it meant they'd take a yacht trip around the world that summer—I was into an ass whupping if I flunked out. This guy said to me, "Frank, you'll never graduate."

When this headmaster was forced to retire because of physical problems,

they had to find another guy, so they brought in Hank Howard, who had retired years before. He was a peach of a guy. It was my junior year. He was very understanding. . . . This guy, Hank Howard, used to put me in his little fucking Volkswagen bug—he and I and his wife—and he would take Mike Goodwein [another ABC student]— he took the black kids, it was just us because we didn't have parents to come visit us on weekends and take us to go visit colleges. Then Hank used to drive us, personally, and t is guy was in his fucking seventies . . . he would drive us around. He liked Trinity. He thought that that was the place I wanted to be. It's a smaller school, pretty good academically, competitive. He thought I could really excel here. And he came down, he visited with me, we visited the admissions folks. He worked with them on financial aid because, fuck, I couldn't afford to go to school. And that's how I ended up at Trinity.

If you ever talk to anybody who has had anything to do with Milbrook, they'll say Hank Howard was a peach.

Though the headmaster or headmistress often sets the tone for what is accepted, and expected, at a prep school, other administrators and individual teachers can have an enormous impact on students. Doris McMillon, a television newscaster, recalls that if the dean of students at the Cushing Academy had not intervened, she would not have been able to attend college. Her mother wanted her to come home and refused to fill out some financial aid forms. She relented only after the dean of students called her long distance and persuaded her to complete and send in the forms. Similarly, other ABC graduates recall particular interventions, or the more general impact, of various prep school administrators or faculty members.

SOCIAL LIFE

For almost all the ABC graduates we interviewed, their social life was either limited or nonexistent while they were in prep school. One former ABC student summed up the views of many: "Socially I thought it was a retarding experience." Most, especially the older graduates, were at single-sex schools, and one of the few opportunities for contact with the opposite sex was to attend "mixers" with students from other schools. In some cases these were voluntary, and a student who wished to participate would indicate his or her interest by signing a sheet on a bulletin board. In other cases, participation was mandatory. In some instances, the students were matched with dates of the same race; more often they were not. Always, it seems, they were matched by height. At a designated time and place, students would meet their preassigned dates. The pair was supposed to remain together for a meal and a dance (and sometimes for additional activities like a glee club concert or a football game). They were not supposed to ditch their dates, though many did. Their memories of these mixers ranged from Eric Coleman's laconic "I don't remember any pleasant experiences" to Frank Borges's description of them as "torture."

Most ABC students went to at least a few mixers but found them to be anything but relaxing or fun. When possible, they socialized with other black students at other prep schools, especially by attending conferences on issues related to minorities. Alan Glenn recalls that during his first three years at Hotchkiss, before it became coeducational, the mixers were not much fun but the conferences were: "These were basically black parties. They called them conferences because there was the guise of, 'Well, we're having these meetings to discuss minority problems at prep schools,' which we did, but that was the small part. After that came the party, which is why everyone really came."

For other students, the network established during the summer program provided contacts and friends. Bobette Reed Kahn recalls that her boyfriend attended another prep school ten miles down the road; he was a middle-class black student she met because he roomed with a male ABC student she had become friends with during the transitional summer program. Some students relied on their summers and their rare visits back home for any real social life. This, however, was problematic in itself, because for many, the longer they were in prep school, the more difficult it was for them to spend time at home. Their new class and style were beginning to drive a wedge between them and their friends and family.

Going Home

As the ABC students adapted to the regimentation and academic expectations of prep school life, they began to change. How much they were changing became apparent to them when they went home. More than one recounted painful experiences that demonstrated the gap between the two worlds in which they found themselves. Sylvester Monroe, the oldest of seven children, remembers trying to get his entire family to sit down and have a formal meal, with all the silverware in the right places, just as he had learned to dine at St. George's, and being told by one of his sisters, "Why don't you leave that St. George's bullshit at St. George's?"

Monroe learned a lesson from that experience. And he became much more cautious about instructing his family and friends to change their behavior. Instead, like many other ABC students, he tried to lead two separate existences. As he puts it, "I dressed, acted one way in Newport, Rhode Island, and when I went home on vacations, I left all of that in Newport." This seemed to work, and his Chicago buddies, most of whom were members of street gangs, accepted him: "These guys knew me and they sort of looked upon me as a nice guy, kind of a bookworm, a smart guy, nice to have around. They sort of gave me a nickname—'Big Time Vest.' I don't know if they understood that I was saying Newport and not New York or whatever, but they would say, 'Vest. Back from the big time!'"

But even for Big Time Vest, accepted by his old street buddies, there wasn't much left in those Chicago friendships after a few years. He still enjoyed returning to Chicago to see his family, and he felt no animosity toward his old friends, but more and more he found that "we'd talk and sort of reminisce about old times, but when we stopped with the old times there was nothing to talk about."

Some did experience hostility from their friends back home. Alan Glenn clearly remembers that going back to Harlem from Hotchkiss was not easy: "There were definitely animosities from people in my community. A lot of my friends looked at it as [though] I thought I was better than they were and I thought I was trying to be white. They wondered why I had to go away to this fancy school. Harlem was good enough for me before—why isn't it good enough for me now?"

Whether or not they encountered hostility on the streets back home, as time passed they had fewer and fewer things in common with their old friends, and they found themselves feeling lonely when they did go home.

Eric Coleman's comments about returning to his hometown of New Haven while he was a student at Pomfret were not atypical:

> I still identified with my neighborhood in New Haven. The biggest problem for me, I guess, was because there had been so much distance and time placed between me and the friends that I had when I went off to Pomfret. By the time that I would come home for a vacation, they were into different things. Some of them had new girlfriends they would spend most of their time with, so I lost contact with them in that way. Guys that I would consider hanging partners had gotten into trouble and maybe were in correctional institutions. Others of them were working full-time, maybe having dropped out of school. Others were just in a different circle. I had lost contact with many of them so that when I came home for vacation it was usually really a kind of lonely time for me.

As he described these lonely feelings, Coleman focused on the loss of one particularly close friendship. One of his best friends had decided against participating in the ABC program. When Coleman came back, the relationship had changed: "There was a little bit of envy, I think, and a little bit of tension." They remained friends and years later, they attended each other's wedding. But the closeness of the friendship, lost when Coleman went to Pomfret, has never been regained.

The way in which speech can drive a wedge between ABC students and their families and friends emerged in a 1974 interview with an ABC student from Richmond, Virginia, who had graduated from Groton and at the time was an undergraduate at Stanford. In response to the questions, "Did you notice a difference in language? Did they [students at the prep school] pronounce any words differently?" he reported on the effect of his newly acquired "British accent" when he went home:

> Yeah, definitely. The first time I came home I was really, people laughed at me. It wasn't like just the people up North would have a northern accent. It was like a British accent from going where I went to school. That was kind of funny coming home, and my brother and a lot of people would just look at me and say, "What's wrong with you," you know, "Where you been?" The language pronunciation was a little bit different I thought. It was northern Massachusetts and yet it was distinct from a northern accent. I think it was close to a British accent. Well, Groton was designed on a British school called

Eton anyway. Some of the professors had gone to England. It was
more like a proper form of English.[38]

As is true for many teenagers during their high school years, and especially during the stressful first few months away from home, these ABC
students had ambivalent feelings toward their parents. Though many had
talked their parents into letting them participate in the ABC program,
others had been encouraged or even pressured by their parents (Jesse
Spikes referred to his involvement in the program as a "conspiracy" between his mother and his homeroom teacher). Many asked themselves
why their parents had sent them away. Harold Cushenberry recalls
"wondering why my parents could possibly do this to me."
In a painfully honest acknowledgment of her feelings at the time, one
woman described her difficulty in adjusting to the world back home while
she was in prep school:

> I had trouble adjusting to my former home. . . . I went through a
> period when I absolutely hated it, and I was ashamed of my parents.
> That feeling lasted probably until I graduated, until I went to college.
> It was painful. All around me, I saw—we lived in a house, a nice
> house—but all around me I saw burned-out buildings and people sit-
> ting along the streets not doing anything, and graffiti. Physically, it
> was ugly and it was a hopeless situation and I didn't want to be a part
> of it. I didn't want to acknowledge that I had been a part of it. On
> some levels I was angry with my parents for not having—it makes no
> sense and I knew it made no sense at the time—I was angry at them
> for not having been like the parents of my classmates at prep school
> who were well-educated and moneyed and always went off on great
> vacations.
> [My parents] were pretty easygoing about it. I think they were
> hurt, but they took it in stride. I suppose my father was more under-
> standing about it and he would talk to my mother and I would hear
> them talking. He would say, "You know, this must be a shock to her
> system. Give her time and she will come out of it." And eventually I
> would. The adjustment—I would go through adjustment periods. In
> the summer I would go through a four-week adjustment period. It
> was kind of like divers coming up from below or something—if you

38. Interview with John King conducted for G. William Domhoff by research assistant Deborah Samuels, September 1974.

come up too quickly you get the bends. I felt weak and depressed and upset for about a month, and then it sort of passed.[39]

The problem of managing the dual identity of prep school graduate and lower-class black is a difficult one. These people did have to wear masks, and it is not likely that we captured the full depth of their feelings in one interview. We will be returning to this issue at several points in our account. For now, though, it is enough to say that most of those we interviewed seem to have dealt with this problem reasonably well.

Still, for some ABC students it was too difficult to try to live in two worlds. They left school, either because they chose to drop out or because they were asked to leave.

Dropping Out

Homesickness, being needed by the family back home, not feeling accepted or content at their new prep schools, or a combination of those factors led some students to pack their bags and go home. Many students who left prep school of their own volition returned home, attended their local public high schools, graduated, and went on to college. Some of the ABC students we interviewed referred to friends who had dropped out of prep school and later gone on to attend selective colleges and earn higher degrees. For example, Bill Lewis mentioned an Andover friend who had decided to quit Andover and go back home to St. Louis. When he finished high school in St. Louis, he went on to Dartmouth. Similarly, Alan Glenn mentioned a friend who didn't like Hotchkiss, so he went back to Brooklyn, finished high school there, and then went on to the University of Pennsylvania and New York University Law School; he's now a successful New York lawyer. Clearly, for some of those who dropped out of prep school (and the ABC program), leaving did not halt their academic achievement or their upward mobility.

39. In his follow-up study of those who had participated in the summer program at Dartmouth, Alden E. Wessman found that many students became critical of their home neighborhoods during their first few years in the ABC program. In response to a question concerning their feelings about their home neighborhoods, 19 percent gave "moderately critical" responses and 22 percent "extremely critical" responses ("Evaluation of Project ABC [A Better Chance]: An Evaluation of Dartmouth College—Independent Schools Scholarship Program for Disadvantaged High School Students" [Final report, Office of Education, Bureau of Research, April 1969, ERIC Document 031549]; 181).

Other ABC students did not choose to leave their prep schools but were asked to leave, generally for one of two reasons: either their grades were unacceptably low, or they got into trouble of some sort. In the early years of the program, not many students were asked to leave because of poor academic performance. The schools and the program appear to have been committed to helping the ABC students catch up, and when necessary they were willing to give the students time and special assistance to enable them to reach an acceptable level of performance. In some cases, however, students did flunk out of prep school. When this occurred, the students were sometimes given a second chance at another ABC school. In *Mixed Blessings*, an autobiographical account of her search for her biological mother, television newcaster Doris McMillon describes a meeting at the end of her first year at the Concord Academy with David Aloian, the school's headmaster. Aloian, she writes, "was sitting at his desk in his office looking at me kindly, trying to find excuses for my disappointing first-year grades." She goes on:

> I looked at him dully. In my heart, I'd already heard the slamming of all the windows *and* doors. I'd screwed up the biggest break of my entire life. I'd justified Mom's worst estimate of my value. I was desperate, miserable, and furious with myself.
>
> "I feel you may do better in another environment—not a lesser environment," he hastened to add, "simply a different environment. One less rigid," he eyed me speculatively, "and old-world. One with a little more give and take. I think you'll flourish with a bit more of the human touch and with your feet flat to the earth.
>
> "Let me tell you something about Cushing Academy," he settled into a gentle propaganda pose. "Cushing's here in Massachusetts, an excellent school, high honors, select enrollment. Unlike Concord, a coed school. Bette Davis matriculated at Cushing." He grinned slightly, then ran through a roll call of names I knew from the headlines, from the movie page, from the arts as well.
>
> He was offering me an honorable second chance, one I was well aware I hadn't proved I deserved. I snatched it, of course.[40]

Two years later she graduated from Cushing. She now works by day for a United States Information Agency Worldnet news program and an-

40. Doris McMillon with Michele Sherman, *Mixed Blessings: The Dramatic True Story of a Woman's Search for Her Real Mother* (New York: St. Martin's Press, 1985), 81–82.

chors an evening talk show on the Black Entertainment Network. She has also served on the boards of both the Cushing Academy and A Better Chance.

Other students were asked to leave because they could not, or would not, adjust to the many rules, restrictions, and expectations at their prep schools. They were thrown out, often following a lengthy period of rebellion that culminated in a decisive event. Eric Coleman remembers one friend who was asked to leave Pomfret: He "had a bit of temper and I guess he had gotten into a couple of run-ins with some of the students there. He was finally expelled from school because one weekend after he had come back from vacation, I guess he had brought a pint of vodka with him, and he stayed in his room and he drank it and ended up intoxicated and was wandering around doing all sorts of foolish things. I guess as far as the headmaster was concerned, that was the last straw for him."

Some of the stories about friends being thrown out had tragic endings. Alan Glenn spoke of a youngster who entered Hotchkiss with him: "He left Hotchkiss halfway through his tenth-grade year. His life just went downhill after that. He was one of those kinds that they say you can't get the street out of him. He didn't want the street out of him, so even at Hotchkiss he was like a somewhat streety person, always getting into the wrong things. You can't run around at Hotchkiss the way you would at a public school here in New York. There are just too many monitors and too many people who care who aren't going to let you do that. Because of that he left Hotchkiss. . . . Later I found out he was in New York selling drugs, next thing I heard he was in jail for having murdered somebody."

Some former ABC students indicated that those of their friends who were more confrontational in their approach to people and issues were more likely to leave or to be asked to leave. Harold Cushenberry reflected on why some friends left Taft and why he stayed: "Some people's personalities were just very different. They were combative. They weren't as willing as I—I have to be honest with myself—to overlook things that I care about. Look, you can be racist and mumble things under your breath and I'm not going to go out and slug you. Some of those type people just had very difficult, very different experiences. They weren't willing to internalize a lot of the stuff that I internalized and sort of use to motivate myself in other ways. And they fell by the wayside." We suspect that many of the students who fell by the wayside had developed the kind of "oppositional identity" described in the first chapter and earlier in this chapter. We will return to this important issue in the final chapter.

However, two studies of the ABC program indicate that in the early years ABC students were no more—and perhaps less—likely to leave prep school than their non-ABC contemporaries. In his 1969 follow-up study of the eighty-two boys who had participated in the summer transitional program at Dartmouth in 1965, Alden Wessman found that during the four-year period, eight students (about 10 percent) had attended a prep school but then dropped out (another seven had either chosen to leave or been asked to leave by the end of the summer transitional program, before they reached prep school).[41] The second study, performed by George Perry and his colleagues, examined the performance of ABC students from 1964 through 1972. The findings indicated that, overall, the attrition rate for ABC students was about 20 percent (of the 1,640 scheduled to graduate by June 1972, 333 had dropped out). Such attrition compares favorably with the estimated 30-percent attrition rate for non-ABC students in the same schools during that time, a figure they derived from information supplied by five representative ABC schools. Though their estimate of 30 percent seems rather high—at Exeter in the late 1970s it was only 5 percent—clearly the large majority of ABC students, like the large majority of non-ABC students in prep school, did not leave school but stayed to graduate.[42]

At the time the Perry report was written, the attrition figures were on the rise for ABC students. By 1972, the figure had reached 28 percent.

41. Alden E. Wessman, "Scholastic and Psychological Effects of a Compensatory Education Program for Disadvantaged High School Students: Project ABC," in *Educating the Disadvantaged*, ed. Edwin Flaxman (New York: AMS Press, 1971–1972), 272–273.

42. Perry, "A Better Chance," 46. The data on Exeter are based on a 1982 study done at Exeter and cited by Robert Sam Anson in *Best Intentions* (155). Robert Thompson, a black student at Exeter in the late 1960s and early 1970s, and now the minister there, notes that things changed dramatically in the late 1970s. When he was a student at Exeter, almost all the black students stayed and graduated. By the late 1970s, when the summer program had been dropped, and ABC was less effective in its recruiting, Exeter began to see a dramatic rise in the attrition rate for blacks.

However, a report that Exeter provided to us, prepared by Verna C. Mayo, adviser to minority students, dated May 19, 1987, and titled "Drop-Out Report of Black Students from 1978–Present," indicated a different pattern. Though the frequency with which blacks withdrew or were asked to leave was higher than the frequency for the total student body, the figures were lower for blacks and higher for whites than Anson reports. The annual drop-out rate for blacks, 1979–85, ranged from as high as 19 percent (1979–80) to as low as 4 percent (1982–83). The figures for the total student body ranged from as high as 8 percent (1978–79) to as low as 4.5 percent (1984–85).

Differences within subgroups of ABC students also began to emerge: females were less likely to drop out than were males; Southern students were less likely to drop out than were students from other parts of the country; white and native American ABC students were more likely to drop out than were black or Puerto Rican students; and students whose parents were together and employed were less likely to drop out than were students who were from broken homes or whose parents were on welfare.[43]

In our attempt to understand what the prep school experience meant to black ABC students in the 1960s and early 1970s, we must keep in mind that even though ABC students may have been under greater strain than other students in the prep school crucible, they were apparently no more likely than their peers to leave in the early years of the program. Although a small but increasing number were leaving prep schools (and the ABC program) for a variety of reasons, most completed prep school and, as we will see, most went on to college.

In his book about Edmund Perry, the ABC student who was killed while mugging a plainclothes white policeman just after he graduated with honors from Exeter, Anson muses: "Other young people had experienced racism, gone to places like Exeter, and lived in two different worlds, and the overwhelming majority of them had survived, their lives and dignity intact."[44] Our findings, based on interviews with ABC graduates and the two studies cited above, support Anson's claim. ABC students no doubt paid a great psychological price at the time for their success, but most of them have done quite well in their adult lives.

The Black ABC Prep School Graduate

Those black ABC students who survived the prep school crucible were not the same people when they graduated that they had been when they

43. Perry, "A Better Chance," 72.
44. Anson, *Best Intentions*, 198. In May 1987 an excerpt from Anson's book appeared in *New York* magazine. The excerpt elicited a spate of letters, including some chastising Anson for not sufficiently emphasizing the many ABC graduates who had faced the same dilemmas as Edmund Perry but had overcome them. As one writer put it, "They encountered some of the same obstacles that Perry did, but these things did not prevent them from moving ahead and achieving their goals" (Henry P. MacConnell, *New York*, June 8, 1987, 8). Sylvester Monroe and his coauthors assert in their book,

arrived. They were not only two, three, or sometimes four years older, and the recipients of excellent secondary school educations. Most had adopted the styles that prevailed in their schools; they dressed like prep school students, they liked the music prep school students liked, and they spoke like prep school students. They bear witness to how rapidly the much-vaunted upper-class style can be acquired. The pressure some felt to change their style when they moved from the prep school world to their world at home caused anxiety; for others, this shift simply resulted in lonely times at home.

Wessman's follow-up study of the males who participated in the 1965 Dartmouth summer program is helpful in considering some of the changes experienced while in prep school. He interviewed and administered a battery of tests to almost all of the eighty-two boys who began the 1965 transitional program. In addition, he analyzed data for a subsample of twenty-three ABC students and twenty-three students in a control group consisting of students who had stayed at their local high schools but were matched with the twenty-three ABC students by race, age, and IQ. He reports that about half of the ABC students interviewed said they had "changed a great deal," mostly in positive ways. The students said they felt more academically competent, more socially aware, more at ease socially, more self-aware, more politically aware, more tolerant, and more articulate.

About one-fourth of the ABC students interviewed also reported feeling greater "tension and anxiety" than when they had arrived. This finding was supported by the data from one of the tests Wessman administered, the Cattell High School Personality Questionnaire (HSPQ). On the HSPQ, students in the ABC subgroup showed increases on all the measures related to anxiety, including measures of "emotionality," "reactivity to threat," "apprehensiveness and worry," and "tension and drive." The students in the control group did not show increases on any of these measures. Interestingly and revealingly, the same ABC students who showed themselves to be more anxious also demonstrated a significant increase on a 10-item scale measuring "casualness"—a testimony perhaps to the pressures at prep school to be, or appear to be, casual.

Wessman also administered the California Personality Inventory (CPI) to all of the ABC students (but not to the control group) and found that

Brothers, that "the great majority of ABC youngsters from the ghettos, the barrios, the reservations, and the white backwaters of poverty in America . . . made it" (280).

their scores had increased significantly on a number of scales. They scored higher on capacity for status (a scale assessing the personality attributes that underlie and contribute to status), social presence, self-acceptance, tolerance, achievement via independence, and flexibility. (They also scored lower on the socialization, self-control, and achievement via conformance scales; lower scores on these scales might be expected of adolescents in the late 1960s.)[45]

When we asked ABC graduates how they had changed as a result of attending prep schools, two responses were prominent. Many said they had become more independent. And many became more aware of the possibilities open to them. Alan Glenn put it directly: "I got to see the other side of the fence. I got to see the jet set, the high flyers, the people that make this country run. I was exposed to a lot of different things. I was exposed to a part of society that, if I had not gone to Hotchkiss, I may have never been exposed to."

Although our interviewees revealed many painful examples of the racism they endured and admitted to much tension or loneliness when they returned home, these negative feelings were far less extensive than we had expected. By contrast, we were surprised by the degree to which the graduates looked back on their prep school days with fondness. They may have felt differently while they were going through the experience itself, but for the most part their memories of their initiation into the elite world of private education form a very positive part of their present outlooks and personalities. The question naturally arises whether they really benefited from their experiences in prep school, but all available indications suggest that they did, contrary to what many skeptics might assume. Wessman's follow-up study showing that they gained in self-confidence and felt more at ease socially and more socially and politically aware corresponds to their responses to our questions and to our impressions of them as well.

For a time we worried that we were not being sensitive enough to the difficulties these young people faced and still face. Then we decided we were being overly sensitive. We do not overlook those who dropped out or were hurt by the experience, but these individuals were no more numerous among ABC students than among the privileged white students. Prep school, after all, is a crucible for power for all the students. Those who do not take our findings at face value are not giving these black stu-

45. Wessman, "Scholastic and Psychological Effects," 276.

dents credit for seizing a great opportunity, making the best of it, and showing resiliency in negotiating between home and prep school identities.

As they headed off to college, then, the world was opening up for these black prep school graduates and offering them new choices: where to go to college, what subjects to study, what careers to pursue, and what travels to undertake. Leaving prep school and entering college in the late 1960s or early 1970s, they could not have had better timing.

4

Black ABC Students
in College

Before World War II the graduates of the country's most prestigious prep schools had a virtual guarantee that the Ivy League college of their choice would accept them. Some prep schools were known to have special relationships with specific colleges. The six boarding schools many consider the most socially exclusive, often collectively referred to as "St. Grottlesex" (Groton, St. Mark's, St. Paul's, St. George's, Kent, and Middlesex) served as strong "feeders" to Harvard. Choate and Hotchkiss had special ties to nearby Yale. Lawrenceville and Hill were closely linked with Princeton.[1] In his book on longtime Deerfield headmaster Frank Boyden, John McPhee provides a glimpse of the special relationship Deerfield had with Princeton: "Until the early nineteen-sixties, the headmaster made an annual visit to the admissions office at Princeton, where he would be told what Deerfield boys Princeton was about to accept. If the headmaster expressed strong approval of other Deerfield boys whom Princeton had decided to reject, Princeton would change its mind."[2]

World War II marked the beginning of a gradual decline in prep school admissions to Ivy League colleges. For example, during the two decades

1. Jerome Karabel, "Status-Group Struggle, Organizational Interests, and the Limits of Institutional Autonomy: The Transformation of Harvard, Yale, and Princeton, 1918–1940," *Theory and Society*, January 1984, 13 (1), 1–40.
2. John McPhee, *The Headmaster: Frank L. Boyden, of Deerfield* (New York: Farrar, Straus and Giroux, 1966), 69.

prior to the war, two-thirds of the graduates of twelve top prep schools attended Harvard, Yale, or Princeton, but by 1973, only 21 percent of the graduates of the twelve prep schools attended these three universities. By the early 1980s, "only" 34 percent of the incoming freshmen at Harvard and 40 percent at Yale and Princeton were from prep schools.[3]

It remains, however, a distinct advantage for an applicant to an Ivy League school to attend an elite prep school. Two studies have shown that students from the best private secondary schools continue to have an advantage over public school graduates when it comes to admission to Harvard. In one of these studies, David Karen, a doctoral student in sociology at Harvard, noted that the Harvard admission staff places applications from certain boarding schools in special colored folders to set them apart from other applications. Karen found that applicants from these schools were more likely to be accepted for admission, even when he controlled for parental background, grades, SAT (Scholastic Aptitude Test) scores, and other characteristics.[4] Persell and Cookson, drawing on data gathered in 1982 and 1983 from more than a thousand seniors at elite schools, demonstrate quite clearly that such an advantage exists throughout the Ivy League. Comparing the rates of admissions to Ivy League schools for applicants from Baltzell's list of the top sixteen boarding schools (the "select sixteen") with rates for "other leading boarding schools" and a national group of applicants, Persell and Cookson found the acceptance rate at each of the Ivy League schools highest for the select sixteen boarding school applicants.[5] Because of the extensive evidence that attending a prestigious college is related to subsequent occupational success, Cookson and Persell refer to attending an elite prep school as a "booster shot" for success.[6]

3. Peter W. Cookson, Jr., and Caroline Hodges Persell, *Preparing for Power: America's Elite Boarding Schools* (New York: Basic Books, 1985), 171–172.
4. David Karen, "Who Gets into Harvard? Selection and Exclusion" (Ph.D. diss., Harvard University, 1985). The second study was by Robert Klitgaard, *Choosing Elites* (New York: Basic Books, 1985), table 2.2. Both are cited in Caroline Hodges Persell and Peter W. Cookson, Jr., "Chartering and Bartering: Elite Education and Social Reproduction," *Social Problems*, 1985, *33* (2), 116.
5. Persell and Cookson, "Chartering and Bartering," 119–121.
6. Cookson and Persell, *Preparing for Power*, 198. The following studies demonstrate the advantages to one's career of having attended an elite prep school: George Pierson, *The Education of American Leaders* (New York: Praeger, 1969); Vincent Tinto, "College Origin and Patterns of Status Attainment," *Sociology of Work and Occupations*, 1980, *7*, 457–486; Michael Useem and Jerome Karabel, "Educational Pathways

Getting In

Early in their senior year, ABC students, like other seniors at their schools, began to prepare to apply to college. All the seniors at elite prep schools had the advantage of highly professionalized college advisory programs.[7] Due to the intense competition to get into the top colleges, the schools had developed elaborate systems of instructing students in how to write effective applications and of training prep school staff in how to recommend them in the best possible terms. Almost all the graduates went on to college. The goal was to get them into the best colleges.

The question that faced ABC students graduating in the late 1960s and early 1970s, therefore, was not whether to go to college, but where to go. Indeed, one of the more remarkable statistics describing the progress of ABC students is that 99 percent of the 1,011 students who had graduated from independent schools by June of 1971 had entered college by 1972. (Ninety-four percent of all students who had *entered* the ABC program, including those who dropped out of the program, had started college.) These figures compare quite favorably with the attendance rates for various other groups. At that time, for example, between 55 percent and 60 percent of all high school graduates entered college, as did slightly fewer than half the students who enrolled in the Upward Bound program. The most revealing comparison, however, is with a "control" group of students who had applied for admission to the ABC program in 1967 but could not be placed because of the cutback in federal funding ABC experienced that year. As part of his extensive evaluation of the ABC program performed in 1972, George Perry matched forty-seven ABC applicants for whom there had not been sufficient funds with forty-seven students who participated in the program "on the basis of academic ability and family background." Of the forty-seven students who had returned to their local high schools, twenty-nine (62 percent) had entered college. In contrast, of the forty-seven ABC students, eight had dropped out of the program and returned to their high schools, and five of these eight entered college. All thirty-nine who had graduated from ABC schools had entered college. Therefore, forty-four of the forty-seven ABC students (94 percent) had entered college. These differences provide clear evidence

through Top Corporate Management: Patterns of Stratification within Companies and Differences among Companies" (Paper presented at the annual meeting of the American Sociological Association, San Antonio, Texas, August 1984).

7. Cookson and Persell, *Preparing for Power*, 177–178.

that the program benefited its students; far too many talented students at public high schools did not continue on to college.[8]

As has been discussed, by the time these early graduates of the ABC program entered the college market, it was more difficult than it had been in earlier decades for graduates of elite prep schools to get into the colleges of their choice. They did, however, have the advantage of another change in the pattern of admission to prestigious colleges and universities: by that time these schools were actively seeking black students. A report by a staff member of the College Entrance Examination Board on the enrollment pattern of blacks in New England in 1965–66 had revealed the embarrassing finding that of all students enrolled in New England colleges, only sixty-nine one hundredths of one percent (0.69 percent) were black. "It is rather clear," the report concluded, "that as far as the main body of American Negroes is concerned, it would not matter at all if New England colleges and universities closed their doors tomorrow."[9] With that finding and the broader pressures stemming from the civil rights era, the battle for black enrollment was on when the first ABC students were applying to college. In an article on college admissions in the *Saturday Review* in 1969, John C. Hoy, then dean for special academic affairs at Wesleyan University, wrote that "the question 'How many blacks will you have in September?' replaced earlier queries concerning athletes, National Merit Scholars, and Scholastic Aptitude Test medians." The search for black students was, according to Hoy, "the fiercest competition for any group of students in the history of American higher education."[10]

But, Hoy went on to write, "the simple fact is that students who even come close to former levels of academic expectations are few." This, then, was the dilemma faced by admissions officers in the late 1960s: how to find black students who could meet the academic expectations of the institution. Not surprisingly, ABC students were much sought after. If they could handle the work at the elite prep schools, which were known to be academically demanding, and if they could withstand the social pressures of the prep school environments (environments not unlike those at many of these colleges), then they were particularly good bets to

8. George Perry, "A Better Chance: Evaluation of Student Attitudes and Academic Performance, 1964–1972" (Study funded by the Alfred P. Sloan Foundation, the Henry Luce Foundation, and the New York Community Trust, March 1973, ERIC Document 075556), 100–101.

9. Cited in John C. Hoy, "The Price of Diversity," *Saturday Review*, February 15, 1969, 96.

10. Ibid., 96.

TABLE 2

Colleges Most Frequently Attended by ABC Graduates

Through 1972		Through 1981	
Harvard	54	Harvard	113
Dartmouth	51	Dartmouth	107
Univ. of Penn.	40	Tufts	103
Tufts	36	Univ. of Penn.	92
Carleton	32	Brown	74
Williams	28	Wesleyan	70
Yale	26	Carleton	65
Brown	24	Williams	63
Stanford	22	Northeastern	59
Columbia	21	Yale	56
Wesleyan	21	Stanford	53
Oberlin	20	Boston Univ.	50
Northeastern	19	Princeton	49
Cornell	17	Oberlin	49
Trinity	16	Cornell	48

succeed in college. Therefore, black ABC students graduating from their prep schools in the late 1960s were in a doubly advantageous position: they had attended a prep school (a booster shot in itself), and they were black at a time when the colleges were competing intensely for black students.[11]

Not surprisingly, then, not only did the early graduates of the ABC program attend college, but they went to very good colleges and universities. Table 2 lists the fifteen schools most frequently attended by ABC graduates cumulatively through 1972 and through 1981. The list includes many elite colleges and universities, including all eight of the top Ivy League schools (Princeton was not on the 1972 list, but by 1981, it was among the top fifteen; Columbia was on the list in 1972 but had dropped off by 1981).

11. Cookson and Persell, *Preparing for Power,* 186–188, find evidence that this double advantage persisted into the early 1980s, especially for those students with high SATs. In a study that controlled for socioeconomic status and for SAT scores, they found that an even higher percentage (89 percent) of those from the lower socioeco-

The value of attending elite secondary schools is perhaps most dramatically reflected in the patterns of college attendance that emerged in Perry's comparison between the forty-seven ABC students and the forty-seven students who would have participated in the program if funding had been adequate. Whereas ten of the ABC students attended Ivy League schools (with five going to Harvard), and many others attended such highly selective schools as Carleton, Middlebury, Oberlin, Tufts, and Wesleyan, only one of the students in the control group attended an Ivy League school (Cornell), and only a few of the others attended highly selective schools.[12]

Many of the ABC graduates interviewed for this book attended the most prestigious colleges and universities. Given the competition for black students at the time, many had been accepted by four or five Ivy League schools. How did they decide which school to attend? Some simply chose the school they thought was the most prestigious. As Monique Burns said in explaining why she decided to attend Harvard rather than Yale or Brown, where she had also been accepted: "I liked Cambridge—also, it's hard to say no to them."

Others chose a particular school because friends had gone there and recommended it, or because they believed it to be particularly strong in a field in which they were interested. Ken Pettis, for example, explains why he chose Brown over a host of other schools that accepted him:

> At the time I was going into the college application process, based on the previous experiences I had had at Taft, I thought I might want to be an engineer, and one of the other black students who had left Taft a couple of years before me had gone to Brown. . . . He would come back from time to time and he had nothing but good things to say about Brown. I through research found out that Brown had a very good engineering department. . . . It was an Ivy League school, and I decided Brown was going to be my first choice. I also applied to every other Ivy League school except for Columbia and one of the other ones, maybe Cornell. Then I also applied to the University of Illinois as a fallback—everybody had to have a fallback. And I also applied to Wesleyan because this woman I knew had applied there. I got into every school I applied to except the University of Pennsylvania.

nomic third of their sample were accepted to the most highly selective colleges than from the top third (83 percent) or the middle third (85 percent).

12. Perry, "A Better Chance," 106.

For some, geographic location was a key factor. Eric Coleman explained his decision to attend Columbia in the following way:

When I was coming out of Pomfret, I had gotten accepted to every school I had applied to—Yale, Dartmouth, NYU, Columbia, Brown, Boston University, Northeastern, University of Connecticut—and my choices came down to Yale and Columbia. I chose Columbia because I didn't really want to go back to New Haven to go to college. I had heard so much about New York City in terms of it being an exciting place to be that I thought it would be a good opportunity to experience New York City. Columbia's reputation as a school was fairly good at that time, and it was an Ivy League school, so I didn't think I would be losing much by going there rather than going to Yale, so I went to Columbia.

Cher Lewis also chose to attend college in New York City, though she made her decision later than most applicants, much more spontaneously, and against the advice of both her parents and her prep school guidance counselor:

I applied to Skidmore, Goucher, Smith (even though I was told I wouldn't get in) and I got into all of the schools I applied to, mainly because my timing was wonderful, I mean with the civil rights movement and the quotas . . . I was applying in 1968. In every place I got scholarships. Then, in April, I came to New York with a friend. We were allowed to sign out for a weekend if someone's parents promised that they would watch over us. I was just totally fascinated and said that this is where I want to come. I had never been to New York. We were down in the Village. I went into NYU, I applied—they accepted me on the spot and gave me a full scholarship. And everyone tried to talk me out of it (at that time, no one from Abbott went to NYU), but I was so excited about being in New York. My parents were heartbroken and thought I was going to be killed.

Some of the southern students returned to the South. Greg Googer, who was from Atlanta, decided to attend Vanderbilt. In addition to his wish to be able to see his family more frequently, his decision was directly tied to his eventual plan to live and work in Atlanta: "I knew that if I wanted to work in Atlanta, there was a cultural tie that I had to make. Atlanta's not one of those types that accepts you readily if you're from the North or have those northern tendencies about you."

But to other ABC students from the South, after having been up

North, going back home seemed risky. During his senior year at the Taft School, Harold Cushenberry, a native of Henderson, North Carolina, was the first black to win a Morehead Scholarship to the University of North Carolina. The much sought-after Morehead pays for all a student's expenses, and since the extent of the financial aid offered by the various colleges was also a consideration for ABC students in deciding which school to attend, Cushenberry was tempted. He visited the University of North Carolina for a weekend, along with all the other Morehead recipients. "My parents," he recalls, "were tickled to death." One of the events of the weekend was a group sing-along. Cushenberry laughs at the memory of the sing-along: "They sang 'Old Black Joe.' Just blatant insensitivity. 'Old Black Joe.' And I'm sitting there, and I said to myself, 'No, it's not time yet. Maybe later.'" So Cushenberry decided not to return to the South. Instead he settled for Harvard, where he had also been accepted with a scholarship, though it was "nowhere near the type of ride the Morehead is."

But not all the students who were accepted ended up going to college. The experiences of one of those who didn't, Christine Dozier, reveal the problems that could arise for ABC students.

Christine Dozier

Christine Dozier—then Christine Harley—grew up in a housing project in Washington, D.C. When she was in the ninth grade, she was recruited to participate in the ABC program. With her parents' encouragement, she decided to leave her close-knit family and familiar neighborhood to spend her high school years at the Abbott School in Andover, Massachusetts. In our interview in downtown Washington, where she now works for the National Science Foundation, she remembered the struggle she experienced as one of four black students at Abbott. The struggle was not academic; she did quite well as a student. Rather, she found living at Abbott to be a frustrating and at times an infuriating experience. Looking back now, she attributes some of her frustration and anger to her own personality and temperament. As she put it: "I've always been somewhat of a rebel, and that rebellious spirit that I showed there got me into a lot of trouble. I was considered a person who was not willing to conform to get along. I said what needed to be said and I did what needed to be done."

In her view, ABC did nothing to prepare the prep schools for the arrival of black students. Though the program provided an orientation for students, there was none for the schools. And the schools, she thinks, very much needed better preparation for the arrival of young blacks from economically underprivileged environments. As a result, she thinks that "they left a lot of scars on these students." She herself emerged from her experience at Abbott "with a lot of resentment" and so unhappy with that academic environment that she never earned a college degree, a decision that "has haunted me in later life."

What upset her most was the assumption on the part of the people at Abbott that culturally she came with nothing of value and that, therefore, the purpose of the experience was to teach her to be like other Abbott girls. "I realized once I got there that was the basic factor that separated me from them: they had and I was perceived to have not. And it was like they were doing me a favor by allowing me to participate in this cultural awakening. They were opening doors to me that I may never have had opened to me had I not gone there. I had gone to museums before I went to Abbott. I had gone to concerts before. I had read books before. . . . The door that you opened to me was the credibility that on my academic record it was going to say that I attended this school, and that gave me some credence. I couldn't get them to understand that the person who came to Abbott was not a person who was there to be molded, but was a person who was there to learn, and to teach, because I thought I had a lot they could learn from me." The institutional racism Dozier describes is perhaps so encompassing as to be called "cultural racism." The experiences and cultures of those not in the dominant majority are seen as irrelevant.

Though highly critical of Abbott, she stayed and she did well. (Why? "Fear of the behind-whipping I'd get from my parents.") When it came time to apply to college, she was ready to be closer to home, so she applied to Goucher and to American University. She was accepted with full scholarships at both; she decided to attend American University so that she could be in Washington. But during the summer between her senior year of prep school and her freshman year of college, she decided she needed a break. She had a job with American Airlines that she liked, and they were glad to have her stay. American University assured her that her scholarship would be waiting for her a year later, but said that they could not hold it longer than that.

A year later, however, her boyfriend of many years had been drafted and was headed for Vietnam. They decided to marry, had a baby, and Christine never used her scholarship to American University. She has since taken college courses here and there, but she has never completed a college degree. Her unhappy experience at Abbott was certainly not the only factor in her not going to college, but in her view, it was a significant contributing factor.

Chris Dozier was strong academically and self-confident in her interpersonal relationships. Other ABC students were not so strong academically, and many lacked the self-confidence that helped Chris Dozier survive. For them the prep school crucible was an often unbearably painful experience. When senior year rolled around and they, unlike so many of their ABC friends, received rejection letters from colleges, the damage to self-esteem could be considerable. Eric Coleman mentioned a friend at Pomfret who he felt had been damaged by the experience of attending that prep school: "One of my good friends probably developed an inferiority complex as a result of being there. He wasn't a great student. He was a hell of an athlete, and I'm sure he got a great deal of gratification out of what he did as an athlete. . . . But most of his classmates probably looked down on him because he didn't do well academically as a student. I think around the time that it came for the members of our class to start receiving acceptances to colleges, it really began to take its toll on him. He wasn't encouraged to apply to the best schools, and even those that he did apply to were either slow in response or when they did respond the results were negative. I think that was the icing on the cake as far as damage to his self-esteem was concerned."

Even though almost all ABC graduates did attend college, some did not, and others may have done so, as Chris Dozier puts it, with "a lot of scars."

Roommates and Friends

As they headed off to college, most ABC students again faced the challenge of living with unknown roommates. Most frequently the colleges matched ABC students with other incoming freshmen, some white and some black. When Jennifer Casey Pierre arrived as a freshman at Carnegie Mellon, she found that she had been assigned to room with a black woman from Pittsburgh (they remain good friends to this day). Ken Pettis's freshman-year roommate at Brown was a white Exeter graduate: "It was an assignment based, supposedly, on interests and background and things like that. Bob and I, as it turned out, had a lot in common, but there is nothing they could have told from an application. We had both gone to prep school and that was about it." The assignment worked out well: though they didn't room together the following year, they did become good friends and stayed in touch after graduating from Brown.

Although Pettis switched from his white Exeter roommate to another white roommate who had also attended Taft, the more frequent pattern was to switch from white roommates to black ones (or, when possible, to single rooms). Frank Borges's experience was not unusual. During his freshman year at Trinity, Borges was the only black in a suite of four males. During the next three years he roomed with blacks. Still, he remained good friends with those he had roomed with freshman year: "Callahan and I played football together, and so we were good friends, and Browse and I were good friends. I socialized with a whole group of folks."

Not only did most of the ABC graduates we interviewed socialize with whites, but many developed close friendships. In some cases, they have maintained these friendships. Alan Glenn described his relationship with a friend from Brown in the following way: "One of my friends is a white guy from Brown. I know him, he knows my family, I know his family. When we have functions, he comes to them; when his family has functions, I go to them. It's a friendship. His family accepts me as Alan Glenn a person, not Alan Glenn, Fred's black friend, and my family accepts him as Fred Cooper, Alan's friend, not Alan's white friend."

In a few cases, those we interviewed said that most of their college friends were white. For example, Barry Greene, at the time of our interview a vice-president with F & M Bank, graduated from the Peddie School and returned to his hometown of Richmond, Virginia, to enroll at the University of Richmond. He was one of very few black students at the school. After some of his friends encouraged him to join Zeta Beta Tau, a Jewish fraternity, he did so. Many of his closest college friends were southern white Jews. As he puts it: "A black Catholic at a southern Baptist school in a Jewish fraternity. It was kind of funny. I enjoyed it."

After graduating from Andover, Greg Googer found that most of his friends at Vanderbilt were not only white but graduates of prep schools. He described his college friends, and the ease with which they recognized their shared prep school backgrounds, in the following way: "The majority of my closest friends were from prep schools—day schools or boarding-school-type situations. Those were my closest friends. . . . The year I attended, there were five of us, I think, from Andover (myself the only black), a bunch of kids from Choate, Deerfield, a bunch of girls' schools out of Virginia like Madeira, schools of that nature. We all knew each other. We could identify each other from just walking around. Or we would hear that this person went to that school and go up and say 'Do you know . . . ?' and play the name game."

He remembered identifying one student as a prep school graduate and even being able to decipher which school he had attended: "I walked up to him and said 'I bet you went to a prep school.' He said, 'Yeah.' I said, 'I bet you went to Lawrenceville.' He said, 'How did you know that?' I said, 'You look like a Lawrenceville prep.' You know, he had a pink shirt on and had khakis on, and long blondish gold hair, and I don't know why, but that seemed to be the uniform of the day at Lawrenceville. He said, 'Well, you're right, I did. I did go to prep school and I did go to Lawrenceville.' That guy and I became very good friends after that."

However, developing and maintaining friendships with white students was not always easy. As was the case for some black students in prep school, many black students in college felt intense pressure from their black friends not to associate with white students. Cher Lewis describes the dilemma she faced when she arrived at NYU in the fall of 1968: "I had a white Jewish roommate who was a real New Yorker, raised in Manhattan. To me she was Miss Savvy, a sophisticate, whom I really adored and thought was wonderful. My resident fellow, I wish I could remember her last name, but her first name was Martha, was totally black power—you know, you shouldn't even speak to white people. In our dormitory at one point a line was painted down the middle of the floor; blacks were to walk on one side. It was very difficult because I had both black and white friends."

Cher Lewis resisted the racial polarization she found at college. Some accepted or endorsed it. Following Sylvester Monroe's freshman year at Harvard, when he had roomed with a white friend from St. George's School, he roomed only with blacks. "After freshman year," he said in our interview, "I led a completely black existence." In his senior year, as he was about to graduate, he wrote "Guest in a Strange House: A Black at Harvard," an article that was published in the *Saturday Review of Education*. In this article, he described the extent of his self-imposed isolation:

> In the spring of my freshman year, during a humanities lecture, I suddenly found myself wondering what possible connection there could be between *Beowulf* (the subject of the lecture) and any solution to the problems of black people in America. Quickly I decided there was none, walked out of the lecture hall, and stopped attending the course. In the same way I canceled my participation in many other black-white activities that seemed to me of no particular value

in preparing to help better the plight of all the black people I'd left back home in Chicago. I stopped eating at mixed dining-hall tables in order to avoid going through the empty motions of talking to white students. I stopped taking courses that weren't taught entirely in lectures, because I didn't want to talk with white teaching fellows.[13]

By his senior year, however, Monroe had come to suspect that some of his actions may have stemmed from insecurity and fear. In that same article, he included comments about black students at Harvard that, he recalled twenty years later, were "very unpopular" with his friends:

But the blame does not belong only to the whites. Blacks have been equally complacent about their own responsibilities as students. More and more young blacks who come here are becoming much too comfortable behind a superficial shield of black solidarity. Somehow they are blinded, it seems, by the small amount of effort it takes to isolate oneself from almost everything that isn't particularly appealing. In essence, too many blacks simply misuse the ideological strength of black solidarity as a kind of cover to dupe the white community into believing that behind their united front of blackness they are mature, self-confident, and functioning black individuals who know exactly what they want and how they will get it. But what I see and hear instead are insecure and frightened young black men and women.

He concluded the article with a painfully honest statement about his own insecurity and confusion: "Quite frankly, I feel very inadequate about my past three years at Harvard, which were lived in an almost totally isolated black vacuum. To be sure, I am thoroughly confused."[14]

Sylvester Monroe was not the only one of those we interviewed who sequestered himself within the black student community during his college years. Most, however, indicated that they resisted the pressure to do so. A number of those we interviewed recalled their refusal to eat all their meals at the all-black tables in the dining hall. Ken Pettis, for example, recalled: "I didn't always eat at the black table, and some people couldn't deal with that. I've always approached that as it's their problem, not mine."

Some reacted angrily to the pressure. Monique Burns, who entered

13. Sylvester Monroe, "Guest in a Strange House: A Black at Harvard," *Saturday Review of Education*, February 1973, 47.
14. Ibid., 48.

Harvard at about the time Sylvester Monroe was graduating, said she too felt the pressure to associate only with blacks:

I *would not* accept that pressure. I refused to. I actively refused to. The reason being, I had some friends from prep school who were white who had come to Harvard, and I was not going to stop speaking to them. I mean, that's absurd. As a human being, that was unacceptable to me. I was asked why I didn't come to sit at the black table and basically it was that if it were the green table or if it were the newspaper table I wouldn't have sat at it every night. I wanted to have the freedom to sit where I wanted. Sometimes I sat with other black students, sometimes I sat with white students, and sometimes I sat with mixtures of them. I hated this idea of sitting at the black table.

Also what angered me was what I saw as hypocrisy, because the students who were sitting at the black table, for the most part, and shouting "black power" and "we're not getting our rights," were actually black students who did not come through ABC but who were of upper-middle-class backgrounds, whose fathers were doctors, lawyers, and professors, and who lived in Scarsdale and other wealthy suburbs. As you know, there are black families of this type. They had not seen anything like what I had seen, so I thought to hell with this hypocrisy, I'll sit where I damn well please. That created some difficult moments as a freshman for me. As time went on I got to know other black students, but on my own terms, and because I liked something in them or in their character or they were friendly or because I dated them—but not because I "had to" or because they were black.

Jeffrey Palmer, now the president of a printing company in Chicago, was the first black to attend the Kimball Union Academy in more than sixty years (a black had graduated in 1903).[15] In our interview with him, he made it clear that he was not about to yield to pressures from either blacks or whites concerning who his friends should be when he got to Yale: "I had never succumbed to any pressures from anybody about anything, so the last thing somebody was going to do was to tell me who I could be friends with. And I have always had friends from every hue and complexion of life that there is, so nobody would even mention that to me. They would probably have had a fight on their hands if they did."

15. "Alumni Achievers' Award," *Kimball Union Alumni Magazine*, Spring 1986, 33.

There is evidence that the tendency of most ABC graduates to reject racial separatism was not atypical for black college students attending predominantly white colleges in the early 1970s. During the 1972–73 academic year, William Boyd (who was soon to succeed Bill Berkeley as president of ABC) oversaw a national study of blacks attending white colleges. With a grant from the Ford Foundation, and assistance in the design and data analysis from Daniel Yankelovich, Inc., he hired 50 college-educated blacks to interview 785 black students at forty colleges and universities across the nation. "Separatism," he concluded, "is the balloon in which the largest amount of hot air has collected." He found that separatism was a "minority viewpoint among black students." Moreover, he found that black students at the more selective colleges were more likely to participate in all extracurricular activities and less likely to prefer all-black housing than black students attending less selective colleges.[16]

Grades and Graduation

Many of those we interviewed did exceptionally well as college students. Some were obviously academic stars. For example, Jesse Spikes graduated magna cum laude from Dartmouth, was elected to Phi Beta Kappa, and won a Rhodes Scholarship. Others did well enough to be accepted into the most competitive law schools, business schools, and other graduate programs in the country. Some we interviewed indicated that they were average students in college, and a few said they were below average. George Perry's more systematic study of the performance of ABC students from 1964 through 1972 again provides a valuable supplement to the information we derived from our interviews.

When Perry did his study in 1972, he was able to obtain college grades for 289 of the more than 1,000 ABC students who had gone on to college. As college freshmen, they had a collective average of 2.3 on a 4.0 scale, the same average reported for black freshmen nationally that year. Furthermore, at three "highly selective" colleges, the grade-point averages

16. William M. Boyd II, *Desegregating America's Colleges: A Nationwide Survey of Black Students, 1972–73* (New York: Praeger, 1974), 13, 35, 74–75. More recent research, which examined the experiences of black college students in the 1980s, suggests that black students are not happy at white colleges. They fared far better at black colleges during the Reagan years. See Jacqueline Fleming, *Blacks in College* (San Francisco: Jossey-Bass, 1989).

for 64 ABC students were compared with those for a control group "matched on the basis of high school grades, SAT scores and family background." At one college, there was no significant difference between the two groups; at another, the ABC students had slightly higher grades than the control group; and at the third, the control group had slightly higher grades than the ABC group. Perry concluded: "ABC students were enrolled in colleges which were more selective than those they would have attended had they not participated in the ABC Program. However, it cannot be claimed on the basis of this study that ABC students' grade point average in college was increased as a result of having attended independent school." [17]

Perry's study also supports our interview finding that after graduating from college, ABC students were likely to attend top graduate and professional programs. He found that among the first ABC college graduates, 40 percent entered graduate school immediately and at least half the others expressed the intention of doing so. They attended excellent graduate programs in a variety of fields. "It is apparent," noted Perry, "that they were continuing in the elite channel which began with their enrollment in independent school nearly ten years ago." [18]

All evidence, then, suggests that the ABC program did a superb job of reaching its immediate goal of enrolling minority students in the best colleges and universities. The vast majority of ABC participants completed the program, almost all of the graduates went on to college, and many attended the most selective colleges, graduate schools, and professional programs in the nation. These results led Gene Maeroff, an education writer for the *New York Times,* to claim in 1982 that when one considers the difference ABC has made in bringing minority students to the nation's most prestigious educational institutions, "the impact of the program is stunning." [19]

The evidence also suggests that most of the ABC students were integrated with white students on the campuses. Although some encountered prejudice and discrimination, isolation from whites was often of their own choosing (or due to pressure from other blacks). At least some integration was possible if they wanted it. After exploring whether this pattern continued after college in terms of friendships, dating, and marriage,

17. Perry, "A Better Chance," 111–116.
18. Ibid., 125–126.
19. Gene I. Maeroff, *Don't Blame the Kids: The Trouble with America's Public Schools* (New York: McGraw-Hill, 1982), 91.

chapter 6 will examine whether ABC students· have achieved the longer-term goal ABC had for them of "assuming leadership roles in business, in the professions, in government and in the community." [20] That is, we will assess whether or not ABC graduates are likely to move into roles in the "power elite," the leadership group that works to preserve upper-class privileges and the economic system on which these privileges are based.

20. "What ABC Is All About," Annual report 1975–76, 1.

5

Relationships

Friendships, Dating, and Marriage

When they headed off to their prep schools as young teenagers, black ABC students were worried about everything from heavier academic loads to how their old friends would treat them when they came home for holidays. It is unlikely that they spent much time worrying about whether or not they would end up marrying upper-class whites from their prep schools.

Worries about interracial dating and marriage, however, may have been very much on the minds of whites who were troubled by the integration of elite prep schools. After all, prep schools were the established meeting ground for upper-class children to find marriage partners. A Swedish observer of "the American dilemma," Gunnar Myrdal, asserted that concern about intermarriage "constitutes the center in the complex of attitudes which can be described as the 'common denominator' in the problem." [1]

1. The quotation from Myrdal is cited in Joseph R. Washington, Jr., *Marriage in Black and White* (Boston: Beacon Press, 1970), 8. In Washington's view, marriage between blacks and whites is "our fundamental fear." He goes on to write that "it is *the* American problem" (1 and 4). In fact, as Andrew Billingsley writes in *Black Families in White America* (Englewood Cliffs, N.J.: Prentice-Hall, 1968), it was not until 1967 that the U.S. Supreme Court struck down "the last legal supports" for the laws that had forbidden "marriage between white persons and black persons" (65). On the origins of laws forbidding marriage between blacks and whites, see John D'Emilio and

In the conclusion to *Philadelphia Gentlemen: The Making of a National Upper Class,* published in 1958, Baltzell depicts the pattern that emerged early in the twentieth century which enabled upper-class boys to meet and later marry upper-class girls:

> The gentlemen bankers and lawyers on Wall Street, Walnut Street, and La Salle Street began to send their sons to Groton, St. Mark's, or St. Paul's and afterwards to Harvard, Yale, or Princeton where they joined such exclusive clubs as Porcellian, Fence, or Ivy. These polished young men from many cities were educated together, and introduced to one another's sisters at debutante parties and fashionable weddings in Old Westbury, Mount Kisco, or Far Hills, on the Main Line or in Chestnut Hill, in Dedham, Brookline, or Milton, or in Lake Forest. After marriage at some fashionable Episcopal church, almost invariably within this select endogamous circle, they lived in these same socially circumspect suburbs and commuted to the city where they lunched with their fathers and grandfathers at the Union, Philadelphia, Somerset, or Chicago Clubs.[2]

In spite of his criticisms of castelike behaviors in the upper class, Baltzell did note that wealthy Jews were gradually assimilated into it. As Jews progressed economically they typically moved from the inner cities to the more fashionable suburbs, and from Orthodox, to Conservative, to Reform religious affiliations. By the second or third generation some who had done exceptionally well economically had married upper-class gentiles.[3] Our research on Jews in the corporate elite also found evidence that the longer Jewish families had been in the highest corporate and social circles, the greater the likelihood that their children would marry out of the faith. Furthermore, as Baltzell had claimed two decades earlier, those who did marry gentiles were particularly likely to marry upper-class Episcopalians and Presbyterians. Over a period of a few generations, then, the descendants of many of the most sucessful Jewish businessmen were less and less likely to be Jewish, and, if they were still Jewish, less and less

---

Estelle B. Freedman, *Intimate Matters: A History of Sexuality in America* (New York: Harper and Row, 1988), 13–14, 34–37, 90–91, 106–107.

2. E. Digby Baltzell, *Philadelphia Gentlemen: The Making of a National Upper Class* (Glencoe, Ill.: Free Press, 1958), 385.

3. E. Digby Baltzell, *The Protestant Establishment: Aristocracy and Caste in America* (1964; reprint, New Haven: Yale University Press, 1987), 65–66.

likely to be involved in the Jewish community.[4] Though many of the pressures to assimilate into the predominantly WASP upper class may be the same for blacks as they are for Jews and other minorities, the visually obvious characteristic of skin color makes assimilation a different matter. Some light-skinned blacks have "passed" for whites,[5] but by and large, blacks cannot assimilate into WASP culture as easily as Jews and other white minority groups. An upper-class woman quoted in Susan Ostrander's *Women of the Upper Class* comments: "I think it would be very hard for me if one of them married a black. Two of my sons dated very nice Jewish girls, and I think that would be something I could live with."[6]

Did the black ABC students become good friends with their white prep school peers? Often they did. Did they date whites? Many did. Did they marry whites? For the most part, they did not. Indeed, many ended up unmarried, perhaps too busy for career and family, perhaps caught between their lower-class origins and their upper-class cultural styles.

Friendships

As already noted, many ABC students developed lifelong friendships with white classmates at their prep schools. This was especially true for those who entered the program in its early days, when they were the only, or one of very few, blacks at their school. Many of our interviewees told us of regular phone calls to and visits with white friends they made while in prep school. Cher Lewis, for example, was one of four black women at the Abbott Academy in the late 1960s. Though she is not in regular touch

4. Richard L. Zweigenhaft and G. William Domhoff, *Jews in the Protestant Establishment* (New York: Praeger, 1982), 81.

5. Washington, *Marriage in Black and White*, chap. 4, "Passing: Mystery, Magic, Mischief, and the Invisible Color Line." For a more current discussion of skin color, see Harriette Pipes McAdoo, "Transgenerational Patterns of Upward Mobility in African-American Families," in *Black Families*, 2d ed., ed. Harriette Pipes McAdoo (Beverly Hills, Calif.: Sage, 1988), 153–154, 165.

6. Susan A. Ostrander, *Women of the Upper Class* (Philadelphia: Temple University Press, 1984), 88. Another woman Ostrander interviewed indicated that when it came to membership in upper-class clubs in her city, black women were more undesirable than Jewish women (though neither were especially desirable). "Of course," she said, "there's racial discrimination. That's the biggest. Then there're religious differences" (101).

with any of the other three black students, she and four white students from Abbott have stayed in close contact for more than twenty years. They were members of each other's wedding parties. They speak regularly on the phone, even though they live in different parts of the country. As Cher puts it, "We're friends and we spend time together."

Interestingly, more than a few of the people we interviewed mentioned that in prep school they had become friends with Jewish students. Greg. Pennington noted: "One of my best friends is a Jewish guy who was one year ahead of me [at Western Reserve Academy]. I spend a lot of time with him now." And Alan Mitchell, a Worcester Academy graduate who now works as an administrator for the Cleveland Board of Education, commented that while a student at Worcester, he had visited the homes of Jewish students. "I'd go home with guys from Chicago who were Orthodox Jews," he recalled (though it's unlikely that Orthodox Jews attended his school; more likely they were Conservative or Reform), "and I'd go to bar mitzvahs and the whole bit, because I was interested. We were good friends and a lot of us still are."

Cecily Robbins, a graduate of Walnut Hill and, at the time of our interview, head of the Big Sisters program in Washington, D.C., explained that it was more than her interest in people of various backgrounds that led to her friendships with Jewish girls. As she put it: "I came from an entirely working-class neighborhood [in Philadelphia]. My mother was born in the house where my family still resides. The neighborhood was not predominantly anything. . . . So when I went to wasp, blond New England, I met some Jewish girls and I formed some real tight friendships with them. I found more ethnicity. I was comfortable with myself and found more ethnicity in some of the other girls. They weren't all wasps. I mean, there's nothing wrong with being wasp, but it's just that when you come from a black, Catholic, West Indian background and you live in an Italian neighborhood and you're thrown into wasp New England, it is a little bit of 'Where do I fit in? I don't.'"

In the previous chapter, we noted that Barry Greene had joined Zeta Beta Tau, a Jewish fraternity, and that among his closest friends in Richmond are former fraternity brothers who are Jewish. Several others also noted that they had become close friends with Jewish students while in college. There were clearly close and lasting bonds established between some black ABC students and Jews. We will return to this theme when we discuss intermarriage; as we will see, when black ABC students did marry whites, they were likely to marry Jews.

Dating

In our interviews, we asked each ABC graduate if he or she had dated interracially while in prep school. Their responses varied.

As we indicated in chapter 3, many ABC graduates found social life at prep school to be somewhere between minimal and nonexistent. One responded to our question about social life by asking in return, "What social life?" Some went on to say that they paid a price when they were in college. Few had anything positive to say about the system of mixers whereby they were paired with opposite-sex students from other schools. Some simply didn't date in prep school. For some ABC students, the only social life they had took place when they returned home for summers and holidays.

Jeffrey Palmer, for example, when asked about his social life at Kimball Union, replied: "At Kimball Union, there wasn't any. It's an all-boys' school. There wasn't any, at least on any basis that would allow me to maintain my sanity. There were dances, but this was 1965, 1966, and there wasn't a whole lot of mixing, at least openly. Obviously there were people sneaking off in the corner, but black people were not received in New England in the social environment very well at that time. So when the Glee Club visited the girls' school, nobody ever said anything to me, but the reception was less than warm. But I had been in that situation before, so it didn't bother me."

Some students, however, especially those who entered prep school a few years after Palmer, when the number of black students had increased dramatically, did lead active social lives, primarily with other black students at their own or nearby schools. Many drew on the social network that sprung up among black students as a result of friendships made during the summer orientation program and at the various ABC conferences that were held.

Some said that while in prep school they dated white students. These relationships rarely progressed beyond the stage of casual dating. Christine Dozier recalled that at Andover, many of the males, both black and white, were challenged by the novelty of interacting with females of a different race: "So there was a lot of that running back and forth. . . . We went to mixers and dances and things like that, but it was always on a very superficial level. Nothing real serious. And the guys were typical teenage guys, you know, one thing on their mind and they didn't care really if it was black or white. It was basically all the same to them, especially in that kind of prep school environment where you go to an all-boys' school or all-girls' school. It always ends up being the focal point of any mixer any time they get together. Socially, I didn't have those kinds of problems, and there wasn't really a lot of time for socializing. Intentionally, it was kept to a minimum." Her former classmate, Cher Lewis, dated both whites and blacks while at Abbott Academy, but she too said of these prep school relationships: "None was intense and they were all short-lived."

Interracial dating, however, was not inevitably superficial, casual, or short-lived. At times, it could be rife with psychological, practical, and long-term complexities. One man recalled spending two prep-school vacations at the home of his white girlfriend. Because of that relationship and his friendship with other white students, he was given a hard time by the other black students; he said his wife still has "problems dealing with" the fact that he dated white women in prep school and in college.

Greg Pennington said that he and his black ABC friends at Western Reserve Academy dated both blacks and whites and that at times this led to uncomfortable situations. One night, he recalled, he and his roommate, Charles, who was also black, got a phone call from two white women they had been dating:

> They wanted to know if we wanted to go to a ball game with them, and I got on the phone and Beth says, "Do y'all want to go to a basketball game?" So I said yes and when I hung up the phone I said, "Ravenna, is that a black school or a white school?" We didn't know, but we decided to go. . . . We took off to this basketball game and there was one black basketball player on the court and all the stands were on one side. . . . During halftime I looked up and saw this group of black students with denim jackets and black leather gloves and shades on and everything. . . . Now at the time I was 160 pounds and my roommate was about 195 to 200 pounds and six foot five. So this group of black students as they walk past look up and see us with these two white girls and one of them says, "Hey," and he gave me the power sign. I looked at Charles to see if he wants to get involved with this potential altercation, and he looked every which way except at these guys, so I gave them back this power sign. . . . The guy says "That's all I wanted to know," and walked out. . . . I was more comfortable going in a white environment with a white date than I would have been going in an all-black or predominantly black environment.

Though Pennington found that his interracial activities were more likely to be challenged by blacks than whites, in some cases, not surprisingly, problems stemmed from the objections of white parents. Glenn Boxx, a financial adviser for the Bell Telephone system in Chicago, recalls that when he was a student at the Shattuck School in Faribault, Minnesota, there was just one black female student at the nearby girls' school, and he did not date her. He found that the students did not seem to be uncomfortable with blacks dating whites, but their parents were. In fact, he recalls dating one woman for a while in his junior year until, as he put it, "We got into a big row with her parents—well, not her parents, her father." He still recalls the graduation ceremony that year. Shattuck was a military school, and traditionally the seniors turned their positions over to juniors for the ceremony. He was given a company to lead in the graduation march. As he passed the parade stand, giving orders to his company, he remembers staring into the eyes of the father of his former girlfriend, who was there to watch the ceremony. His girlfriend's father seemed surprised to see him in a position of such authority, sending his (mostly white) men through their military paces.

Many indicated that if they wanted to date they had to date whites simply because there were so few blacks in their schools. The following comment by Greg Googer, describing his experiences dating white women while a student at Andover, reflects the practical nature of these relationships (it also reflects how far he and other prep school students were from considering marrying the women they dated): "Dating at Andover was kind of hard. . . . I went out with some of the girls at Andover. There was a limited number of black females there. There was not always an opportunity to go out with them. Someone else would have ties with those people. Sometimes when you went to a dance you would go with a white female, or go alone. I chose not to just go alone. Sometimes, I chose to go to a dance with white people. . . . We all were really dating what was available to us. It wasn't that I was going to take this girl home and marry her and have mixed babies. It was no big deal. It was basically I had to have a date."

The wish for more social contact with other blacks was reflected in a number of anecdotes. Janice Peters recalled a mixer she and her Milton Academy classmates went to at a New England boys' school. She was one of just two or three black students at Milton; the school they were visiting had twenty or thirty black students. When she and the other black women got off the bus, all of the black students at the host prep school— gathered to see the arriving women—broke into applause. Similarly,

Frank Borges recalled that he and the other black students at Milbrook loved to play sports against Windsor Mountain, a coed school in the Berkshires, because the school had some black women students: "We used to love to go up there to Windsor Mountain because for about two minutes we got to see a black female."

Though many indicated that they continued to date whites as well as blacks in college, by the time they left college, relatively few black ABC graduates continued to date whites. Some attributed this to less tolerance of interracial relationshps in their working environments than in their college environments. Alan Glenn, for example, said that he had dated both whites and blacks while at Hotchkiss and at Brown but had not dated whites since graduating from Brown: "I haven't dated a white woman since Brown, not because I don't think I should but because I haven't run into any white women that I wanted to date. But I also think that is due to the fact that in corporate America I don't think that is readily accepted as it is in the academic world. Not at all, to be quite honest."

Others, like Greg Googer, attributed their change from dating both whites and blacks to dating only blacks to having found a context in which there was a larger group of black women. Googer found very few black women at Andover and relatively few at Vanderbilt. Atlanta, where he now lives, has a large community of college-educated black women. (Googer referred to the many "Bumpies"—Black Upwardly Mobile Professionals—in Atlanta.)

Marriage

Before turning to a consideration of marriage among the ABC students, we wish to note a few relevant findings from the extensive literature on marriage patterns in American culture.

- Research by social psychologists and sociologists for the past fifty years has shown that people are most likely to marry those who live nearby. This phenomenon, which social scientists have called "residential propinquity," holds for friendship as well as marriage patterns; it was first systematically applied to marriage in 1931, when sociologist James Bossard examined marriage license applications in Philadelphia. He found that the members of one out of every four couples lived within two blocks of each other, and the proportion of marriages decreased as the distance between marrying partners increased. This pattern, which came to be known as

Bossard's Law, has been found more recently in cities throughout America (and in other countries).[7]

- People who marry tend to share many similarities, including religion, social class, attitudes, and values. They also tend to be of the same race. In spite of an increase in interracial marriages that occurred during the civil rights movement of the 1960s, the proportion of interracial marriages in the total population has remained quite small. Through 1965, fewer than two out of every thousand marriages in this country were between whites and blacks. By 1970, that figure had increased but only to seven out of a thousand; by 1980, it had climbed to thirteen out of one thousand. The most frequent intermarriage pattern is of a black male with a white woman; in most minority groups, the women outmarry more often than the men.[8]

- Research on "marital timing" (the age at which people marry) indicates that both black men and black women marry later than white men or white women. Moreover, for women, black or white, those who enroll in four-year colleges or universities marry later than those who do not.[9]

About 60 percent of the ABC graduates we interviewed had been married at one time or another (some more than once), but only 50 percent were married at the time they were interviewed. Almost all—but not all—married blacks, but no simple pattern emerged. Some married

7. Zick Rubin, *Liking and Loving* (New York: Holt, Rinehart and Winston, 1973), 194. Rubin says that the term *residential propinquity* is another example of "the inimitable jargon of the social scientists who brought you 'interpersonal attraction' and 'mate selection.'" For evidence of the importance of residential propinquity in friendship formation, see Leon Festinger, Stanley Schacter, and Kurt Back, *Social Pressures in Informal Groups* (New York: Harper, 1950) and L. Nahemow and M. P. Lawton, "Similarity and Propinquity in Friendship Formation," *Journal of Personality and Social Psychology*, 1975, *32* (2), 205–213.
8. Rubin, *Liking and Loving*, 197, George E. Simpson and J. Milton Yinger, *Racial and Cultural Minorities: An Analysis of Prejudice and Discrimination*, 5th ed. (New York: Plenum Press, 1985), 298–299, and David Heer, "The Prevalence of Black-White Marriage in the U.S., 1960–1970," *Journal of Marriage and the Family*, 1974, *35*, 246–258.
9. Jay D. Teachman, Karen A. Polonko, and Geoffrey K. Leigh, "Marital Timing: Race and Sex Comparisons," *Social Forces*, 1987, *66* (1), 239–268. Their finding that blacks marry at a "slower pace" than whites is based on longitudinal data from a national sample of twenty thousand respondents tested initially in 1972 and followed up in 1973, 1974, 1976, and 1979.

friends they had known growing up or had met when they returned home to visit or live. Some married people they had met in college or graduate school. Some married people they met once they entered careers. And some married whites. But not all patterns were equally satisfactory. We will examine each of these marriage patterns separately.

MARRIAGE PARTNERS FROM BACK HOME

Almost 20 percent of the ABC graduates we interviewed married people they knew from their neighborhoods. One of these marriages ended seven years later when the partner drowned tragically in a boating accident. All the others ended either in divorce or separation.

Jeffrey Palmer, who left Steubenville, Ohio, to attend Kimball Union and then Yale, married a woman he had grown up with in Steubenville. They remained together for six years before divorcing. He continues to be somewhat puzzled by the whole relationship: "To tell you the truth, I don't know how the hell that happened. I have often tried to figure it out. . . . You would think there would be no rational reason that I would marry her. All of the sociological things—people say, 'Well, this guy has gone away, and done this, and this is where he is headed'—you put all those things in a line and it wouldn't equal me marrying her. But, at the same time, we were happy for a while and I was never sorry that I did it. But I go back and look at it and it seems bizarre. We didn't have anything in common."

Another of those we interviewed described his marriage to a woman from his hometown. After graduating from prep school and college, he returned to live in the town in which he had grown up. There he met and married a woman four years younger than he—she had just graduated from high school. They thought they could overcome their various differences, including their differences in age and education; they couldn't and divorced after five years.

Cecily Robbins, who grew up in Philadelphia and then attended Walnut Hill and George Washington University, did not marry someone from her own neighborhood, but she did marry a man with whom she had little in common. He had dropped out of high school and had very different views than she had. Though their differences were partly what attracted her to him initially, she found that ultimately these differences made it impossible for them to stay together. As she explained in our interview, shortly before the divorce was final: "He was a police officer when I met him. I had decided that all these nice little middle-class men in suits were a drag, and I figured why not become involved with someone who was more along the lines of a blue-collar person. His background was not anywhere near mine. That's one of the problems that we had. Educationally, sociologically, ideologically, politically—should I go on? I thought we were going to complement one another, but we did not. We ended up clashing a lot."

COLLEGE (OR GRADUATE SCHOOL) ROMANCES

Slightly more than one-fourth of the ABC graduates we interviewed met their partners while in college or graduate school. Most of these marriages remain intact. For instance, LaPearl Winfrey met her husband when they were both undergraduates at Oberlin. Despite the strains of a three-year period when she was in New York doing doctoral work in psychology while her husband and daughter remained in Chicago, their marriage has survived. She recalls with a measure of pride that although "nobody expected our marriage to last, we managed." Greg Pennington, also a psychologist, met his wife when he was an undergraduate at Harvard and she was an undergraduate at Wellesley. And Alan Mitchell met his wife when they were both studying at Case Western Reserve (he was studying architecture, and she, having graduated from Wellesley, was working on a master's degree).

Some of the ABC graduates, almost all of whom were from backgrounds that included unmistakable poverty, married partners whose parents came from the black middle class. One of those we interviewed said that his wife's background was very different from his own. Her parents, both of whom worked, "knew what they wanted for their kids and they did everything they could to get them there." He added that as a result of her parents' efforts, "If you'll excuse the expression, my wife is a Black JAP [Jewish American Princess]."

Others saw such differences as potential problems and consciously chose to marry blacks who had economic backgrounds similar to their own. One of those we interviewed noted that while in college he had almost married a black woman who had a middle-class background but decided against it. He had gone home with her to visit her family and found himself uncomfortably aware of how different her background was from his. He worried that she might not understand or be sympathetic toward his mother, who was struggling on her own—his parents were divorced—

to make ends meet for a large family. He broke off the relationship. He later married another black woman he met in college who was from a family that, like his own, had struggled economically.

Though none of those we interviewed had married other ABC students, we did hear about such marriages. In one case, two ABC students fell in love while in prep school, applied to and attended the same university, and married during their undergraduate years. In another, perhaps more expected pattern, two people who met originally as ABC students during the summer program began to date seriously when they were students at the same college, fell in love, and married.

DEGREES FIRST, MARRIAGES LATER

Many of those we interviewed—almost a third—did not marry until they were out of school and in the working world. For the most part, these ABC graduates, with their degrees (and often advanced degrees) from prestigious schools, married other people who were well educated. For example, Doris McMillon, the newscaster, married a Haitian physician, and Calvin Dorsey, who has degrees from Stanford and the University of Mississippi, married a black woman he met in Atlanta who was a third-generation college graduate. In some cases, ABC graduates met their husbands or wives through their work. For example, Jeffrey Palmer met his second wife (who had graduated with honors from the University of Illinois) when he was in the advertising business; she is the creative director of a small, black advertising agency.

MARRYING WHITES

In writing about the "reciprocal attraction" that often occurs among those in "the fraternity of the successful," C. Wright Mills asserted that there is a wide range: "On the slight side, it is a sort of tacit, mutual admiration; in the strongest of tie-ins, it proceeds by intermarriage. And there are all grades and types of connection between these extremes."[10] As we have shown, some ABC students established more than "tacit, mutual admiration" with their white prep school classmates. Others developed close friendships with white students, and many have maintained these friendships. Some have developed and maintained close relationships with whites

10. C. Wright Mills, *The Power Elite* (New York: Oxford University Press, 1954), 281.

with whom they've worked. And some have established what Mills called the "strongest of tie-ins:" they married whites.

We have noted the relative infrequency of marriages between blacks and whites in America (in 1980, slightly more than 1 percent). Few black ABC students married whites, but they did marry whites more often than occurs in the country at large. We estimate that between 5 and 10 percent of the ABC graduates married whites.

Bobette Reed's marriage to Jeffrey Kahn is particularly intriguing because it highlights quite clearly both their differences and their similarities. After graduating from Williams College in 1973 with a degree in religion, Bobette Reed entered the Harvard Divinity School. While there, she worked at two jobs in order to support herself. The first was at the Divinity School Bookstore and the second was with the Harvard University police department. She started as a security guard for the police department and was soon promoted to a position in which she supervised the security patrol. It was in this capacity that she met Jeffrey Kahn. Not long before, Harvard's Fogg Museum had been broken into and valuable paintings had been stolen. Jeffrey Kahn—a student at the Harvard Business School—had set up a new computer system that was being used by the Harvard police. Like Bobette, he was working part-time for the Harvard University police department to help pay for his schooling. Unlike Bobette, he had experience in criminal work as a former New York City policeman. And unlike Bobette, an Episcopalian soon to be ordained as a deacon, Jeffrey Kahn was Jewish. He had grown up in Hartford, had attended a New England prep school (Loomis), and had received his bachelor's degree from Yale.

Though they were married by a rabbi, there was never any discussion of Bobette's converting to Judaism. Bobette received counseling from her priest. She described their conversation: "When I went to my priest, he said, 'Bobette, is it the same God?' and I said, 'Of course it is.' He said, 'Well, what's the difference?' I said, 'You know what the difference is. The Jews believe that Jesus Christ is not the Messiah, and indeed, if there is a Messiah, he is yet to come.' And he said, 'Well, yes. Would you have any problems raising your children as Jews? Is there anything besides that that you do not believe in?' I guess if I were picky there would be some things, but I said 'No.' And he said, 'Well, then, I have no problem.'"

At the time of our interview, they had not yet had any children. Bobette attends church every Sunday, and Jeffrey attends temple periodically (not every week, but more often than just during the High Holidays of Rosh Hashanah and Yom Kippur). Though it might appear that they have vast differences to overcome, Bobette's view is that they have many important things in common: "Even though we come from very different kinds of socioeconomic backgrounds, they're really not that different. When you look at the private school, when you look at the colleges, when you look at the graduate schools, they really begin to merge."

Notably, Bobette Reed Kahn was not the only ABC graduate we interviewed who is married to a white, Jewish man. Recall Cher Lewis, born in Richmond, educated at the Abbott School, NYU, and the Columbia School of Business, who married Josh Feigenbaum. Neither Lewis nor Feigenbaum has changed religion. "We are of different religions," she explained. "We celebrate some Jewish holidays, we celebrate public holidays. So we sort of do both." Their twin daughters, Emma and Zooey, three-and-a-half at the time of the interview, were being raised "so far with almost no religion." The children were attending a neighborhood nursery school run by the First Presbyterian Church ("We haven't told his mother the name of the nursery school," she confided), but they had just been accepted into a private nondenominational school for gifted children.

Of the thirty-eight people we interviewed, three married whites, and two of the three married Jews. The third interracial marriage was between a black male and a white woman he met in college; about four years later they were divorced.

In order to gain a larger picture of the patterns we were interested in— not just marital patterns but friendship and career patterns—we asked each ABC graduate to tell us about other ABC students he or she knew from the summer program, prep school, or college. This provided us with information about a much larger sample of ABC graduates—a few hundred instead of thirty-eight. On the basis of this larger but less direct sample, we can draw the same general conclusion that we have drawn from our interview sample: most black ABC students did not marry whites, but the rather small percentage who did is surely greater than the national figure of about 1 percent. The indirect sample reinforces our estimate that between 5 and 10 percent of the black ABC graduates married whites. And this indirect sample also provides supporting evidence for our finding that when intermarriage did occur, the white partner was likely to be Jewish.[11]

---

11. It is not surprising, then, that the first interracial couple described in *Newsweek*'s special feature "Colorblind Love" consisted of a black and a Jew—Chuck and Lois Bronz (Barbara Kantrowitz, "Colorblind Love," *Newsweek*, March 7, 1988, 40–41).

STILL UNMARRIED AFTER ALL THESE YEARS

About 40 percent of both the men and the women we interviewed had never married. For the most part, the men did not express concern about this but the women did.

Many of the men who had never married indicated that they had been so dedicated to their careers that they had not had the time for, nor were they willing to make a commitment to, marriage. Jesse Spikes is an example. "People used to ask me," he said, "'Why have you never gotten married?' I never had time. There were things I wanted to do, and there was no time in my life for this the way I saw it. There were things I had to do." Other men said that they were currently involved with particular women and that they expected to marry and begin families within the next few years.

In what at times were painfully honest self-analyses, some of the female ABC graduates we interviewed indicated that because of loneliness, or the feeling that time was running out on their childbearing years, or both, they were reassessing their commitment to their careers. One made it clear that her commitment to her career, especially as a black woman, had taken its toll "in sleepless nights, in stress, and in breaking down of social life." The day we spoke with her, she acknowledged that she was "feeling a little lonely and alienated." As she explored the nature of her alienation, she eventually discussed marriage:

> At different points of my life I have felt different kinds of alienation. Initially, when I was first at prep school, I felt a kind of alienation from my parents. There have been other kinds of alienation. What I feel to the greatest extent now, oddly enough, even though I have a number of friends who are from that prep school world, and from [college], is that I feel a certain social alienation and I think I'll always have that. I'll never be here nor there. I'll never be a full member of that club. Yes, I can have friends that are from prep school and yes, I can have friends from college. We can have very warm relationships and we do. Some of my friends are married and I feel close to their husbands and children. But, on many levels, there are times when I just feel that I don't fit in. And yet, on so many other levels, I do feel like a part of that world, and that world is largely a white world. I've never talked so much about black and white as I have with you today. . . . Socially, I'm beginning to think about things now, like marriage. In some ways it would be very natural for me to

marry someone who was white and of a certain class and educated. Some ways that would cause all kinds of difficulties and does create difficulties for me.

Another of the women we interviewed was also reassessing the nature of her social life. When asked if she was married, she responded by saying: "I'm single. Oh, God, sometimes I think I always will be. I hope to not always be. I'd like very much to get married." She had been involved with a man for ten years and was in the midst of asking herself (and presumably him) questions about the future of this relationship. Ten years earlier, she had met the man she refers to as her "preferred mate." They dated for three years while both were in the same city, but he subsequently moved. Despite the distance, they continued to see each other.

She acknowledged that for a long time the intermittent nature of the relationship had been just what she wanted because it allowed her to pursue her career, a career that required long working hours. But she wasn't so sure that long-distance love was what she wanted in the future. In her mid-thirties, she was thinking more and more about getting married. As a result, she was having second thoughts about the relationship and was "sort of aggressively pushing for some change." Recently, she had been seeing this preferred mate less often than in the past. Though they still talked on the phone a few times a week, they were seeing each other only every other month or so. As she put it: "Time is still an element, a major, major element. [He] is my preferred mate. As long as I have any hope of having him, then I don't really want to bother with anybody else. But at some point you cut your losses. That's a horrible thing to say, but ten years is a long time."

In exploring relationships with friends and marriage partners, we have seen the first evidence of crosscutting tensions in the lives of ABC graduates. Half of those we interviewed are divorced or have never been married, and at least some of those who have not married feel caught between two worlds. The sheer time pressures of making it big have also taken a toll on their social lives.

Interracial friendships are relatively common and long-lasting; interracial marriage is rare. For both types of relationships, another marginal group within a predominantly WASP elite, Jews, appear to be more likely than chance would indicate to be the white partners. We agree with those social scientists who would argue that this is because those who are mistreated by a society develop a healthy skepticism about its culture and pretensions. They develop "double vision" and as a result are able to discern sham and hypocrisy more readily. Jews and blacks may share a common perspective on American society that brings them closer despite other cultural differences.

Given the elite cultural styles of many of the ABC graduates, along with their frequent interactions with whites, the small number of intermarriages is evidence that at the top levels of the American melting pot class similarities cannot counteract racial differences as they do religious ones. This finding reinforces what has been shown at the middle levels of American society, where Hispanics and Japanese Americans are far more likely to marry Anglos than blacks are.[12]

The picture that is emerging, then, reveals that the further we move into adult life, the more difficult the class-assimilation process becomes. But what about the world of corporations and government? How are these people doing in their careers, and will any of them attain seats of power?

12. Thomas F. Pettigrew, "Integration and Pluralism," in *Modern Racism: Profiles in Controversy,* ed. Phyliss A. Katz and Dalmas A. Taylor (New York: Plenum Press, 1988); see also Joe R. Feagin, *Race and Ethnic Relations,* 3d ed. (Englewood Cliffs, N.J.: Prentice-Hall, 1989).

6

Careers and Power

At the same time that Sylvester Monroe, Cher Lewis, and the other early ABC students were receiving the best (and the most expensive) prep school and college educations available in this country, the job market for educated blacks was undergoing dramatic changes.

Prior to the 1960s, career choices for blacks with advanced degrees were severely limited. Education was the major most frequently chosen by black college students, and black college graduates who did not pursue careers in education were most likely to go into social work. A select few went on to become doctors or dentists, and an even smaller number became lawyers; these black professionals usually lived and practiced in black neighborhoods.

Blacks with very strong educational credentials in business or economics had a very difficult time obtaining jobs with large corporations. In a 1986 interview study of seventy-six top-level black executives with *Fortune*-500 firms in Chicago, sociologist Sharon Collins found that fewer than half of the twenty-nine interviewees who entered the labor force before 1965 were able to find positions in the white private sector. Most had to begin their careers in government, black businesses, or black community agencies. Those who were hired by mainstream corporations were often given such jobs as stockroom or billing clerk, jobs well below their level of education. The only good jobs "came from companies that were sensitive to government oversight."[1] The president of an insurance subsidiary of a major corporation, who holds an M.B.A. from a prestigious university, told Collins how he finally landed his first job as an accountant with a large government contractor: "I wanted to be in the investment banking community, but there was no opportunity at all. I finally settled on a job as an accountant at [an aerospace firm]. [The] company stacked the roster, they wanted lots of graduate degrees and they wanted minorities, despite the fact that there were not the obvious or blatant kind of regulations. And I was [underutilized], not doing work [at] the level of an M.B.A."[2]

The New Black Middle Class

However, by the mid-1960s, the media were helping to overcome this rank discrimination by providing what sociologist James Blackwell refers to as "secondary role models." As he wrote in *Mainstreaming Outsiders: The Production of Black Professionals:* "The United Negro College Fund's advertising campaign showed Black students in a variety of settings; commercials from oil companies, engineering and computer firms, and business and industry in general began to depict Blacks in diverse occupational roles. Some commercial television programs utilized Black actors in what was for the industry 'nontraditional' occupational characterizations. Hence some Blacks were physicians, dentists, nurses, lawyers, and athletes. All of these factors contributed heavily to the changing career choices of Black students."[3]

Surveys of employment patterns in the mid-1970s revealed that blacks had entered new occupational territory. Sociologist Bart Landry concluded on the basis of his research on this issue, "There were not simply more white-collar jobs to be had, there was greater diversity." Landry continued: "Unlike the old black middle class, which was restricted to serving the needs of blacks ignored by indifferent or even hostile white professionals, the new black middle class was becoming, like whites, a class of salaried white-collar workers. By the mid-1970s, this new black middle

1. Sharon M. Collins, "The Marginalization of Black Executives," *Social Problems,* 1989, *36* (4), 320; also see her "Pathways to the Top: Black Mobility in the Business World" (Ph.D. diss., Northwestern University, 1988).
2. Collins, "Marginalization of Black Executives," 320.
3. James E. Blackwell, *Mainstreaming Outsiders: The Production of Black Professionals* (Bayside, N.Y.: General Hall, 1981), 24.

class was no longer confined to the few professional occupations of teacher, minister, doctor, dentist, lawyer, and social worker. A national sample of the black and white middle classes that I collected in 1976 turned up no less than 65 different job titles held by black males, including accountant, engineer, sales manager, policeman, scientist and architect."[4]

Landry's use of the terms *old* and *new* black middle class reflects his belief that the expanding career opportunities of the 1960s and 1970s were part of a much broader set of changes. The black middle class, in his view, has gone through three phases. The period of the "old mulatto elite," in which individuals of light complexion rose to leadership positions within the black community, lasted from Emancipation until 1915. The period of the "old black middle class" occurred between 1915 and 1960. Faced with the prejudices and indignities of life in a segregated society, most members of the old black middle class worked, lived, and socialized within the confines of the black community. The third phase, that of the "new black middle class," began in 1960 and continues to the present. This phase, which Landry argues came about only because of the "chance simultaneous occurrence" of the civil rights movement *and* economic prosperity, brought members of the black middle class into a different relationship with the white community. Whereas the normative climate during the phase of the old middle class was designed to "keep blacks in their place," the civil rights movement and the new laws brought about a very different climate: "Whites, South as well as North, who discriminated became 'racist' rather than regular guys, and those who attempted to block the access of blacks could no longer count on success, instead running the risk of losing face rather than being heroes."[5] Members of the new black middle class are much more likely to work and socialize in integrated environments than their predecessors were.

Landry's general findings on the new black middle class are reinforced and supplemented by Collins's interviews with black executives in Chicago. Whereas those managers who entered the job market before 1965 were lucky to find any kind of job in a white-controlled corporation, those from the post-1965 era received many good offers and were often given responsibilities involving interactions with white employees or customers. Even more than Landry, however, Collins stresses that these advances were dependent on both government and community pressures.

---

4. Bart Landry, *The New Black Middle Class* (Berkeley: University of California Press, 1987), 88.
5. Ibid., 83.

Indeed, a significant minority of the jobs were in affirmative action or personnel units that dealt with government agencies or in public relations or community relations units that dealt with black communities.[6]

As black ABC students entered the job market in the late 1960s and early 1970s with undergraduate and graduate degrees from schools like Harvard, Dartmouth, and the University of Pennsylvania, they could not have been better prepared to take advantage of the changes that had taken place in the job market and in the black middle class. Even when the economic prosperity that had been so important to the emergence of the new black middle class grew more slowly, and even when the recession of 1973 reversed some of the gains blacks had made in narrowing the income gap between blacks and whites, those with degrees from selective schools continued to be in demand. Blacks with advanced degrees were particularly sought after. In a 1976 report prepared for the Carnegie Commission on Higher Education, Harvard economist Richard B. Freeman wrote: "At the top of the educational hierarchy black workers with graduate training obtained increases in income far above those of comparable whites, with the result that the economic incentive for black investments in post-bachelor's study came to exceed that for white investments."[7] Put simply, in terms of future income, it was a good investment for whites to continue their education beyond the bachelor's degree, but an even better investment for blacks to do so.

More recently, Jomills Braddock and James McPartland, two sociologists at Johns Hopkins, surveyed the employment practices of more than four thousand employers in 1983. Among other things, they found that various personality and attitudinal traits such as "leadership potential" and "proper attitudes about work and supervisors" were critical factors in deciding whether or not to hire an applicant. They also reported that employers gave "special credibility and weight to minority graduates of suburban schools" as opposed to graduates of inner-city black schools.[8] Given the quality and prestige of the schools ABC students attended, as well as the rigorous training they received in interpersonal skills, it is not surprising that when the time came to enter the working world most ABC graduates did quite well.

Most, but not all, ABC graduates entered what Landry calls the new

6. Sharon M. Collins, "The Making of the Black Middle Class," *Social Problems*, 1983, *30* (4), 369–382, and Collins, "Marginalization of Black Executives," 317–331.
7. Richard B. Freeman, *Black Elite: The New Market for Highly Educated Black Americans* (New York: McGraw-Hill, 1976), 37.

black middle class. Before turning to a discussion of where these graduates are now in their careers and how they got there, let us consider certain particularly valuable social assets that many of them acquired while attending elite prep schools.

Charm and "Networking" as Cultural and Social Capital

For years, sociologists have argued—and convincingly demonstrated—that those at the top of the class structure transmit their advantageous positions to their children. They do so in a variety of ways. Most directly, parents can and usually do see to it that their wealth goes to their children (this parental assistance is, of course, encouraged by lenient inheritance taxes and by ways of getting around the taxes that do exist).[9] There are also less direct ways of insuring that one's children are able to maintain the economic comfort into which they were born. As is evidenced by the considerable emphasis placed on having them attend "the best schools," providing them with a quality education is a less direct but important component of an upper-class child's "inheritance."

French sociologist Pierre Bourdieu has written extensively on the importance of both cultural knowledge and connections for maintaining one's position in the class structure. He has transformed the commonplace ideas about "being classy" and "having connections" into high-status concepts by referring to them as "cultural capital" and "social capital."[10] He argues that one way those at the top of the class structure maintain their position is by monopolizing access to cultural capital, especially in the context of an ostensibly meritocratic system. This can entail controlling access to knowledge per se; it can also refer to controlling access to the techniques for creating new knowledge. Bourdieu explains how writ-

8. Jomills Henry Braddock II and James M. McPartland, "How Minorities Continue to Be Excluded from Equal Employment Opportunities: Research on Labor Market and Institutional Barriers," *Journal of Social Issues*, 1987, *43* (1), 13 and 19.

9. For a summary, circa 1956, of the various ways the wealthy avoid taxes, see C. Wright Mills, *The Power Elite* (New York: Oxford University Press, 1956), 146–170. For a more recent summary, see Michael Patrick Allen, *The Founding Fortunes: A New Anatomy of the Super-rich Families in America* (New York: E. P. Dutton, 1988), 154–184.

10. Pierre Bourdieu, "Cultural Reproduction and Social Reproduction," in *Power and Ideology in Education*, ed. J. Karabel and A. H. Halsey (New York: Oxford University Press, 1977), 487–511.

ing enabled particular groups to practice "primitive accumulation of cultural capital," because only those who could read and write could gain access to the knowledge in written texts. Along these lines, Persell and Cookson discuss the widespread and rapid adoption of microcomputers at elite boarding schools as an example of upper-class institutions adapting to technological innovation to enhance cultural capital and thus preserve their position in the social structure.[11]

It is in this context that we can explore some of the subtler benefits the ABC students received as a result of having attended elite prep schools. In the earlier chapters, we explored the nature of prep school life and the academic experiences of ABC students in prep school and college. As we spoke with ABC graduates about their careers, it became apparent that in addition to the formal education they had received, many had acquired at least two skills that became part of their cultural and social capital: the ability to talk with anyone about anything, and the ability to benefit from the access to influential people they had gained as a result of attending elite schools.

Prep schools pride themselves on their graduates' ability to interact comfortably with a wide variety of people. The early training in conversational skills at the sit-down dinners during the summer transitional program was designed to prepare ABC students for similar situations at prep school, where they would be expected to converse with fellow students, faculty members, and visitors on diverse topics. Those who ran the elite prep schools did not assume that such conversational skills and the other interpersonal skills that combine to make an individual attractive came without effort. As Anson, whose son attended Exeter, notes: "On the whole, Exeter students were charming; it was one of the things that set them apart from other teenagers, and the Academy's adults worked hard at maintaining the difference."[12]

During our interviews, a number of the ABC graduates referred to their ability to feel comfortable in a variety of settings. Some noted that they had developed this quality while they were ABC students. For example, William Foster, at the time of our interview employed by Xerox Educational Publications in Connecticut, described his behavior with some friends of his wealthy white in-laws: "I have such eclectic taste in so many

11. Caroline Hodges Persell and Peter W. Cookson, Jr., "Microcomputers and Elite Boarding Schools: Educational Innovation and Social Reproduction," *Sociology of Education*, 1987, 60, 123.

12. Robert Sam Anson, *Best Intentions: The Education and Killing of Edmund Perry* (New York: Random House, 1987), 108.

things. I mean, I'm able to converse with anybody on almost anything. I went to someone's house, a marvelous home, and I felt a little out of place until I saw they had some Oriental prints, and I was saying, 'Isn't this from the such and such dynasty?' The guy perked right up. It worked out well. I felt very comfortable."

Maccene Brown, now a lawyer in Durham, North Carolina, explained how her prep school experience as the only black student in her class at Miss Hall's contributed to her ability to work effectively with and feel comfortable around whites: "When you've gone to school with people who are truly rich, you just don't get impressed with things as easily as other people are. . . . It made me wiser to white people in a lot of ways. . . . You tend not to put the people of another ethnic group on a pedestal. You feel that you can compete if you have to." She then added a very important and revealing comment that we heard echoed in other interviews: "You're comfortable in the presence of folks who are not of your own ethnic group—and a lot of black people are still not comfortable around white folks." Although black prep school graduates may be more likely to notice this discomfort, other blacks who are aware of it would probably be unlikely to mention it to a white interviewer.

Greg Googer observed that his years at Andover helped him in "learning the games, the rules, of what to say, of what not to say, and how to say it." He went on to conclude, "I attribute most of the things I've learned to my Phillips Academy background." Perhaps there is no more important cultural capital for blacks than to feel comfortable interacting with whites on an equal basis; this is a major contribution of the ABC program to its graduates.

When the earliest ABC graduates were prep school students, the term *networking* was not yet in vogue, and Bourdieu had not yet coined the phrase *social capital*. The concept, however, had been around for a long time. What is now called networking or social capital was previously referred to as having, developing, or using "connections" or taking advantage of "the old boy network." For example, in *The Late George Apley*, John Marquand's classic novel about the upper class in late nineteenth-century America, the title character gives the following advice to his son: "You must bear in mind that the friendships and associations which you are now making at Harvard will be with you for the rest of your life. In my experience there is no truer axiom than that 'a man is known by the company he keeps.' Besides this, the connections you are now forming are of definite importance to your subsequent career."[13]

By dint of having attended elite prep schools and colleges, graduates of the ABC program had formed valuable connections, and they had become part of a number of networks. For example, graduates of Choate knew Choate schoolmates who, like themselves, had entered the working world; moreover, they knew that because they had gone to Choate they could, with carefully placed phone calls or letters, gain access to thousands of Choate graduates they did not know personally. The director of development at Choate has stressed the valuable entree a Choate education provides: "There is no door in this entire country that cannot be opened by a Choate graduate. I can go anywhere in this country and anywhere there's a man I want to see . . . I can find a Choate man to open that door for me." [14]

ABC graduates were also part of networks that included all those who had attended their colleges, and many were also part of law school, business school, or graduate school networks. Such connections might well prove valuable for getting an interview for a job, getting the job itself, or gaining certain advantages once in a job. For example, Alan Glenn, at the time of our interview working for Manufacturers Hanover, described his ongoing friendship with a Hotchkiss classmate: "One of my best friends from Hotchkiss is Mike Carroll. He's white. He's from a middle-class Irish background here in New York, and we became very good friends. He's now a writer for the *American Banker*. And we stay in contact, get together and go out for drinks every now and then, have breakfast or lunch, whatever the case may be. Sometimes it's mutually convenient because he works for the *American Banker*, so he feels he can grind me about what is going on here at Manufacturers Hanover, and I can grind him about what's going on in the banking industry in general. So it's mutually beneficial for both of us."

Glenn also noted that such contacts turned up at unexpected moments. At one point, he was riding a subway and saw a familiar Hotchkiss face: "I didn't even know he was in New York. I said, 'God, that looks like

13. John P. Marquand, *The Late George Apley* (New York: Pocket Book Edition, 1945), 60–61. Such advice from parent to child echoes through the years. Karen K. Russell, the daughter of former Boston Celtic great Bill Russell, recalled asking her father why he had encouraged her to attend the Harvard Law School even though he himself had faced "the worst kind of unbridled bigotry" in Boston. He told her: "I wanted you to have the best possible education and to be able to make the best contacts" (Karen K. Russell, "Growing Up with Privilege and Prejudice," *New York Times Magazine*, June 14, 1987, 23).

14. Peter S. Prescott, *A World of Our Own: Notes on Life and Learning in a Boys' Preparatory School* (New York: Coward-McCann, 1970), 67.

Chuck.' I walked up to him and started talking, and it was Chuck. We exchanged business cards and we've been in contact since then."

These networks remain intact even if they are unused for years. When Doris McMillon was in Minnesota promoting a book she had written, she called Alida Rockefeller, an old friend from the one year McMillon had spent at the Concord Academy. Though they had not seen each other for years, Alida "came over to the hotel. She picked me up, she took me to her house, we sat and we talked and we ate cookies."

Doris McMillon is forthright about the nature of her relationship with Alida Rockefeller: "We don't call each other or anything, but we write letters to one another, and I know some of the things personally that are happening to her, or that have happened to her. She knows what's going on with me, and we stay in touch. But I know that if I'm in a position where I have to call her for something, I can call her and say, 'Alida, if you can't help me with this, will you tell me who can?' And if she should ever need me for anything, she can call me."

And, McMillon candidly explained, Alida Rockefeller is part of a much larger network to which she, as an alumna of both the Concord Academy and the Cushing Academy, now has access. In our interview, she said that she had just given a talk to current ABC students: "I keep trying to explain to the kids, 'This is an opportunity for you to meet the folks who are out there making decisions in the business world. I went to school with the Cartiers, the Pillsburys, the Rockefellers, the Fishers. Tony Fisher's family, the Fisher Brothers in New York—I think they've just built every high rise, every skyscraper, that's up on Park Avenue and Fifth Avenue. But I got a chance to meet those kind of people. Well, what I found out ultimately is that they get up in the morning and get out of the bed and go to the bathroom like I do. So it's no big deal. However, they are who they are, and if they can help you, they will."

ABC graduates are also part of a network that includes others who participated in the ABC program. Many ABC graduates have kept in touch with friends they made while in the program, and, as is often the case with networks, even if they haven't been in touch with these friends lately, they know where they are or how to find them. The more interviews we did, the more the same names came up. By the end of our research, when we asked participants to recommend others, they often suggested we talk to people we had already interviewed.

In some cases, ABC graduates tapped into this ABC network when they made or sought to make career moves. Upon returning to Atlanta after working in the Middle East, Jesse Spikes joined a law firm that included Oliver Lee; the two had become friends as young teenagers when they participated in ABC's first Public School Project at Hanover High School in New Hampshire.

A corporate lawyer we interviewed described how the father of a former prep school classmate had become a valuable contact for him when he was interviewing for his current job. He had been invited for an interview at the largest firm in the city in which he grew up. Knowing that the father of a woman he had gone to prep school with was a partner at another large law firm in that same city, he called him up and told him of his forthcoming interview. His friend's father asked for his résumé and then arranged for him to be interviewed while he was in town. The ABC graduate ended up joining that firm.

The process of networking refers not so much to being a member of a network as to knowing how to use various networks to accomplish one's goals. Using a network does not guarantee that one will be hired, but by opening doors, it increases the chances that one will be talked to, looked at, and seriously considered. As a result, being able to use networks increases the chances one will be hired. Doris McMillon gave a casebook description of how to draw on various networks to obtain a desired job. McMillon had heard that Worldnet, a worldwide telecommunications network that is part of the United States Information Agency (USIA), was about to expand. At the time she was hosting a half-hour evening talk show for the Black Entertainment Network. The network was about to go on "hiatus" from June to September, so she knew she would have some extra time. She turned first to her pastor, H. Beecher Hicks. "Pastor Hicks," she recalls saying to him, "there's a job coming up. Now we can pray about this job. But do you have any connections?" It turned out he did. He called Reverend Garrett, a special assistant to Vice-President Bush, who in turn called Mel Bradley, a special assistant to President Reagan. After meeting with Doris McMillon, Bradley sent a letter and one of her videotapes over to Charles Wick, the head of the USIA, asking him to take a careful look at her.

This was not the only message Charles Wick was to receive about Doris McMillon. A few days later, McMillon happened to run into Bill Gray, a black congressman from Philadelphia whom she had interviewed on her show for the Black Entertainment Network. She told him that she had applied for a job at the USIA, and the next day, Gray called Wick to recommend McMillon.

McMillon is a devout Christian who hopes someday to be a television evangelist. "The Lord," she told us, "did not put me into this profession to do bad news. Gospel means good news." When she mentioned her interest in the USIA job to Senator Paul Tribble's wife, Rosemary, a member of her Tuesday morning prayer group, Rosemary Tribble wrote Wick "a glowing letter of recommendation," as did Jim Quello, a commissioner for the Federal Communications Commission whom she had known since her radio days in Detroit. After all these recommendations came into the USIA, the next thing she knew, McMillon was broadcasting news around the world for Worldnet.

ABC Graduates at Work:
Stars, Professionals, and Hidden ABCers

How effectively have ABC graduates used the formal educations they obtained and the cultural and social capital that accompanied their formal education? On the basis of our interviews with ABC graduates, in which they described not only their own careers but the careers of other ABC students, we have concluded that most fall into one of three categories: stars, professionals, and "hidden ABCers."

THE STARS

By ABC stars, we are referring to people who have done exceptionally well in their chosen fields, people who have gained regional and, in many cases, national recognition for their success. These ABC graduates are on the cutting edge. Many have risen to occupational heights in fields that have long been dominated by whites.

More than a few of those we interviewed, and others we heard about, fall in this category. Sylvester Monroe, the writer for *Newsweek,* is surely a star, as is Monique Burns, who graduated first from the Concord Academy and then from Radcliffe College, and who at the time of our interview was a senior editor at *Travel & Leisure.* Eric Coleman, a state legislator from Hartford, is a rising political star in his home state, as is Frank Borges, at the time of our interview the treasurer of the state of Connecticut. Doris McMillon falls into our star category, as does Harold Cushenberry, the youngest judge on the superior court in Washington, D.C. Many other stars have emerged from the ABC program. Rather than list the occupational accomplishments of all of them, we have chosen to profile two: Jesse Spikes, the Dartmouth graduate who was a Rhodes Scholar and is now a corporate lawyer in Atlanta, and Linda Hurley, who at the age of thirty-three became one of the highest-ranking women in minority banking in the country.

Jesse Spikes. Jesse Spikes's upward movement through the competitive worlds of academia, law, and business has been continuous and rapid. After graduating—as one of the best athletes and one of the best students—from Hanover High School, Spikes enrolled at Dartmouth. Majoring in English, he took advantage of the opportunity to spend one semester during his sophomore year in France and the winter term of his senior year in Nairobi. He was editor of Dartmouth's Afro-American Literary Society magazine; he played football one year and ran track all four years; he was elected to Phi Beta Kappa; and he graduated magna cum laude. No one was surprised when he won a Rhodes Scholarship in the fall of his senior year.

Spikes spent the next two years at Oxford studying comparative politics and philosophy. When he entered Oxford, he had decided that he would go to law school, but he had not yet decided where to apply. Having spent six years in New Hampshire and two in England, he was leaning toward returning to the South and was seriously considering the University of Virginia. But his Oxford philosophy tutor told him bluntly that to do the things he wanted to do, it would be useful to have the contacts Harvard would provide. "You need to know those people," the tutor told him, and Spikes, finding it hard to disagree, applied to and was accepted at Harvard.

After three years at Harvard, Spikes did return to the South to work for an Atlanta law firm that had employed him during the summer after his first year of law school. But offers kept coming his way, some of which took him a long way from his home state. In fact, although each job change marked a step up in his career, he changed jobs so often that some colleagues questioned his ability to stay with one job.

After only two months with the law firm in Atlanta, Spikes was offered a job as clerk with Damon Keith, a federal judge in Detroit, Michigan. Eight months later he took this job. Keith had been appointed by President Carter to the U.S. Court of Appeals, Sixth Circuit. During the next thirteen months, Spikes and Judge Keith commuted back and forth from Detroit (where they lived and did some of their work) to Cincinnati, the site of the Court of Appeals for the Sixth Circuit.

Having completed his clerkship, he returned again to Atlanta. A friend from Dartmouth was a lawyer in a newly formed firm. Spikes began working there in October 1979. But less than a year later, he was lured away, this time to become general counsel for the Atlanta Life Insurance Company. At the time, he says, Atlanta Life was "from the standpoint of capital the largest black-owned enterprise in America."

He stayed with Atlanta Life for less than a year. Although he enjoyed the work and was making no effort to seek another job, another opportunity arose through his networks, and he could not resist.

Andrew Young, after serving as Jimmy Carter's representative to the United Nations, had returned to Atlanta and been elected mayor. Young was eager to see Atlanta develop as a great international city and began cultivating some of the contacts he had made while working at the United Nations. One of those was the chairman of the Al Bahrain Arab African Bank, a bank in the Middle East with international investments. One Sunday in June 1981, in the hope of persuading that bank to invest some of its capital in Atlanta, Young sponsored a luncheon to introduce a representative from the Arab African Bank to a group of Atlanta businessmen. During that lunch, Ebrahim Al-Ebrahim, the envoy from the bank, mentioned to Andrew Young that he was looking for an American legal adviser. The bank did a lot of business in New York and needed someone who could represent their interests. The person would need to relocate to the Middle East but would travel extensively to Europe and America.

Jesse Spikes had not attended that luncheon. Three days later, however, sitting in his office at Atlanta Life, he got a call from Prentiss Yancey, a black lawyer at an Atlanta law firm where he had worked during the summer after his second year of law school. Yancey described the job and asked if Spikes knew anyone who might be interested. As Spikes suggested various classmates from law school and other lawyers he knew, Yancey rejected each one in turn. Finally it became clear that Yancey was calling to see if Spikes would apply for the job; Spikes agreed to give Ebrahim Al-Ebrahim a call in New York.

Things happened quickly after that. Al-Ebrahim suggested Spikes fly to New York that evening, which he was able to arrange. "I met him for breakfast the next morning and chatted for twenty minutes. He offered me the job. I thought about it for four days, called back, and accepted."

The primary attraction was the opportunity to make a lot more money than he was making in Atlanta and, as a result, to help his family out. Spikes had thought he was going to be able to do that when he returned to Atlanta, but things had not worked out that way:

My family was in very humble circumstances. I'd always wanted to do things that my family—my mother and father, brothers and sisters—were not able to do for themselves. I had assumed that would be true by virtue of all this education I'd gotten. I came out of law school in 1977. The going salary was $20,000 a year in the major law firms. To me that seemed like a lot of money. Well, I went out and got an apartment, and I bought a car, and a few furnishings for the apartment, and basically I was going home for meals by the time I got through paying my monthly obligations. So what I realized very quickly was that even though theoretically I was making a lot of money, it didn't go very far, and I could pretty much forget about the dreams I had for doing things for my family because of the limitations of what I could do for myself. So the one thing that really struck me about the prospects of going to the Middle East was the financial wherewithal because the financial rewards were substantial. And I saw it as an opportunity—I wanted to do things for myself, but all these things that I'd always dreamt about doing for my family became quite immediate, and that was the good part. Yes, I wanted the experience, I wanted the exposure, but I saw the opportunity to do things that, until then, where I stood then, would for some time remain just dreams.

The work was interesting and lucrative, but life in the Middle East proved lonely. Even after the business pace slowed down a bit and he moved from Bahrain to Cairo, Spikes still found himself feeling isolated. "The people were very friendly, very nice, but not very open to outsiders. I think that part of my situation was being single. People tend to socialize in coed, family groupings, and a single, foreign male really has no place in that social setting. So I found that most of my social life there was with friends who came over from the States to visit. I met a number of people from the American Embassy, or people who were there doing other things, and I belonged to a sporting club. I was learning to play tennis, and so the people around the tennis court were people I started to spend time with. So, yes, it was lonely and I think towards the end that was the thing that really made me decide to give it up."

He had earned enough while working in the Middle East to afford a long break when he returned to Atlanta. He came back in December 1985 and for the next ten months spent most of his time with family and friends (especially with his mother, who passed away five months after his return). He had bought an old house in 1979 in a predominantly black, working-class neighborhood in southwest Atlanta and upon returning in 1985 he spent a lot of time remodeling it. After being an outsider in Cairo, at the time of our interview he was enjoying the feeling of being a part of his neighborhood. And though he had been tempted by some trendier, more exclusive homes, he felt an obligation to remain where he was.

> I live there by choice. It's a working-class neighborhood. The people there work for a living. They're not young professionals that have moved back in to take over these nice great houses to upscale them. These are their homes. And I've thought about moving to other areas—there's a house on a lake, for instance, that I've looked at, at a decent price—and I really would like to do that from a personal standpoint. One of the things that keeps me where I am is my neighbors. I grew up in Henry County. I never knew a black doctor. I never knew a black lawyer, except I remember one Sunday the school or one of the churches sponsored LeRoy Johnson, who was the first black person in the Georgia Assembly since Reconstruction. And it's important to me to be there. On my street, I'm known as the lawyer. If people are looking for me, they may not know my name, but they'll say "Oh, you must be looking for the lawyer." They know where I live. My neighbors look out for my house to the extent that that's necessary. It's important to me that the kids on my street have a lawyer living on their street to see an example of what they can do, but also to understand that I, too, am just a person like their parents and everybody else around there. There's no real mystique about it. I mow my lawn. I prune my trees. I plant dogwoods.

Almost a year after returning to Atlanta, Jesse Spikes went back to work with his old firm—the firm that includes his ABC friend from high school days in New Hampshire, Oliver Lee. When Spikes originally joined the firm in 1979, it employed twenty lawyers. When he joined them again, late in 1986, the firm, through a series of lateral mergers, had expanded to include seventy lawyers (a "medium-sized" law firm for Atlanta).

So, twenty years after leaving a small Georgia town outside Atlanta to enter the ABC program, and after a journey that took him to New Hampshire, Nairobi, Oxford (England) and Cambridge (Massachusetts), Detroit, Bahrain, and Cairo, Jesse Spikes is back in Atlanta, working in a corporate law firm, living in a big old house, thinking about getting married and having a family. Jesse Spikes's name has appeared with some regularity in ABC newsletters and yearly reports over the years, for his is one of the success stories of which the program is understandably proud.

Linda Hurley. Linda Hurley's rise to ABC star status was less continuous and less predictable than Jesse Spikes's. From the outset of her relationship with the ABC program, her path was unusual.

When Linda was about to enter the ABC program, her older brother was just completing the program as a boarding student at Kimball Union, a prep school in New Hampshire. His experience at Kimball Union had not been a good one, and he consequently counseled his younger sister to avoid boarding-school life. He even looked into the options available to her, suggesting that she continue to live at home with her mother and two younger brothers in the Franklin Field Public Housing Development in Dorchester, Massachusetts, while commuting daily to the Commonwealth School, a progressive private school in downtown Boston. She took his advice.

Although she liked the Commonwealth School enough to stay, she remained somewhat of a loner, partly because she was a commuting student and partly by inclination. There were about a dozen other black students, but many of them, like most of the white students, seemed to be from another world. "It appeared that most of the black students there . . . were able to pay a significant portion of their way through. That put them in a radically different class. I lived in Dorchester in a housing project; they lived in Roxbury on something that's called The Hill. And even though you hear that Roxbury is a slum, there is a very elite section. I mean, one of my classmates was the daughter of a television announcer. Yes, she was black also, but I had about as much in common with her as I did with some of the whites there whose parents were professors at Harvard."

Academically, she recalls, she was a lazy student, not very likely to push herself. "If I could get by with reading every other chapter," she recalls, "that's what I did." Still, she did well enough to be accepted at both Wellesley and Wesleyan. She decided to attend Wellesley, partly because it was closer to home and partly because the campus was so stunningly beautiful. At Wellesley, she majored in psychology and black studies. She spent the summer prior to her junior year at the University of Ibadan in Nigeria, and she spent her junior year as an exchange student at Spelman College in Atlanta, Georgia. She did fine at Wellesley, but she was not an academic standout. As graduation approached, she knew she was ready to leave the Boston area, but she was not at all sure where she wanted to be or what she wanted to do.

One of her friends—a black woman from Chicago—was planning to pack her stuff in her car and drive to Chicago when the semester ended, and Linda decided to accompany her friend and help with the driving.

She liked what she saw of Chicago and thought she might stay there. First, however, she decided to spend some time with a Morehouse student she had met while she was a student at Spelman during her junior year. As she recalls: "He was living in Memphis and said, 'Why don't you come spend the summer?' And, so, I went down there and spent the summer doing absolutely nothing. It was the first summer I could remember that I did nothing, because I usually worked. I did nothing but swim all day and dance all night."

But when the summer ended she decided to return to Chicago. She moved back in with her friend's mother and sister (her friend had left Chicago) and to help pay for room and board got a job at Marshall Fields. After working there for four months she had a serendipitous conversation with a stranger on a bus that changed the course of her life. "Did you know," he asked her, "that banks are *the* major employer in Chicago?" She didn't know it, but she decided to take her résumé around to some banks the next day. Within weeks she had been hired by the Continental Illinois National Bank and Trust Company.

Though she did not realize it at first, she started out "grossly underemployed." Having come out of a liberal arts background, with no real business experience, and having walked in off the street rather than come through the bank's management recruitment program, she was trained in the personal banking area, the next step up from being a teller. Within a few months, she realized that this would be a dead end. She also realized that others with her background were in the management-training program. "I looked at my peers in personal banking, got a feel for their background, their academic background at least, and many of them didn't have college degrees. Those who did were from—I don't mean to take anything away from these schools in the Midwest—but they weren't Wellesley."

She applied for and was accepted into the management-training program, went through that program, and was assigned to the New York regional office as a commercial loan officer. There, over the next three and a half years, she managed portfolios of corporate customers with annual sales of between $20 million and $2 billion; performed credit analyses; negotiated, priced, and structured loan agreements; marketed noncredit services; and managed leveraged buy-outs. Though Continental was encouraging her to specialize—one of her supervisors told her he wanted her to be "sharp as a pin and just as broad"—her inclination was to broaden her banking experience. By this time she had decided that she wanted to be the chief executive officer (CEO) at a bank and knew that in order to do that she would have to widen, not narrow, her expertise. She also knew that she would not become the chief executive officer at Continental, one of the ten largest commercial banks in the country at the time.

She therefore left Continental to work for Highland Community Bank, which is also in Chicago. As she put it: "I left a forty-billion-dollar bank to go to a forty-million-dollar bank." Though Highland is black-owned, that was not what attracted her. What did attract her was the opportunity to have broader responsibilities than were available at a larger bank. She was given the title of vice-president and director of marketing, and though her main responsibility was to bring in corporate business, she handled everything from local advertising to dealing with the Federal Reserve. In a feature article about her in the *American Banker,* she explained to the reporter that she kept her various responsibilities straight by having a separate notebook for each task. "People would say to me, 'You wear a lot of different hats,' and I'd say, 'No, I carry a lot of different notebooks.'" [15]

During her second year at Highland, this formerly "lazy student" decided to apply for entry into Northwestern's Executive Master's Program. In order to be accepted, one must be in senior management and have had ten years' work experience. Though Linda Hurley had only nine years of work experience, Northwestern waived that requirement, noting that by this time she was the number two person at her bank.

After attending classes all day on alternate Fridays and Saturdays for two years, she received her M.B.A. in June 1987, an accomplishment of which she is obviously proud. Despite the extraordinary demands on her time during this period, she remained active in professional and civic organizations.

In January of 1987, Hurley left Highland to join Seaway National Bank of Chicago, the nation's largest black-owned bank. Her appointment as a senior vice-president made her one of the highest-ranking women in minority banking. At the time of our interview, she was vice-chairperson of the board of the National Bankers Association and still looking forward to becoming the CEO of a bank. When asked if that meant that she would

---

15. Andrea Bennett, "Building up Bank Unity for Big Business Bids: Linda Hurley Harnesses Minority Bank Power," *American Banker,* August 23, 1985, 25.

either stay in Chicago or move back to New York, she said it did not: "It can really be anywhere—and I'm not just looking at the minority banks. I almost don't care who owns it. I'd like an ownership interest, thank you very much. And I don't care who has it or anything like that. But even just looking at the minority banks, there are 109 minority-owned banks. That includes women, Hispanic, black, Asian. There are 39 black-owned banks in thirty-two states. I mean, I could be anywhere."

Jesse Spikes and Linda Hurley are but two of many ABC graduates we consider to be stars. It is impossible to know precisely what percentage of the early graduates would fall into our star category. On the basis of comments made by the ABC graduates we interviewed, including what they told us about others who participated in the ABC program, we estimate that 15 to 20 percent of the early graduates could be called "stars"; this figure dropped by the mid-1970s, when the program was not as selective in its recruitment, nor as effective in its preparation of students, as it had been in its first decade. In our view, far more ABC graduates—probably half of the program's graduates—fall into the second of our three career categories, that of the professionals.

THE PROFESSIONALS

Almost all those who completed the ABC program went on to college. Most completed college, and many received graduate or professional training. As a result, hundreds of graduates of the ABC program work as doctors, lawyers, professors, bankers, journalists, accountants, or in other white-collar jobs. We have chosen to call these people "the professionals." Some of them may be on their way to becoming stars, but by and large, they have joined what sociologist Landry has called the new black middle class, a class that now includes a much wider variety of occupational alternatives than ever before.

To demonstrate some of the intricacies of the star category, we presented fairly detailed profiles of Jesse Spikes and Linda Hurley. In order to suggest the variety of experiences of those we are calling professionals, we will provide briefer depictions of four ABC graduates who fall into this category.

Jennifer Casey Pierre. Born in Baltimore, Jennifer Casey Pierre entered the ABC program in 1968. After successfully completing the summer program at Carleton College, she attended the Baldwin School outside of

Philadelphia. Because of her interest in engineering, she decided to attend Carnegie-Mellon University in Pittsburgh, a school known for math, science, and engineering. When she found her first physics course boring, she decided to switch her major to math, and to minor in business.

While a student at Carnegie-Mellon, she spent her summers working for General Foods. As a result of that work, she won a minority fellowship that paid for her to attend Columbia University's Graduate School of Business. After receiving her M.B.A. in 1977, she went to work for General Foods in White Plains, New York, as an assistant products manager. In 1981, after two years with General Foods and two years with the American Can Company in nearby Greenwich, Connecticut, she accepted an offer from R. J. Reynolds in Winston-Salem, North Carolina.

At the time of our interview, she had been working for Reynolds for six years and had been promoted twice, first to assistant manager and then to brand promotion manager. Single at the time of our interview (she has since married), she owned a condominium in a complex that is mostly white and was active with the National Urban League's Black Executive Exchange Program and with the Forsyth County Court Volunteer Program.

Kenneth Pettis. When we interviewed Kenneth Pettis in his New York office at Bankers Trust he was vice-president and "team leader" of the Global Syndications Group, which manages primary and secondary asset sales within the bank's New York division.

Pettis first heard about the ABC program as a junior high school student in Chicago. Knowing that he was scheduled to attend a high school with one of the worst reputations in the city, he was enthusiastic when a counselor asked him if he would like to go away to a prep school. He had never been east of Gary and had never been on an airplane until 1970, when he flew east to participate in the summer program at Williams College in Williamstown, Massachusetts ("the smallest town I'd ever seen").

After four years at the Taft School and four more at Brown University, where he majored in economics, Pettis was ready to enter the business world. While at Brown, he had held many jobs, including student manager of the college bookstore, projectionist for the film society, and housekeeper for a family in Providence. As he made his plans for what he would do after graduation, he knew one thing: "I decided I wanted some of the things I'd seen. I decided it was time to start making some money."

Employment recruiters were streaming into Brown looking for ambitious young talent. Pettis decided to go with Bankers Trust, mainly because they offered the most money, but also because he believed they had a good training program and because the people he spoke with from Bankers Trust were "enthusiastic." So after graduating from Brown, he came to New York and went through a twelve-month management-training program with twenty other trainees (according to his résumé, he ranked sixth in the class of twenty-one). His title upon completing the training program was official assistant. A year later he was promoted to assistant treasurer; then, two years later, to assistant vice-president; two years later he was again promoted, this time to vice-president, the position he held at the time of our interview. He lives with his wife, a black graduate of Smith College who is also a banker, in Jersey City.

LaPearl Winfrey. After finishing the ninth grade in her hometown of Richmond, Virginia, LaPearl Winfrey attended the Masters School in Dobbs Ferry, New York. Three years later she entered Oberlin College, where she majored in psychology and graduated in three years. (When she arrived at Oberlin, she realized that if she took the usual four years, she and her two younger sisters would all be in college at the same time; to avoid this drain on family finances, she went to school each summer and finished in three years.)

During her second year at Oberlin, she met her future husband, a black student from Chicago who had started at Oberlin in 1964, dropped out of school to go into military service, and subsequently returned to Oberlin. When he graduated, a year before she did, he returned to Chicago to work as an advertising representative for one of the newspapers there. She joined him in Chicago after she graduated, worked for a year, and then entered a master's program in psychology at Roosevelt University. After completing the program and working for another three or four years, she decided it was time to get her Ph.D. in clinical psychology.

Her husband thought he was going to receive a promotion that would send him to New York City, so LaPearl Winfrey applied to doctoral programs in the New York area. As it turned out, he did not get the opportunity to move to New York, but she was accepted at Stony Brook. She decided to go anyway, leaving her husband and their two-year-old daughter in Chicago, and commuting back to Chicago when she could. After three years at Stony Brook she returned to Chicago, where she now works as a clinical psychologist in a practice with five other therapists (four women and one man), all of them black. She, her husband, and their daughter live in a predominantly black neighborhood.

Calvin Dorsey. In autumn 1968, Calvin Dorsey, the youngest of six children, left Clarksdale, a city of 20,000 in northwest Mississippi, to attend the Mount Hermon School. After three enjoyable years there ("It was just a wonderful experience"), he attended Stanford University, where he majored in political science and minored in communications.

After graduating from Stanford, he returned to the South to enter a master's program in communications at the University of Mississippi. He earned his M.A. and then lived in his hometown of Clarksdale, where he worked first as a disc jockey and then started his own record promotion company.

He left Clarksdale to sell advertising for Cox Communications. After two years in Chattanooga, he was transferred to Atlanta. At the time of our interview, he had been working for Cox in Atlanta for five years and was living with his wife in a renovated home they had recently purchased in a predominantly black neighborhood on the south side of the city.

Jennifer Casey Pierre, Kenneth Pettis, LaPearl Winfrey, and Calvin Dorsey are representative of the many ABC graduates who are professionals. They all have at least a B.A. degree, and three of them have advanced degrees. Although none could be called wealthy, they all earn good money, own their homes, and have entered what Landry calls the new black middle class.

THE HIDDEN ABCERS

There is a third category, one that the ABC program doesn't talk a great deal about. This category includes those who dropped out of the program, either during the summer program or after starting prep school, and those who have not been successful. Some of these individuals have run into trouble with the law. Yet this group also includes graduates of the program who, by any external measure, seem to be doing fine but have come to believe that they have not lived up to the high expectations that the program had for them or they had for themselves. These are the hidden ABCers, those who, over the years, have chosen not to maintain contact with the program.

In our interviews, we heard many stories about ABC students who had dropped out of the program. As we indicated in chapter 3, some of these dropouts went on to do well at their local public high schools, and some attended prestigious colleges; others ran into trouble with drugs or the law, and some are no longer alive.

Certainly the most publicized case of an ABC graduate running into trouble was that of Edmund Perry. The 1985 graduate of Exeter was killed late one night on a dark street in Harlem while he and his brother, Jonah, were in the process of mugging a jogger who turned out to be a plainclothes policeman. As we indicated in our first chapter, the widespread publicity generated by the death of Edmund Perry has skewed the impression casual observers have of the ABC program and its graduates. Much of the publicity suggested, at times explicitly and at times implicitly, that even when given the prestigious education of a school like Exeter, A Better Chance students are likely to bungle the opportunity to improve their lot in life.

Though Perry is not the only former ABC student to run into trouble with the law,[16] we are convinced that very few ABC graduates have faced such difficulties. But, as we have indicated, there are others who also fall into the category of the hidden ABCer.

It was Linda Hurley, one of our stars, who used the term *hidden ABCers* during our interview to refer to "people who won't come forward because they don't feel they've lived up to the standards of ABC." The most poignant example she had of such a person was her older brother, who attended the Kimball Union Academy, dropped out of college, and is now a successful dancer living in Europe.

> He is living a very happy and successful life, but is it what ABC prepared him to do? Well, probably ABC didn't care, but there is this image we have that I am supposed to be the next black Einstein, if you will, or something because I've been given the chance. But there are a whole lot of people who are so afraid to identify themselves as ABCers because they felt, "I'm the ABCer who fell in the crack," or "I'm the one that didn't conform," or "I'm the one who never even finished the ABC program." And I think that's unfortunate. There's no reason for us to have pressure on us for the rest of our lives just because we got this opportunity and somehow didn't live up to our interpretation of what it was trying to do for us. . . . I talk to my

16. In response to an excerpt from Robert Sam Anson's book, *Best Intentions*, which appeared in *New York* magazine, former ABC student Michael DeVeaux wrote a letter to the editor from prison. "I attended the Hotchkiss Preparatory School for Boys in Lakeville, Connecticut," he wrote. "I understand Edmund Perry. I have lived his life. I have thought his thoughts. Like Perry, I was not prepared for the psychological and emotional trauma of the white-prep-school experience. Unlike Perry, though, I am alive, and I, too, have a story worth telling. In another sense, though, I, too, am dead. I have been convicted of murder and am serving an indeterminate life sentence. My sepulcher is a cell at the infamous Sing Sing prison" (*New York*, June 15, 1987, 11).

brother sometimes about Kimball. We used to go up there to visit and he used to come home all the time. But there is still this pain, and Jesus, my brother has been out of high school forever.

In the course of our interviews, we heard about various other people who had not followed the traditional path to success. One name came up twice: Spencer Armstead. His name was first mentioned during our interview with Barry Greene, a banker in Richmond. Greene had gone to junior high school with Spencer Armstead; then he had gone to the Peddie School and Armstead to the Cushing Academy. Greene had seen Armstead at a softball game in Richmond a year or two earlier but wasn't sure how to contact him. A few months later, during an interview in Washington, D.C., television newscaster Doris McMillon mentioned Armstead while listing the names of other black ABC students who had been at the Cushing Academy when she was there. She didn't have an address for him but provided the name of someone at Cushing who might know more about him. That person told us Armstead was indeed in Richmond, where he was working as a chauffeur, and gave us his address and phone number. After a few letters and phone calls, we drove to Richmond to interview Armstead.

Spencer Armstead . . . but, now, Spencer Edward Jones, III. When we met Spencer Armstead, a stocky, five-foot, six-inch former halfback with a light complexion and a close-cropped beard, we asked him, as we asked each of those interviewed, whether he minded if we taped the interview. Like all but one of those interviewed, he agreed. When we then asked whether he preferred that we use his name or refer to him anonymously, he said he didn't mind if we identified him, but pointed out that he had legally changed his name five years earlier. He wrote his new name—Spencer Edward Jones III—on the file folder on which we had written the name Spencer Armstead.

Earlier than he can recall, his parents had split up and his mother had married Andrew Armstead. Though Spencer knew his real father was named Jones, he grew up using his stepfather's surname. In spring 1966, when he was in the tenth grade, he was asked to participate in the ABC program.

That summer, Armstead attended the summer program at Carleton College. Like so many who went through the summer program in those early years, he has very fond memories of that summer. He worked hard and learned new things, but mostly he remembers the intense camaraderie that developed over the eight weeks he and the other students spent in Minnesota. The parting scene was particularly memorable: "When it was time to go, everybody cried. I mean, everybody. The tough guys. It was real moving. Because we were so raw, and we were away from home, many for the first time, it was like, why couldn't we just take this whole group and go to one school? It was like nobody wanted to leave, people were pulling each other apart, and the advisers and stuff were crying. It was very, very moving."

His experience at Carleton was so positive that three years later, when he graduated from Cushing Academy (though he had finished his sophomore year back in Richmond, he had been asked to enter Cushing as a sophomore), he decided to go to Carleton. Like other ABC students who had attended the summer program at Carleton, he chose to return there for college in part because of Fred Easter, a black administrator who ran the summer program. Armstead recalls Easter as "beyond unbelievable," someone who would challenge students to take full advantage of the opportunity they were being given: "He was the disciplinarian. The big guys, he was the one who would go up to 'em and collar 'em and tell 'em: 'Look here, man, don't blow this.' He'd say: 'You got brothers back in the ghetto, turning junkies and whatever, and here you are, you got all this, white folks are going to take care of you, pay for this, all you got to do is learn.' You could relate to him."

The transition from Cushing to Carleton was dramatic. At Cushing, Armstead had been a star athlete (a halfback on the football team, a guard on the basketball team, and an outfielder on the baseball team), popular, and a decent, though not particularly good, student. In his view, you had to be "really dumb" to get poor grades at Cushing because your behavior was monitored so carefully that at the slightest drop in performance, teachers would be on your case, pushing you to do your work. As he put it: "The academic part of it, I could keep up. I wasn't at the head of the class, but I wasn't a dummy, I could keep up. I never got bad grades. Really, if you got bad grades at Cushing you was really dumb, because the teachers . . . lived in the dorm. If you was messin' up, the teacher would come knock on your door at eight o'clock after dinner, and sit down with you, and say 'Now what's the problem?'"

At Carleton, however, no one was monitoring him on a daily basis, and the temptations were many: there were women living in the same dorm; it was the late 1960s, and there were lots of drugs available; and you didn't even have to go to class if you didn't want to. "Carleton was just like a country club. It's a great school—I have nothing but the best to say for it.

It was so liberal—I mean, women were living right next door to me. That blew my mind after coming from Cushing. . . . So I just got there and said, 'Wow.'"

By his senior year, he was asking himself a lot of questions about how he wanted to live his life. He had gone to see some recent graduates who were out in the working world and realized that the lives they led were not what he wanted for himself: "It was like they had no freedom. They were already locked into nine-to-five junior executive jobs, they already had the ulcers, they already were in debt over their heads. It frightened me, and I realized that's not what I wanted to be."

He decided he also didn't want to be in college, so during his senior year he dropped out. He spent the next few years

hanging around and traveling, some in Minnesota, some in Denver, Oakland, Reno, Vegas, Tiajuana, I had a ball. It was a collection of us. About three or four of us just up and left school, and we formed what you could call, I guess, a little mutual admiration society. It was that dropout mentality. A couple of them lived out there, so we just kind of hung around, and when things died there, we went some-where else. It was fun times. We were our own people, didn't have any responsibilities. Whenever we'd want gratification for what we were doing, we'd go back and see some of these people who had graduated. These guys, they were, like, "Well, I can't drink but one beer because I got to go to bed at nine o'clock cause I got to be up by six to go to work at eight."

By 1975 he was back in Richmond, and by 1976 he was in jail. Over the years, he had, as he puts it, "been in and out of trouble," but he had never been to jail. One night he and some buddies had gotten into a fracas out-side a neighborhood store, and when a policeman came, his friends ran and he didn't. When the policeman pulled his gun, Armstead blew a fuse: "He didn't need to pull his pistol. When he pulled his pistol, that's when I went off. I said, 'I'm going to take that pistol from you and whip your ass.'" The policeman immediately put out an all-points bulletin. Within minutes, a slew of other police had arrived, and after what Jones now calls "a little tussle," he was arrested and subsequently convicted for disorderly conduct and resisting arrest. He spent the first half of the bicentennial year in jail.

He came out of jail with plans to fight a legal battle associated with some property he had inherited from his grandmother, to get and keep a job, and to stay out of jail. He did all three. Richmond was in the process

of a renewal project that involved tearing down the commercial, industrial, and residential property in his neighborhood. When all but three
houses, one of them the house he had inherited, had been torn down,
Armstead decided to sue the city. He lost the initial rounds at the local
and state level but won at the federal level; the city had used federal
money for its project but had not prepared the required environmental-
impact statement. Because of the outcome of the lawsuit, the city of Richmond has to rebuild the community it leveled, and Spencer Jones is now
chairman of the Fulton Project Area Committee. The city, he says, has
to go through his organization. As he put it, "I'm trying to rebuild a
community." [17]

He has also achieved the occupational stability he sought. For more
than ten years, he has had his professional chauffeur's license. He is now
the head taxi driver for an upscale Richmond transportation company
that provides both limousine and taxi service.

He has also stuck to his third goal: he has not returned to jail.

Jones does not regret his participation in the ABC program. In fact, he
believes that, like the many ABC graduates who became "stars" and
"professionals," he benefited from the experience. And once again, the
emphasis is on interpersonal skills and self-confidence in dealing with
whites: "I feel like I'm a better person from the ABC program. I think
that the main thing that helped me was that [the program gave me] my
ability to handle or understand white folks. . . . The experiences that I
learned in the ABC program helped me to deal with what *I* wanted to do
in life."

More specifically, he is convinced that his ABC experience helped him
in his legal battles to save his house and in his current role as head of his
neighborhood organization. As he put it:

> Everybody told me when I first started, "You'll never beat City
> Hall." I knocked them on their ass. That kind of strength came from
> all the people I've been dealing with: the ABC students, Carleton
> students. . . . All you gotta do is walk through that door. Just cause
> it say for white only, you go through there, see what's happening and
> face issues and people face to face, they have to deal with you. They
> knew what I was talking about and they knew I was right. It was the
> urban renewal thing. They just leveled the whole community, right?
> The oldest community in Richmond. And I got up in front of City

17. See "Fulton Roots," *Richmond News Leader*, November 19, 1977, 1.

Council and started making noises, and they said, "Hey, we got to listen to him." And they found out where I had been educated at and it was a thing of like, "He didn't graduate but he ain't no dummy."

I've always been real appreciative to the ABC program for giving me that opportunity. I could have been a lawyer. That's what I wanted to be. But it wasn't because of what ABC did that I *didn't* become a lawyer, it was because of what I wanted to do after I saw what being a lawyer could turn you into. . . . I don't think I cheated the program. I believe in my mind that I'm a success, though not by traditional standards. I think that I've succeeded because my mind is straight now."

Spencer Jones is but one hidden ABCer, and though his experience differs in some ways from that of others in this category, his account reminds us that some ABC students did not "make it" in traditional terms but still feel that they benefited from participating in the program.

What percentage of those who participated in the ABC program fall into this category of hidden ABCers? Linda Hurley estimated that it might be as high as 40 percent. We think it's probably closer to a third, but we have no way of knowing with certainty. We stress, again, that this is not a category of failures. Indeed, we agree with Spencer Jones's self-evaluation that he is anything but a failure. There are others in this category who by any objective standard (including academic degrees or income) have done quite well, but who *feel* they have not lived up to expectations. According to most standards, many of these people are leading successful and productive lives. When we add them to the stars (15 percent to 20 percent) and the professionals (50 percent), we conclude that the vast majority of those who participated in the ABC program have emerged, years later, as productive members of society.

Corporate America Is No Picnic for Blacks

Being a productive member of society is one thing. Being headed for the very top is another. In this section we explore one of the key questions that animated this research—can blacks with an upper-class style and education make it to the top in corporate America? Can they become part of the power elite?

We define the power elite as the leadership group of the upper class. This concept is very similar to what Baltzell and others call "the establishment," but it has a little sharper edge to it because it rightly gives the impression that the power elite is involved in defending a structure of upper-class privileges that involves the subordination of others. Moreover, the concept of a power elite is narrower in that it focuses on actual decision-makers within corporations and their closely related policy-oriented institutions. The establishment, on the other hand, is a more general term encompassing all those who are comfortably ensconced in all elite institutions related to and nourished by the upper class, including museums, art galleries, up-scale publishing ventures, and prep schools. The concept of a power elite, then, locates power in top-level positions in institutions controlled by the upper class. These institutions include corporations; banks; law, accounting, brokerage, marketing, and advertising firms; foundations; trade associations; policy-discussion groups; and think tanks. All these institutions have their roots in the upper class, and all strive to serve its interests in one way or another.[18]

In spite of the upper-class orientation of the power elite and the considerable number of upper-class members who are a part of it, many people born at the middle levels of the social structure work their way into the power elite. Usually such people have acquired some elite schooling along the way, and they become even more assimilated into upper-class styles as they move up the institutional ladders. Many corporate leaders fit this pattern. ABC graduates are now reaching the point in their careers where they are ready to become part of these inner circles. Many could be said to be part of the establishment on the basis of their prep school and Ivy League educations and connections. But will they move up to the power elite?

By and large, those we interviewed who work for corporations and their supporting institutions experienced few difficulties at the entry level. Indeed, many, especially those with law degrees or M.B.A.'s from prestigious universities, indictated that they were much in demand when they entered the job market. Kenneth Pettis, the vice-president of Bankers Trust profiled earlier in this chapter, told us that as a senior at Brown, he never had to interview off-campus because so many recruiters came to the campus in search of the most promising seniors.

---

18. Our definitions are based on case studies summarized in the following books: G. William Domhoff, *Who Rules America* (Englewood Cliffs, N.J.: Prentice-Hall, 1967), *The Higher Circles* (New York: Random House, 1970), *The Powers That Be* (New York: Random House, 1979), and *Who Rules America Now?* (Englewood Cliffs, N.J.: Prentice-Hall, 1983).

However, once they had worked for a while in these large, predominantly white, male institutions, many became dissatisfied with their rate of promotion and with what they saw as their opportunities in the future. One person who did express satisfaction was Bill Lewis, a graduate of Andover with a B.A. and an M.B.A. from Harvard. At the time of our interview he had been with Morgan Stanley for seven years, and his title was vice-president. How have things gone for him at Morgan Stanley? "Great. Promoted. Top of my class. Making a lot of money. Having a lot of fun. Working in the mergers and acquisitions department."

When we mentioned that in an earlier study of graduates of the Harvard Business School women and blacks reported that they seemed to reach a "cap-off point" beyond which they were not going to be promoted,[19] he responded in the following way:

> This is a service business. Your performance is gauged with others around you. There are a lot of subjective factors—it's not like we're making widgets on a production line where somebody can come by and monitor your performance. We're doing analysis, providing services. . . . In any sort of service business, interpersonal relationships are major in determining how successful you are. . . . I, fortunately, have been able to develop sufficient relationships and do a sufficiently good job to be promoted right along and to do well. Whether that will continue or not, who knows; but to date I haven't had any problems. . . . I certainly haven't received any indication that I'm capping off, but I don't know. Call me in four years.

Much more frequently, when we asked our interviewees about the level of their satisfaction with their work and their future plans, those in large corporate institutions lowered their voices, sometimes asking not to be quoted, and stated that they were thinking of leaving their current employer. In a number of cases, when we tried to call these people back months after the interview to ask further questions, we learned they had indeed left. For example, when we asked one ABC graduate what it was like working for a major New York bank, he responded:

> It has its ups and downs. Being black in corporate America is no picnic. Regardless of how well you are educated or how strong your

19. Richard L. Zweigenhaft, "Women and Minorities of the Corporation: Will They Attain Seats of Power?," in *Power Elites and Organizations*, ed. G. W. Domhoff and T. R. Dye (Beverly Hills, Calif.: Sage, 1987), 51.

background, there are still biases and prejudices in corporate America. . . . I don't feel I've been treated as I should at ———. When I went into the training program, I was near or at the top of my class. Every position that I have been put into, I've always been told I've done well. I've been told that I've done well verbally but when it comes to putting it on paper, it loses something in the translation. Then it is always explained to me as, "Well, you have to realize that I'm a tough grader" or this or that and it doesn't float. You tell me how great a job I do, say that on paper. . . . I see many blacks leaving the corporate ranks.

When we tried to call him a year later, we were told: "He's somewhere out in California."

Some of those we interviewed indicated that they were shocked when they first encountered racial prejudice where they worked. Monique Burns, an editor at *Travel & Leisure,* told us that she had not experienced prejudice at Concord Academy or at Radcliffe, but she did when she entered the working world:

I was the first black editor here. There was one other that had lasted about six months. I understood quickly why. I was treated as someone who was not as skilled as my colleagues, even though I was (and in some cases I was more skilled). Someone had lost a Cross pen, and I had been given a Cross pen by my brother. This woman's pen had her initials on it, mine didn't. She came into my office and started talking about this stolen Cross pen. She picked up my pen and looked at it. I felt hurt, and I don't think she would have done it otherwise, but she had heard that black people steal. It was incredible because I thought the people I was working with were pretty intelligent, and I was just amazed to find these prejudices. . . . I didn't have these experiences in prep school. . . . I hadn't really encountered it in college—it may well have been there, but I didn't notice it.

Some of those we interviewed made it clear that they were planning to go out on their own at some point. "In five years I won't be working for ——— I'll tell you that," one of those we interviewed told us. "I'll be in my own business." Another had this to say about his plans: "I see a plateau for myself that I may have reached already, not only in this organization, but in any large corporation. . . . I don't see a long-term career for myself in the large corporate world, because I think that requires certain compromises which I am not willing to make. So, I'm going to have to at some point strike out on my own. . . . One has to have the capital to jump into something like that, and I'm not in that position yet and won't be for another several years."

This same person noted that his "bitterness level" had increased as a result of his experience in the corporate world. As an example, he told the following story:

The president of this [corporation] is a good-old-boy. I don't know if you know him or not, his name is . . . and his family is very big, I think with . . .—his father or grandfather was head of . . . one of the big Southern colleges—but anyway that is just background. . . . Our [corporation] has been getting a lot of press, because we're doing very well, we're going through some structural changes which the market seems to really like. There was an interview with him and he was not quoted, but an anecdote was told about him. They were trying to get a flavor for the type of individual he is, and in the article they said here is a man who refers to blacks as "coloreds," sometimes correcting himself and sometimes not. Now it was not a direct quote; however, having met the man and having heard some of the internal anecdotes about him, things that he has reportedly said and done, I believe it. And what bothered me more was that after this came out he issued no statement to the population as a whole or the black officers in this [corporation] to try to smooth what he had to have known would be ruffled feathers. That disturbs me a bit. Therefore, I wonder. If indeed that is how he feels, and if indeed he is now trying to mold this bank into the image that he wants it to be, what is to say that his lieutenants and their lieutenants are not going to share these types of attitudes? And, therefore, what's in this for me?

Jeffrey Palmer decided to leave a large elite institution for a black company. He recalled the irony of some of the changes he had made since his undergraduate days as a student activist at Yale. After receiving his M.B.A. from the University of Chicago, he was hired by Needham, Harper and Steers, an advertising agency and assigned to work on the Recipe Dog Food account. "It was so bizarre," he laughed. "One day I had hair out to here and was saying 'Power to the people!' and the next day I had a job selling dog food." He "was doing very well" at Needham but after five years had not become a supervisor. When the J. Walter Thompson Co. offered him a job as an account supervisor, with a substantial pay increase and significant responsibilities to run the Quaker Oats account, he accepted.

He did very well at J. Walter Thompson too but was becoming dissatisfied: "I was on the fast track at Thompson. They put me in all these special things that they had going for their rising stars. . . . I was at a retreat one time and I was talking to the Chairman of the Board of J. Walter Thompson and he said, 'Well, why are you thinking about leaving?' And I said, 'It's very simple, actually. When I came into this company, I looked up and saw the ceiling. The white guy that came in the door right next to me looked up and saw a skylight. Quite frankly, I'm having to bend over to stay in this room I'm in. And it's time for me to move on.' So, he understood that. I told him, 'I can't have your job. How high can I go? Either I'm dissatisfied today or I'm dissatisfied tomorrow.'"

So, after three and a half years with J. Walter Thompson, Palmer left to work for Burrell Advertising Agency, the largest black-owned agency in the country. He is now in business for himself as co-owner and president of the Accent Printing Company, which employs forty people. He has no doubt that he made the right decision: "When I went into the advertising business in Chicago as an account executive, there were—in all of the agencies in Chicago, particularly the ones up and down Michigan Avenue, the cream of the crop in the agency business—there were three black account people in the entire agency business. I was the first black account person ever to work at Needham, Harper and Steers. In 1987, eighteen years later, there are three black account people on Michigan Avenue. And there is one at Needham, Harper and Steers."

Our findings are very similar to those of black investigators who have studied the careers of black executives in corporate America. In three different survey and interview studies, two based on data gathered in the 1970s and the third based on data gathered in the mid-1980s, sociologist John Fernandez found blacks and Hispanics reporting that they were being passed over at the middle levels of corporations. Moreover, they provided him with numerous examples of individual, cultural and institutional racism.[20]

20. John P. Fernandez, *Black Managers in White Corporations* (New York: Wiley, 1975), *Racism and Sexism in Corporate Life: Changing Values in American Business* (Lexington, Mass.: Lexington, 1981), and "Racism and Sexism in Corporate America: Still Not Color- or Gender-Blind in the 1980s," in *Ensuring Minority Success in Corporate Management*, ed. Donna E. Thompson and Nancy DiTomaso (New York: Plenum Press, 1988), 71–99. For a discussion of individual, institutional, and cultural racism, see James M. Jones, "Racism in Black and White: A Bicultural Model of Reaction and Evolution," in *Eliminating Racism: Profiles in Controversy*, ed. Phyliss A. Katz and Dalmas A. Taylor (New York: Plenum Press, 1988), 127–131.

Collins also found that many of the black executives she interviewed in Chicago were on shaky ground. One-third of the top executives in her study who entered the labor force after 1965 were recruited for dead-end positions in personnel or public relations, even if they had such technical skills as accounting or engineering. More generally, she found in 1986 that 38 percent of her seventy-six interviewees were doing "racially oriented" work in their present position or had done so in the last job they held before leaving the company, meaning work in which they interacted primarily with black customers, civil rights agencies of government, or black communities. Not only were many of these jobs dead ends, they were being downgraded or eliminated in an atmosphere of social apathy and intense foreign economic competition. "The lack of a strong push by government on the one hand, and the need to reduce staff costs on the other, will eradicate these positions," she concluded.[21]

However, two-thirds of the black executives were not doing racially oriented work at the time they were interviewed by Collins. One-third had always held positions where they interacted primarily with non-blacks, and one-third had been able to escape from racially oriented jobs, usually because they had gained generalizable experience and skills through sales or marketing to black customers.[22] Nevertheless, Collins is not optimistic that many blacks will rise to the top in major corporations because of the persistence of racism inside and outside the corporate community.

Support for this pessimism can be found in the work of management consultant Edward W. Jones, Jr., a former assistant to the president of AT&T. In a survey of hundreds of black managers with M.B.A.'s from five of the highest rated business schools, more than 90 percent said they had encountered subtle forms of racism and felt they had less opportunity to advance than whites; two-thirds had the strong impression that many whites in corporations persist in the belief that blacks are intellectually inferior.[23]

The discouragement and pessimism coincide with the small number of blacks who have become senior managers in *Fortune*-1,000 companies.

21. Collins, "Marginalization of Black Executives," 329.
22. Ibid. For a more complete presentation of all Collins's findings, see her "Pathways to the Top," esp. 177–178, 227, and 248–257.
23. Edward W. Jones, Jr., "Black Managers: The Dream Deferred," *Harvard Business Review*, 1986, *86* (3), 85; see also Jones, "What's It Like to Be a Black Manager," *Harvard Business Review*, 1973, *51* (4), 108–116, and Joe R. Feagin, *Race and Ethnic Relations*, 3d ed. (Englewood Cliffs, N.J.: Prentice-Hall, 1989), 228.

Jones reports that a 1979 study by Korn Ferry International found that out of 1,708 executives in the highest ranks, only 3 were black. A similar survey by the same organization in 1985 revealed that out of 1,362 senior executives only 4 were black.[24]

In March 1988, *Business Week* named four black executives who might become chief executive officers in the next decade: Jerry O. Williams, president and chief operating officer of AM International; Frank Savage, a senior vice-president at Equitable Life; Herman Cain, president of a Pillsbury subsidiary, Godfather's Pizza; and A. Barry Rand, a group-level president at Xerox, responsible for thirty thousand employees. At the same time, the article noted that only a handful of blacks had moved beyond middle management. Moreover, in the 1980s fewer and fewer blacks earned the M.B.A.'s that are becoming increasingly important for top positions. A comment by Williams of AM International provides the right context for the possibility that he and three others have a chance to become chief executive officers: "I read a lot more stories today about blacks at the top in corporations. But it's always the same five or six people."[25] Ironically, seven months later, Williams suddenly resigned after a conflict with the chief executive officer of AM International over the future direction of the company.[26]

The studies conducted by Collins and Jones include many black executives over the age of forty. This suggests that those ABC graduates we interviewed who are in the corporate world, most of whom had not reached their fortieth birthday at the time of our interviews, are in for even bigger disappointments than they have experienced so far. When the far greater number of whites competing for the few top slots as CEOs and directors is combined with the biases created by personal and institutional racism, it seems unlikely that more than two or three blacks will make it to the very top of a *Fortune*-1,000 corporation in the next two decades, even with the cultural capital of prep school and Ivy League educations. In any case, the next five to ten years will tell the tale for early ABC graduates in the corporate world.

For now, our most confident prediction is that the black men and other males of color, and women of any color, who are invited to join corporate boards of directors will continue to reach these seats of honor via avenues

24. Jones, "Black Managers," 84.
25. "The Black Middle Class," *Business Week*, March 14, 1988, 63.
26. Alfred Edmond, Jr., "Williams Bids Farewell," *Black Enterprise*, 1989, *19* (6), 14. See also "J. Williams Resigns Posts at AM International Inc.," *Wall Street Journal*, October 10, 1988, B5.

other than a rise through management. Instead, they will be appointed from top positions in universities, nonprofit community organizations, and government, or from the world of hype and celebrity. Many will serve as tokens or ornaments. This is what we found for many Jews on corporate boards, and it has also been shown for blacks and women now on corporate boards.[27] It does not seem likely that the pattern will change. The middle levels of American society will become more integrated, and so to some extent will the establishment as we have defined it, but not the power elite.

The large majority of ABC graduates have entered the new black middle class. They are a success. They have made the most of their opportunities. However, what captures our attention at this point are the barriers faced by the highest achievers and the problems encountered by those who withdrew from or resisted the program. From these two ends of the continuum we can learn more about the reasons for success and failure, and thus about modern racism and how black people react to it. It is to these issues, and to the general conclusions we have reached about race and class in America, that we turn in the final chapter.

27. Richard L. Zweigenhaft and G. William Domhoff, *Jews in the Protestant Establishment* (New York: Praeger, 1982); Thomas Dye, *Who's Running America: The Reagan Years* (Englewood Cliffs, N.J.: Prentice-Hall, 1983); M. Moskowitz, "The 1982 Black Corporate Directors Line-up," *Business and Society Review*, Fall 1982, *43*, 51–54; Ann M. Morrison and Mary Ann Von Glinow, "Woman and Minorities in Management," *American Psychologist*, 1990, *45* (2), 200–208.

7

Race and Class in America

We began our study well aware that class has proved again and again to be the primary determinant of social identity and behavior at the top of the social structure. Although religion may remain a salient component of social identity for many upper-class Americans, and ethnicity remains salient for some members of the upper class, such as Jews, we believe that both religion and ethnicity are far overshadowed by class identifications within the upper class.

This recognition led us to undertake this study of ABC and its graduates, to explore to what extent class identification could displace racial identification among those blacks who had the educational background, cultural styles, and social connections to make it to the very top in America. We thus found ourselves in the middle of a long-standing and recently heated debate concerning the relative importance of race and class in the United States, a debate that has taken place mostly in terms of the middle-, working-, and underclass of American society. In this final chapter, we draw on our findings and the best ideas we could discover for explaining them to deal with the second and more difficult of the orienting questions posed in the first chapter—the relative importance of race and class in America.

Historically, the mainstream position has been that race is of far more importance than class in understanding the situation of black Americans. According to this view, blacks have faced deep-seated prejudices and discrimination simply because of their color, not because they were poor and lower class. A few relatively conservative adherents of this viewpoint have sometimes seemed to lose sight of the fact that blacks were brought here as the slaves of a ruling planter class. Even more often some of those endorsing this view have ignored the fact that anti-black prejudices and discriminations built into American culture and laws have been pathetic rationalizations and crude sanctions that have served to keep blacks economically subordinated.

Perhaps ironically, it was great black scholars such as W. E. B. DuBois in 1935 and Oliver Cox in 1948 who argued that the situation of blacks was rooted in a profit-driven class system with a strong and enduring incentive to find the cheapest labor possible, whether free or slave. From this perspective, any personal or cultural prejudice toward blacks that was not based on the desire to exploit their labor power was of relatively minor importance.[1]

But DuBois and Cox were Marxists, and Marxists in America are usually out of fashion whatever their color, so the emphasis on class in the study of race relations was a minor one in the prosperous decades following World War II. Class did not receive much notice again until the mid-1970s, when the black middle class was growing by leaps and bounds and all indications were that blacks would be increasingly involved in the higher education system. Even then, what class analysis there was concerned social classes along a continuous stratification ladder rather than the Marxist view of two contending classes characterized by constant conflict.

The potential significance of class in understanding modern race relations was brought to the attention of social scientists by a black but non-Marxist sociologist, William J. Wilson, who used the provocative title *The Declining Significance of Race* to make his point. Wilson's key argument was that increasingly the fate of black Americans was decided by their level of education and their work skills, and therefore class had come to be more important in their lives. From this observation he took the next, and controversial, step, claiming that race was not as important as it used to be.[2]

1. W. E. B. DuBois, *Black Reconstruction in America 1860–1880* (1935; reprint, New York: Russell & Russell, 1956) and Oliver Cromwell Cox, *Caste, Class, and Race* (Garden City, N.Y.: Doubleday, 1948).
2. William Julius Wilson, *The Declining Significance of Race: Blacks and Changing American Institutions* (Chicago: University of Chicago Press, 1978).

Most black sociologists thought Wilson was wrong, but many whites who study social stratification tended to believe he was probably right.[3] There were exceptions to this black-white dichotomy, of course, and some who said that Wilson was both right and wrong; Pettigrew, for example, argued that Wilson was right to say that class was becoming more important but wrong to think that race was declining in importance.

In Pettigrew's view, a new relation between race and class had emerged. The situation was no longer "either-or." The influence of race and class variables now mixed and interacted in complex ways on different issues. Indeed, the interaction of race and class was important up and down the social ladder. For example, being black and poor has more negative consequences than being white and poor. However, within the middle ranges of corporations and government, as we noted earlier, a good education has come to have a greater short-term payoff for a black than for a white person.[4]

Most of the information for this renewed debate comes from studies conducted in the 1970s and involves the middle and lower levels of the class structure. We think our findings may throw new light on the issues because they include the highest levels of the class system. Moreover, we are able to interpret our results in the context of new information from the 1980s showing a declining percentage of blacks (especially males) going to undergraduate colleges and graduate schools. We now know that high-aptitude black students do only as well in public school as blacks of average aptitude and that middle-class black students do not do as well as white students from the same educational and income levels.[5] In addition, there is often a fairly sudden decline in performance between junior and senior high school. Clearly, the relationships among race, class, and education need further analysis, and the experiences of ABC graduates may provide a good starting point.

---

3. For the viewpoint of many black sociologists and a few white ones, see Charles V. Willie, *The Caste and Class Controversy* (Bayside, N.Y.: General Hall, 1979).

4. Thomas F. Pettigrew, "Race and Class in the 1980s: An Interactive View," *Daedalus,* 1981, *110* (2), 233–255, and Joe R. Feagin, "The Continuing Significance of Race: Discrimination in Contemporary America" (Paper presented at the Association of Black Sociologists Meeting, San Francisco, August 1989).

5. John U. Ogbu, "Class Stratification, Racial Stratification, and Schooling," in *Race, Class and Schooling: Special Studies in Comparative Education,* ed. L. Weis (Albany: State University of New York Press, 1988).

Patterns of Achievement

Both the complexities of human achievement and the relatively small size of our sample make it difficult to pinpoint the factors that have led ABC students to become either stars, professionals, or hidden ABCers. How did Doris McMillon, who had a very troubled relationship with her mother and who flunked out of the first prep school to which she was assigned, become a highly successful television commentator, seen not only nationally but internationally? And what led her former classmate, Spencer Jones, to find himself, in the first half of 1976, a college dropout in a Virginia jail? What caused Linda Hurley to change from a "lazy student" at the Commonwealth School and Wellesley to an ambitious banker, willing to go to school for two years on weekends to earn her M.B.A.? There are no simple answers to these questions. Human behavior is influenced by situational factors, personal qualities, and congenital temperamental patterns, all interacting and sometimes changing dramatically in their importance over the span of a lifetime. However, some patterns seem to be related to particularly high or low levels of achievement on the part of ABC students.

Most ABC students were the first members of their immediate families to attend college. However, the few whose parents had gone to college, even if they did not graduate, seem to have had a distinct advantage. Moreover, whether or not their parents had gone to college, those who thrived in the program and afterwards were especially likely to have had parents who emphasized education and who liked to read. Linda Hurley's mother, for example, never attended college, but she had been a schoolteacher in rural South Carolina. Linda's mother remained "very academically focused." She encouraged her children to read and saw to it that they had dance, acting, piano, and violin lessons.

Similarly, Jeffrey Palmer's father, a postal worker with three years of college, was widely read and, as his son put it, "one of the brighter people I've ever met." Palmer also noted that his grandmother, though not formally educated, "read extensively." Monique Burns mentioned that her father, whose last year of formal education was the eighth grade, worked as a printer and loved to read. "I suppose," she told us, "being a printer, the written word was very important to him, so he gobbled up all kinds of books on history and philosophy and literature, and he educated himself."

Pettigrew has suggested a concept that may help account for the encouragement received by Hurley, Palmer, and several other successful

ABC graduates. He argues that within the economic black lower class there has always been a "hidden middle class," comprised of poor people who have middle-class values and participate in activities typically engaged in by members of the middle class.[6] Chicago psychologist LaPearl Winfrey described her background in a way that fits this concept very well: "I always found myself in a rather curious kind of position, because I think the typical picture of an ABC student is someone who came from a very poor and very deprived family, and I don't seem to fit that mold at all. I was very poor but I don't think I was deprived in that sense. I think that without ABC many people would not have gone to college and never taken a foreign language and would have wound up farming in the back woods of Georgia or someplace. . . . My family was very poor but it was middle class in a sense. We had piano lessons, and we went to camp through church and that kind of thing. Education was very, very much stressed in my family, and I never even considered that I would not go to college."

In some cases, other relatives provided important role models. Although neither of his parents had attended college, Ken Pettis's uncle Ernest had gone to college after his discharge from the navy. "In my family," he recalls, "I was always the one. . . . I was Kenneth who was like Ernest, Ernest being my uncle who had gone away to college. People had expectations for me." And, as we know from a wide range of research, especially that of social psychologist Robert Rosenthal, expectations do matter greatly.[7]

6. Thomas Pettigrew, personal communication. Sociologist Hyman Rodman has suggested a related concept, that of the "middle class value stretch." In his view, many poor people hold the dominant middle-class values and aspirations, but their repertoire of values and aspirations is broad enough to adapt to their circumstances. See his "The Lower-Class Value Stretch," *Social Forces*, 1963, 42 (2), 209.

7. R. Rosenthal and L. Jacobson, *Pygmalion in the Classroom: Teacher Expectation and Pupils' Intellectual Development* (New York: Holt, Rinehart and Winston, 1968); R. Rosenthal and D. B. Rubin, "Interpersonal Expectancy Effects: The First 345 Studies," *Behavioral and Brain Sciences*, 1978, 2, 377–415; R. Rosenthal, "From Unconscious Experimenter Bias to Teacher Expectancy Effects," in *Teacher Expectancies*, ed. J. B. Dusek, V. C. Hall and W. J. Meyer (Hillsdale, N.J.: Erlbaum, 1985).

In his study of the families of five high-achieving and five low-achieving black high school students, Reginald M. Clark (*Family Life and School Achievement: Why Poor Black Children Succeed or Fail* [Chicago: University of Chicago Press, 1983]) found that the parents of the high-achieving students demonstrated persistently encouraging dispositions toward their children's schooling. Whereas the parents of the five low-achieving students had little confidence in the chance of success for themselves or for

Also noteworthy was the frequency with which ABC stars and professionals mentioned individuals at their local junior high schools or in their communities who played important roles as mentors in encouraging and supporting them when they needed it. Bobette Reed Kahn spoke fondly of a favorite English teacher and of an assistant principal at her junior high school in Cleveland, both of whom encouraged her to consider the ABC program and helped her with what turned out to be a difficult interviewing process. Jeffrey Palmer recounted how important Art Kobacher, a businessman in his hometown of Steubenville, Ohio, had been in his life; not only did Kobacher tell him about the ABC program and encourage him to apply, but a few years later, Kobacher flew Palmer and his father to New Haven in his private plane to look at Yale. More than a decade later, Palmer and Kobacher became business partners. Linda Hurley referred gratefully to a guidance counselor at her junior high school who was "an incredible resource" for her family and who guided her older brother and herself into the ABC program.[8]

A "hidden middle class," role models, and mentors, although significant, do not go far enough in explaining the success of many ABC students for several reasons. First, it is important to note that most of the siblings of ABC students did not attend college. The few who did, almost without exception, went to local schools, not selective ones. If being from a hidden middle-class family were enough, many more of these siblings should have gone to college. Second, most black families put a strong em-

their children, the parents of the high-achieving students tended to believe in the importance of school achievement for success in later life.

For an exceptionally fine review of the literature on the many societal, community, family, school, and individual factors that affect black students' academic achievement, and the relationships among these factors, see *Black Student Eligibility: A Review of the Literature* (Berkeley: University of California, Task Force on Black Student Eligibility, Office of the President, 1990).

8. See Wilhelmina Manns, "Supportive Roles of Significant Others in Black Families," in *Black Families*, 2d ed., ed. Harriette Pipes McAdoo (Beverly Hills, Calif.: Sage, 1988), 270–283. Despite the title, Manns looks at significant others who were *not* related as well as those who were. More than half of the significant others identified by her twenty black adult respondents were not relatives. The largest group of these were teachers, counselors, and school administrators, both black and white. These findings are in keeping with the work of Patricia Gurin and Edgar Epps, *Black Consciousness, Identity, and Achievement: A Study of Students in Historically Black Colleges* (New York: John Wiley and Sons, 1975). In this study of black students at all-black colleges and universities, they found no relation between family background (including father absence) and grades, test scores, or measures of achievement motivation (394–395).

phasis on the value of education; there are many more families that stress the importance of education than there are successful black students. Finally, as we stated in the introduction to this chapter, there is evidence that even students from the black middle class itself have more trouble in school than their white counterparts. All this suggests that something may be undercutting the strong emphasis on education in most black families, whether middle-class, hidden middle-class, or lower-class. One clue to the problem may be found in those ABC students who did not do well in school and who have not been successful by traditional white cultural standards.

We found that those who were particularly rebellious and who had the most difficulty accepting authority were the most likely to run into trouble in school. The late 1960s and early 1970s were years of considerable youthful rebellion, of course, and many ABC students challenged the status quo; indeed, many were challenging the status quo by their very participation in A Better Chance. But some students were more rebellious than others. As we indicated in chapter 3, some of those who dropped out of the ABC program were individuals who were unable or unwilling to adjust to the prep school regimen. As banker Ed McPherson said of one of his friends who left Andover during his first year there, he "was the kind of person who would only accept Andover on his own terms."

Three of those we interviewed had graduated from their prep schools but emphasized that their rebelliousness had made their experiences more difficult. Christine Dozier, the only ABC graduate we interviewed who did not go directly on to college, recalled that during the summer she spent at Mt. Holyoke before attending the Abbott Academy, one of the Mt. Holyoke students on the staff recommended that she be dropped from the program "because I had a very independent and aggressive attitude. I was very outspoken and in the small school environment that I was going to, I might be perceived as being very rebellious. And she was very astute in recognizing those things, because it was true. It was like putting a firecracker in Abbott."

Another ABC graduate we interviewed had been fired from his job, had difficulty finding another, and had recently been thrown out of his mother's house. He was living with a friend (but looking for his own place) and supporting himself by parking cars for an expensive restaurant. Looking back on the conflicts he had in prep school, college, and in various jobs, he said: "I don't tend to do well with authority. . . . I'm funny about who I take orders from." And Spencer Jones, who ran into trouble with the Richmond police in 1976, also recounted earlier run-ins with people in authority. For example, after playing basketball during his first two years at Carleton, he left the team because he and the coach had "differences in philosophy": "I liked to show off on the basketball court. You know, play that ghetto ball. He didn't want me to play that." Jones also had conflicts with Fred Easter, whom he met during the summer session at Carleton College and so liked and admired that he decided to attend college at Carleton. Even though Easter was black, he was in a position of authority, and this meant, as Jones put it, "Sometimes you hated him because he was 'the man.'"

How can this rebelliousness be understood? Has it been pervasive among black students in recent years? We think the answer to these questions can be found by looking at research on minority education in other countries, then focusing on the particular experience of black students in inner-city American schools. In this context we can see the continuing and pervasive influence of racism and understand just how important programs like ABC may be.

Stigmatization and Oppositional Identity

In genteel Sweden, where Finnish people are considered inferior, Finnish children fail in school far more often than Swedish children. In Australia, however, where they are perceived as positively as other Scandinavian immigrants, Finnish children do as well as anyone else. By now it is fairly well known that Japanese American children do as well as or better than most white students in California high schools. What is not so well known is that some of these fine Japanese American students are descendants of the Burakumin, a group whose members are considered genetically inferior by other Japanese and often fail in school in Japan. Similarly, Koreans who live in Japan do poorly in school, but Korean immigrants to the United States do quite well. Finally, blacks who immigrate to St. Croix in the Virgin Islands from nearby non-American islands do better in school than blacks who are natives of St. Croix, and blacks from Jamaica do better in one Washington, D.C., high school under study than do the blacks who grew up in the ghettos of the nation's capital.[9]

9. The findings on Finns are summarized in Jim Cummins, "Empowering Minority Students: A Framework for Intervention," *Harvard Educational Review*, 1986, 56 (1), 19, 21–22. The findings on Burakumin in America and Japan, and on Koreans, are summarized in John U. Ogbu, "The Individual in Collective Adaptation: A Framework for Focusing on Academic Underperformance and Dropping Out among Invol-

What are the implications of these findings that an ethnic or racial group will do well in school in one country but not in another? First, they suggest that any genetic or racial explanation of school failures by minority groups is highly unlikely, even though there remains the slight possibility that different groups or classes of Finns, Koreans, and blacks may be going to different host countries. Secondly, these findings suggest that any explanation of school failures in terms of some cultural "deficiency" loses credibility because most immigrant groups are clearly "deficient" in terms of their knowledge of the folkways of the host country. Instead, when the international pattern of minority successes and failures is viewed in conjunction with the varying relations of dominance and subordination in the home and host societies, another explanation emerges. We learn first of all from such comparisons that it is "involuntary" minorities—those who were conquered or enslaved—who do poorly in school. Members of such minorities are stigmatized from birth as inherently inferior to the dominant group, which then treats them as outcasts by excluding them from the better jobs and restricting social contact with them.[10]

untary Minorities" (Paper presented at the annual meeting of the American Educational Research Association New Orleans, April 5–9, 1988). The findings on students in St. Croix can be found in Margaret A. Gibson, "Race Gender, and Social Class: The School Adaptation Patterns of West Indian Youths," in *Minority Status and Schooling: Immigrant vs. Nonimmigrant,* ed. Margaret A. Gibson and John U. Ogbu (New York: Garland, forthcoming). The findings on students in Washington, D.C., can be found in Signithia Fordham, "Afro-Caribbean and Native Black-American School Performance in Washington, D.C.: Learning to Be or Not to Be a Native" (Lecture, School of Education, Harvard University, April 1984) and are summarized in Gibson, "Race, Gender, and Social Class."

10. John U. Ogbu, *Minority Education and Caste: The American System in Cross-cultural Perspective* (New York: Academic Press, 1978), 101–103; John U. Ogbu and Maria Eugenia Matute-Bianchi, "Understanding Sociocultural Factors: Knowledge, Identity, and School Adjustment," in *Beyond Language: Social and Cultural Factors in Schooling Language Minority Students* (Los Angeles: Evaluation Dissemination and Assessment Center, 1986), 90–91. For a discussion of the concept of stigma and how it can apply to a social group such as black or poor people, see Thomas F. Pettigrew, *Racially Separate or Together* (New York: McGraw-Hill, 1971), 91–92, 179–182, 263–264, and 285–287; Pettigrew, "Social Psychology's Potential Contributions to an Understanding of Poverty," in *Poverty and Public Policy: An Evaluation of Social Science Research,* ed. V. T. Covello (Boston: Hall, 1980), 189–233; Irwin Katz, *Stigma* (Hillsdale, N.J.: Lawrence Erlbaum Associates, 1981); and Robert Page, *Stigma* (London: Routledge & Kegan Paul, 1984).

For a very similar analysis of the situation of black Americans in a path-breaking

However, members of such involuntary minorities, whether they are Caucasians, Asians, or blacks, do much better in school when they move to a country where they are not stigmatized and dominated, thus exploding the claim that they are genetically inferior or culturally deficient. Finns are a stigmatized minority in Sweden, for example, because Sweden controlled Finland in the past, and Koreans are looked down upon in Japan because they used to be brought there as menial laborers after Japan colonized Korea. This line of reasoning also may explain the mixed success of Mexican Americans in the United States, particularly in the Southwest, for the Mexicans there were subjugated and stripped of their land as recently as 1848. New immigrants from Mexico to the United States may thus be viewed as a defeated minority in the cultural traditions of at least some areas of the country.[11] This framework can also explain the dire educational situation of native Americans.

Immigrant groups, by contrast, are often successful in schools in their adopted countries, especially in the first generation.[12] There appear to be several reasons for this contrast. Most important, the immigrants have usually immigrated with the hope of improving their lives; this optimism allows them to overlook much of the hostility they face. Some even arrive with plans to return to their home country after saving enough money, which also makes it easier to endure discrimination. Then, too, immigrants seem to measure their current status against their past situation in their home country, not their current situation in their host country; they therefore may not perceive their oppression and exploitation as deeply as the involuntary minorities do. Finally, many of the insults and slights do

---

book on urban sociology. see Jonathan Logan and Harvey Molotch, *Urban Fortunes* (Berkeley: University of California Press, 1987), 124–134.

For a parallel argument by a psychologist who asserts that bicultural pressures put black youth in a quandary, see A. Wade Boykin, "The Triple Quandary and the Schooling of Afro-American Children," in *The School Achievement of Minority Children*, ed. U. Neisser (Hillsdale, N.J.: Erlbaum, 1986).

11. Maria Eugenia Matute-Bianchi, "Ethnic Identities and Patterns of School Success and Failure among Mexican-Descent and Japanese-American Students in a California High School: An Ethnographic Analysis, *American Journal of Education*, 1986, *95* (1), 233–255. For a good account of how the position of Mexican Americans differs in New Mexico, Texas, and California, see Joan W. Moore, "Colonialism: The Case of the Mexican Americans," *Social Problems*, 1970, *17*, 463–472.

12. See Ogbu, *Minority Education and Caste;* Ogbu, "Individual in Collective Adaptation"; Matute-Bianchi, "Ethnic Identities"; and Gibson, "Race, Gender, and Social Class."

not wound them as deeply because they still find their identities within their own language and culture; they may not even fully understand some of the more subtle abuse.[13]

The differences in attitudes between immigrants and involuntary minorities can be seen in the conflicts in Miami, Florida, between the 80,000 black immigrants from Haiti and the 310,000 indigenous black Americans. Haitians speak of black Americans as lacking in ambition, as having given up. On the other hand, American blacks are annoyed that Haitians are willing to accept menial jobs, often below the minimum wage. "They'll do anything the man wants," complained a black American carpenter. American blacks think Haitians are naive, and they point out that in Miami more Haitians than black Americans live below the poverty line. What both sides do seem to agree on is that Haitians are more optimistic. "Haitians don't come here with the sense of racism and white dominance that American blacks have," according to sociologist Alex Stepick. "Haitians still believe in the American dream, while American blacks do not," said Ginette Dreyfuss Diederick, a Haitian psychiatrist in Miami. There are still no studies of school performance, but at the local high school American blacks ridicule the Haitians as obsequious—which probably means that they do not yet share the oppositional culture that makes school and its authorities something to be resisted.[14]

13. Ogbu, *Minority Education and Caste*, 27–28; Ogbu and Matute-Bianchi, "Understanding Sociocultural Factors," 87–88. This pattern has not escaped the notice of successful immigrants. Mark Mathabane, a black South African "discovered" by tennis player Stan Smith, came to America to attend college on a tennis scholarship. His first book, *Kaffir Boy* (New York: Macmillan, 1986), became a best-seller after he appeared on the "Oprah Winfrey Show." In a sequel, *Kaffir Boy in America* (New York: Charles Scribners and Sons, 1989), Mathabane recounts that in his senior year at Dowling College, a small liberal arts school on Long Island, he became the first black editor of the school newspaper. Though unable to persuade American blacks to join him on the newspaper staff, he did get the eager support of two blacks from immigrant families. "Both were children of immigrant blacks from the West Indies," he observes. "They confirmed a phenomenon I had encountered before. I had discovered that most black students from immigrant families were less inclined to allow white racism to prevent them from realizing their dreams. They were hardworking, and came from stable families which adhered to strict values of respect, discipline, pride, and success. They knew that racism existed in America; they everywhere confronted obstacles and setbacks; yet they kept fighting, and eventually succeeded in spite of bigotry" (105).

14. Stepick and Diederick are cited in Jeffrey Schmalz, "Miami's New Ethnic Conflict: Haitians vs. American Blacks," *New York Times*, February 19, 1989, 1. See also Alejandro Portes and Alex Stepick, "Three Years Later: The Adaptation Process of 1980

Given the contrasting treatment voluntary immigrant minorities and involuntary minorities receive and their varying perceptions of themselves as a consequence of this differing treatment, it is not surprising that immigrants everywhere in the world tend to do well in school whereas involuntary minorities tend to do poorly, whatever their racial backgrounds. Thus, any understanding of black successes and failures in the educational system must begin with the fact that they cannot be compared to immigrant minorities and then criticized for not doing as well in school because most immigrants, with the partial exception of some Mexican Americans, came to the United States by choice. They were able to overcome the discrimination practiced against them more readily because of their immigrant identities and because they had not been stigmatized as a conquered minority from birth. But blacks, like native Americans, are an involuntary minority, and they are treated very differently as a result.

As an involuntary minority, blacks have been excluded from good jobs outside the black community until very recently; this job ceiling clearly discouraged performing well in school. In addition, legal and extralegal barriers to black advancement exist. For example, the exclusion of blacks from housing programs was official government policy from 1935 to 1950, and unofficial policy until 1962.[15] Although that exclusion was eliminated in the 1960s, recent studies by the *Atlanta Journal and Constitution* have shown that even middle-class blacks face great discrimination

(Mariel) Cuban and Haitian Refugees in South Florida," *Population Research and Policy Review,* 1986, *5* (1), 83–94; Tekle Woldemikael, "Opportunity versus Constraint: Haitian Immigrants and Racial Ascription, *Migration Today,* 1985, *13* (4), 7–12; Raymond Mohl, "An Ethnic 'Boiling Pot': Cubans and Haitians in Miami," *Journal of Ethnic Studies,* 1985, *13* (2), 51–74.

In her fascinating book, *Between Women: Domestics and Their Employers* (Philadelphia: Temple University Press, 1985), Judith Rollins notes that some white women choose to hire foreign-born women as "domestic servants" rather than American black women because the foreign-born women are perceived as more likely to be "submissive" and American black women are perceived as more likely to be "angry." Rollins writes: "Foreign-born women, more vulnerable and less 'angry' (or, at least, less apt to show it), are attractive to employers also because of their docility and more subservient manner. . . . Such behavior is appreciated and encouraged by employers. Employers' preference for foreign-born help not only emanates from their desire to pay as little as possible but is another indication of their wish to have a certain kind of relationship with the domestic" (130).

15. Pettigrew, *Racially Separate or Together,* 20.

in obtaining home loans from private financial institutions.[16] Blacks in many parts of the country are still subject to unexpected and unprovoked attacks in downtown areas and to police searches in white neighborhoods. Throughout the 1980s newspapers provided accounts of the houses or churches of blacks being burned to the ground. All these actions serve as constant reminders to blacks that they remain stigmatized as a group.

Moreover, most blacks are exposed to recurring humiliation of a sort that most white people do not even recognize. Many social psychology experiments have demonstrated the subtle and not-so-subtle ways whites treat blacks differently.[17] These daily insults hold true even for educated and highly successful middle-class blacks, as Landry points out: "Lingering racist attitudes find expression in subtle as well as overt ways, subjecting blacks to embarrassment and humiliation. It is perhaps the many expressions of unconscious racism and persistent stereotypes of blacks that are most annoying since they have a way of causing 'slips of the tongue' among whites who would never think of calling a black person 'nigger.' The possibility of encountering these inadvertent slips or conscious racist slurs [is] an ever-present reality to middle-class blacks and a source of strain that whites would have difficulty imagining."[18]

The work of sociologist Stanley Lieberson has provided a strong empirical basis for emphasizing present-day discrimination against blacks in understanding their lower levels of educational achievement and employment. Comparing various generations of southern, central, and Eastern European immigrants to comparable generations of blacks on a variety of educational and economic indicators, Lieberson refutes claims that the "legacy" of slavery, family instability, or the alleged lack of the proper norms or educational values account for any differences between blacks and the various white immigrant comparison groups. In the specific area of educational attainment, he presents a strong argument that the "hard-

16. Bill Dedman, "The Color of Money: Home Mortgage Lending Practices Discriminate against Blacks," *Atlanta Journal and Constitution*, May 1–4, 1988.
17. For a good summary of these studies, see Thomas F. Pettigrew and Joanne Martin, "Shaping the Organizational Context for Black American Inclusion," *Journal of Social Issues*, 1987, *43* (1), 41–78.
18. Bart Landry, *The New Black Middle Class* (Berkeley: University of California Press, 1987), 114. See Joe R. Feagin, *Race and Ethnic Relations,* 3d ed. (Englewood Cliffs, N.J.: Prentice-Hall, 1989), 14–16, for a useful discussion of the differences between overt, covert, and subtle racism.

ening of attitudes toward blacks" in the North led to a widening gap between blacks and the immigrant comparison groups.[19]

Lieberson argues that blacks face a very different situation than any white or non-white immigrant group did, for two reasons. First, there is "an exceptionally unfavorable disposition toward blacks due to the slave period and the initial contact with blacks."[20] This is true in comparison to either white or Asian immigrant groups. Second, blacks face a different situation than the non-white immigrants because there are far more blacks than, say, Chinese or Japanese immigrants, whose numbers were limited by Congress. This means that outside the South blacks constituted a far greater threat as competitors for educational and job opportunities than did the Asian immigrants, who were able to move quietly into specialized economic niches. In 1970, for example, there were 22,580,000 blacks but only 591,000 Japanese and 435,000 Chinese.[21]

Drawing on the work of earlier anthropologists and educational researchers, as well as their own field work in American high schools, anthropologists John Ogbu, Gini Matute-Bianchi, Signithia Fordham, and Margaret Gibson argue that the kind of harsh discrimination against blacks demonstrated by Lieberson leads blacks to form an "oppositional social identity" and an "oppositional cultural frame of reference." By an oppositional social identity they mean a sense of peoplehood or collective fate defined in opposition to the majority and its views. This oppositional social identity is more important than any other group identification they may make (that is, class, religion, occupation) because of the consistently negative treatment blacks receive regardless of their situation in life. As Fordham and Ogbu write:

> Subordinate minorities like black Americans develop a sense of collective identity or sense of peoplehood in opposition to the social identity of white Americans because of the way white Americans treat them in economic, political, social, and psychological domains, including white exclusion of these groups from true assimilation. The oppositional identity of the minorities evolves also because they perceive and experience the treatment by whites as collective and enduring oppression. They realize and believe that, regardless of their

19. Stanley Lieberson, *A Piece of the Pie: Black and White Immigrants since 1880* (Berkeley: University of California Press, 1980), 234–237.
20. Ibid., 368.
21. Ibid., 382.

individual ability and training or education, and regardless of their place of origin (e.g., in Africa) or residence in America, regardless of the individual economic status or physical appearance, they cannot expect to be treated like white Americans, their "fellow citizens"; nor can they easily escape from their more or less birth-ascribed membership in a subordinate and disparaged group by "passing" or by returning to "a homeland."[22]

The closely related concept of oppositional cultural frame of reference refers to those beliefs and practices that protect black people's sense of personal identity against the insults and humiliations of the dominant white group. Since these beliefs and practices provide a defense against racism, they necessarily exclude certain white cultural traits as inappropriate, and some of these oppositional practices help to keep whites at a distance when need be. Thus, this oppositional cultural frame of reference creates unconventional ways of moving, gesturing, talking, and thinking that are viewed as irrational and frightening by whites. Ironically, the oppositional culture created as a protection against white racism is then used as the primary rationalization by whites for rejecting black people—they allegedly lack the proper "culture," so they can't be trusted. Once again, a full statement of the concept by Fordham and Ogbu explains it more completely:

> Along with the formation of an oppositional social identity, subordinating minorities also develop an oppositional cultural frame of reference which includes devices for protecting their identity and for maintaining boundaries between them and white Americans. Thus subordinate minorities regard certain forms of behavior and certain activities or events, symbols, and meanings as *not appropriate* for them because those behaviors, events, symbols and meanings are characteristic of white Americans. At the same time they emphasize other forms of behavior and other events, symbols, and meanings as more appropriate for them because these are *not* a part of white Americans' way of life. To behave in the manner defined as falling within a white cultural frame of reference is to "act white" and is negatively sanctioned.[23]

22. Signithia Fordham and John U. Ogbu, "Black Students' School Success: Coping with the 'Burden of "Acting White,"'" *Urban Review*, 1986, *18* (3), 181.
23. Ibid.

Not the least of the valued traits in this oppositional culture are a suspicious, confrontational attitude toward authority and a casual stance toward education.[24] Both make it difficult to perform well in the classroom. To take school seriously—to be successful in school—involves "acting white," which means breaking with a black identity based in part on ignoring white values. Field observations in high schools in California, the Virgin Islands, and the District of Columbia suggest that most black teenagers, but certainly not all, experience a clash between their educational values and their desire to remain part of their peer culture. They fear being called a "brainiac" or, even worse, a "pervert brainiac."[25]

Some of the most poignant examples of the tensions faced by black students can be found in Fordham and Ogbu's intensive study in the early 1980s of thirty-three eleventh-graders in the District of Columbia. Some of their subjects used to be very good students; a few still were. But all these students dreaded being singled out for their academic achievements. The few who were still doing well had developed coping strategies to fend off peer rejection while keeping up with schoolwork.

They describe Martin, for example, a good student who graduated tenth in his junior high class and earned one A−, three B's, and a D for his work in the tenth grade. He attends school regularly and is viewed positively by his teachers. But Martin is very concerned that he not be labeled a brainiac. Fordham and Ogbu had the impression that because of this he did not study as hard as he could have. Moreover, Martin has adopted the strategy of "lunching"—clowning around—to avoid ridicule:

> *Martin:* Okay. Lunching is like when you be acting crazy, you
> know, having fun with women, you know. Okay, you still be

24. For an excellent and graphic account of how young urban blacks regard "the man," see Herbert L. Foster, *Ribbin', Jivin', and Playin' the Dozens* (Cambridge, Mass.: Ballinger, 1974). In addition, for an analysis of the specific social and linguistic behaviors of low-income black children in elementary schools that lead teachers to conclude they have a "bad attitude" and to leave them out of advanced learning groups, see Perry Gilmore, "'Gimme Room': School Resistance, Attitude, and Access to Literacy," *Journal of Education*, 1985, *167* (1), 111–128.

25. Fordham and Ogbu, "Black Students' School Success," 190–194. Not all blacks, of course, are in schools where this is the dominant ethos. See, for example, James A. Banks, "Black Youths in Predominantly White Suburbs: An Exploratory Study of Their Attitudes and Self-concepts," *Journal of Negro Education*, 1984, *53* (1), 3–17. Banks studied ninety-eight black students between eight and eighteen, mostly from the upper-middle class and with highly educated parents. He found that they were

going to class, but you—like me, okay, they call me crazy, 'cause I'll be having fun. . . .

Anthropologist: Do they say you're "lunching"?

Martin: Yeah. Go ask [my girlfriend]. She be saying I'm lunching 'cause I be—'cause I be doin' my homework, and I be playin' at the same time, and I get it all done. I don't know how I do that.

Anthro: So it's important to be a clown, too—I mean, to be a comedian?

Martin: Yeah. Yeah, a comedian, because you—yeah.

Anthro: A comedian is a male? There's no doubt that a comedian is a male?

Martin: A male, un-huh! 'Cause if you be all about [concerned only about] your schoolwork, right? And you know a lot of your *friends* not about it, if you don't act like a clown, your friends gonna start calling you a brainiac.

Anthro: And it's not good to be called a brainiac?

Martin: Yeah, it's—I don't want nobody to be calling *me* one, 'cause I know I ain't no brainiac. But if they call you one, you might seem odd to them. 'Cause they'll always be joning on you. See? When I was at Kaplan [Junior High School], that's what they called me—"brainiac," 'cause I made straight A's and B's.[26]

Rita, another student they studied, who scored at the 96th percentile on the pre-SAT (Scholastic Aptitude Test) test, attempted to resolve her conflict by cutting classes and by sometimes doing poorly. In the tenth grade she received four C's, two D's, and one B, but the next year she had three A's, three B's, and one C. Rita was also one of the few high-achieving female students to use the comedy cover; she was often called "that crazy Rita."[27]

As part of his work for a master's degree, William Foster, one of the ABC graduates we interviewed, has written about his journey from the inner city of Philadelphia to the ABC program. Though he had sufficient academic promise to be selected to participate in the ABC program, this promise was hidden below the surface of "class clown." He writes, "I had given up on education, and was wasting my tenth-grade year at Overbrook [High School]. I don't think I cracked open a book all year. I never

---

positive toward both blacks and whites, though slightly more so toward blacks, and that they were very assimilated in their attitudes.

26. Fordham and Ogbu, "Black Students' School Success," 194.

27. Ibid., 197.

studied for tests and was fast on my way to becoming the top banana in the annals of Class Clowndom. My grades were a disaster. I had decided to quit school within a year's time anyway. What difference did it make? If the white man didn't want me to succeed in school, I'd succeed some place else."[28]

Not all black students reject school or adopt paralyzing strategies that try to span two worlds. Within the overall context of an oppositional culture, some students develop individual strategies that allow them to succeed. For example, a few students take the painful route of becoming "raceless," leading to isolation from their peer group. They quietly accept individualistic achievement values and make an effort to identify themselves as "people" and not as members of a racial group. Fordham suggests there are usually heavy psychic costs to this strategy.[29]

Another type of successful student, termed an "emissary" by Ogbu, is able to "play down Black identity and cultural frame of reference in order to succeed in school and mainstream institutions without rejecting Black identity and culture."[30] Their motto seems to be "Do Your Black Thing But Know the White Man's Thing." One of the most important aspects of this strategy is an emphasis on the fact that any success achieved by the individual contributes to the general advancement of black people. This strategy is more likely to be adopted at a time of heightened political consciousness, such as during the civil rights movement.

One recent ABC participant who read an earlier version of this book told us that in high school he consciously invoked the names of Dr. Martin Luther King, Jr., and Malcolm X when his peers started to criticize him for "acting white" by taking school seriously. He would reply that Martin Luther King must not have been black, then, since he had a doctoral degree, and that Malcolm X must not have been black either since he had educated himself while in prison. This student also took an openly political stance against discrimination toward blacks in the school setting, thereby making clear his complete identification with the black community.

Finally, some students succeed through balancing their acceptance of school demands with their participation in certain "black activities" and

28. William H. Foster III, "Bookin' . . . An Odyssey" (M.A. thesis, Wesleyan University, 1986). In April 1990, "Bookin'" was performed at Wesleyan University as a "chorea poem" to raise funds for the homeless.
29. Signithia Fordham, "Racelessness as a Factor in Black Students' School Success: Pragmatic Strategy or Pyrrhic Victory?" *Harvard Educational Review*, 1988, *58* (1), 54–84.
30. John U. Ogbu, "Individual in Collective Adaptation."

thus shielding themselves from peer criticism. Such activities include sports and cheerleading, but also the "lunching" and "acting crazy" adopted by Martin and Rita in the earlier examples.

Rather clearly, then, some students succeed within the context of the oppositional culture. Thus, what is needed is not an attack on the oppositional culture, which we see as an inevitable adaptation to racism, but to find ways of defining education so that it is not seen as part of "white" culture. The political and group stances adopted by the "emissaries" offer the most promising approach, for they allow for educational achievement within an oppositional identity that openly challenges white racism and maintains close ties with the black community.

That an ambivalence toward learning need not be part of an oppositional identity is suggested by the fact that the earlier, Southern-based oppositional identity adopted by American blacks held a positive attitude toward education. This earlier oppositional identity, rooted in an outward deference and seeming passivity, defined success in school as a possible avenue to greater freedom. This attitude toward education persisted among blacks who moved to the North in the years after World War II but seems to have been transformed in the 1960s by the experience of new forms of racism in the inner city. Perhaps the fact that blacks in the South controlled their (segregated) schools, whereas whites dominated northern schools, also contributed to the change in attitude toward education.

Although many young black women do poorly in school because they do not want to be accused of "acting white," even more males have a problem with their ambivalence toward education. This finding of a sex difference in school performance owing to the development of a stronger oppositional identity on the part of black males helps to explain why the number of black males enrolled in higher education fell from 470,000 to 436,000 between 1976 and 1986 whereas the number of black women increased from 563,000 to 645,000. It is not the whole story, but it is part of it.[31]

Support for the notion that differences in the academic achievement of black men and women can be understood in terms of the ideas put forward by Ogbu and Fordham can be found in a detailed attitudinal survey

31. For a discussion of gender differences in school performance, see Gibson, "Race, Gender, and Social Class," and Fordham "Racelessness as a Factor in Black Students' School Success." For the figures on black enrollment in higher education between 1976 and 1986, see *Minorities in Higher Education* (Washington, D.C.: American Council on Education, 1989).

in Los Angeles high schools by Roslyn Mickelson. In a study showing that blacks are just as positive as whites in their abstract belief in the value and importance of education, but far more likely to doubt that education will have any practical value for people such as themselves, Mickelson found that the gap between these "abstract" and "concrete" attitudes was smaller for middle-class black women than it was for black men of either the middle or working class. Further, she found that concrete attitudes are better predictors of school achievement for all the students she studied and that "being female is much more important in achievement for blacks than for whites." These findings, Mickelson argues, reflect the different occupational realities that black men and women face, for "middle class black women receive the best returns on higher education of any black cohort."[32]

Given the importance of the prohibition against "acting white," perhaps it is not surprising that ABC graduate Greg Pennington would recall after visiting ABC students at twenty prep schools in 1982 and 1983 that he suffered "culture shock" when he went off to prep school for the first time: "In general, the phrase refers to the experience that results when two different cultures are placed together. The culture shock for me began while shifting from an inner city public school in which my major challenge was how to get good grades without letting my classmates know that I was studying, to a school in which the group norms were far more supportive of achievement goals, and even meal times were supposed to be academic exercises."[33]

We do not want to make the idea of an oppositional identity an all-or-nothing matter, or to claim that only black students develop such a stance. There is evidence that Mexican Americans and native Americans sometimes experience peer pressure against "acting white."[34] There is also evidence that some working-class white youth in England and the children of unemployed whites in the United States can develop an oppositional stance.[35] However, the problem does not affect as many white stu-

32. Roslyn Arlin Mickelson, "The Attitude-Achievement Paradox among Black Adolescents," *Sociology of Education*, 1990, *63* (January), 56, 59.

33. Gregory Pennington, "The Minority Student Experience in Predominantly White High Schools" (Report for the Whitney M. Young Foundation and A Better Chance, December 1983), 2.

34. Fordham and Ogbu, "Black Students' School Success," and Matute-Bianchi, "Ethnic Identities."

35. Paul Willis, *Learning to Labor* (London: Gower, 1977); Jay MacLeod, *Ain't No*

dents, and we do not believe it cuts as deeply for them. Thus, over and beyond the obvious and well-documented effects of poverty, overcrowded schools, and other overt problems that negatively influence the performance of black students, we think that the concepts of oppositional social and cultural identities help to explain what differentiates black students from immigrant minorities who were once lower class and badly treated by everyone.

Put another way, these concepts provide part of the answer to those who might think that the ABC program was not important because its students were the "cream of the crop" and would have graduated from high school and gone to college anyhow. Such a claim disregards Perry's finding from his 1972 study that ABC graduates attended far more prestigious colleges than the control group of students who were accepted to ABC but could not attend because of the unexpected reduction in Office of Economic Opportunity funds. More important for our purposes here, it also overlooks Perry's finding that 94 percent of the ABC sample went to college as opposed to only 62 percent of the public school sample.[36] This loss of one-third of the talented students in the public school control group strikes us as dramatic and tragic, and it suggests that at least some of these promising students may have come to see success in school as "acting white."

The problems faced by black youth in school and the need for programs to help them until such time as white racism is eradicated can be seen most starkly when their situation, and that of working-class whites, is contrasted with the upbringing and education of children of the upper class. It is to this comparison that we now turn.

Makin' It (Boulder, Colo.: Westview Press, 1987). *Ain't No Makin' It* compares two small groups of teenagers in a low-income housing project in a large northeastern city. Ironically, the predominantly white group has an oppositional attitude, whereas the predominantly black group accepts an emphasis on achievement and education. The predominantly black group is unusual in that their families are relatively new to this majority white housing project and see it as a step upward from the ghetto; moreover, two of the seven boys in the group are immigrants from the West Indies (130–133). Another boy won a scholarship to a local prep school starting in the fourth grade. One of the seven members of this group is white. In short, the findings in *Ain't No Makin' It* concerning the predominantly black group do not contradict our analysis because the sample is so small and atypical.

36. George Perry, "A Better Chance: Evaluation of Student Attitudes and Academic Performance, 1964–1972" (Study funded by the Alfred P. Sloan Foundation, the Henry Luce Foundation, and the New York Community Trust, March 1973, ERIC Document 075556).

Go to School, Learn to Rule

Children of the upper class are born to a certain destiny. Because of the wealth and social position enjoyed by their families, people have deferred to them and honored them since birth in such a way that they are suited for leadership roles when their time arrives. "Any member of the ruling class is a man of divine right," wrote the philosopher Jean-Paul Sartre. "Born into a class of leaders, he is convinced from childhood that he is born to command, and, in a certain sense, this is true, since his parents, who do command, have brought him into the world to carry on after them." [37]

The psychiatrist Robert Coles, best known for his gripping account of black youngsters growing up in the South during the 1960s, has interviewed the children of the rich as well. He was struck by their sense of "entitlement," their assurance by their teenage years, after some doubts in middle childhood, that they had a right to their many privileges. [38] Similarly, several interview studies with adult members of the upper class have revealed a feeling of specialness that is best characterized as a sense of superiority. "What do you think are the unique feelings or attitudes held by the upper class?" a wealthy Easterner in her mid-thirties was asked. "That's a hard one," she replied. "I think you get a sense that you are better than most other people. It's hard to imagine what better involves. Here's what I think. The unique thing you get from being upper class is this: it's that you're not a nobody. If somebody starts to push you around you can say, 'You can't do that to me!' You have some sense that you have rights and privileges which other people can't trample over." [39]

Similar thoughts are expressed by an upper-class woman who rejects her class, Abby Rockefeller, the feminist daughter of David Rockefeller, the former chairman of the Chase Manhattan Bank. She says her cousins

37. Jean-Paul Sartre, "Materialism and Revolution," in *Literary and Philosophical Essays* (New York: Collier Books, 1955), 224. We would add that women of the upper class are also born to rule, although their domain has been limited by upper-class sexism. See G. William Domhoff, "The Feminine Half of the Upper Class," in his *The Higher Circles* (New York: Random House, 1970); Susan A. Ostrander, *Women of the Upper Class* (Philadelphia: Temple University Press, 1984); Arlene K. Daniels, *Invisible Careers* (Chicago: University of Chicago Press, 1988).

38. Robert Coles, *The Privileged Ones: The Well-off and the Rich in America* (Boston: Little, Brown, 1977), 361–409.

39. Interview conducted for G. William Domhoff by research assistant Deborah Samuels, February 1975; see also Gary Tamkin, "Being Special: A Study of the Upper Class" (Ph.D. diss., Northwestern University, 1974) and Joanie Bronfman, "The Ex-

"don't want to get down to the sense of superiority they all feel. So instead of rooting that out, they use guilt as a shield to obscure it. That's why they are so willing, even eager, to express their guilt: guilt is socially acceptable; arrogance is not."[40]

This deep-seated feeling of superiority often has its origins in youngsters being catered to by servants and local merchants. Learning the history and importance of one's extended family certainly strengthens the feeling, as does attendance at private schools. "At school we were made to feel somewhat better [than other people] because of our class," one retired man said. "That existed, and I've always disliked it intensely. Unfortunately, I'm afraid some of these things rub off on one."[41]

From a middle American or underclass point of view, it might seem that the rich kids had it all handed to them, that they were given every break. But the rigor and discipline of the private schools are exacting. Our analysis leads us to believe that members of the upper class are very proud, in retrospect, of how hard they worked at their private schools. They feel that the suffering in compulsory chapel or in Latin classes, along with the regimentation of daily life, the tight schedules, and the limited weekend privileges, forced them to earn their degrees. They recall that some of their friends folded under the pressure, becoming druggies or dropouts. The prep schools are indeed crucibles of power, as Cookson and Persell state.[42]

Put another way, prep schools help to "stigmatize" their students as forever superior. The resulting superiority complex aids them in maintaining class domination, for they are confident and smooth in interpersonal interactions. Even the negative aspects of a superiority complex, and there are many in terms of personal growth and happiness, are useful in ruling others. For example, people with a superiority complex have a strain of detachment and aloofness that tends to generate awe and deference in others. Then, too, the coldness and isolation of their personalities

---

perience of Inherited Wealth: A Social-Psychological Perspective" (Ph.D. diss., Brandeis University, 1987).

40. Peter Collier and David Horowitz, *The Rockefellers: An American Dynasty* (New York: Holt, Rinehart and Winston, 1976), 590. In her book *Women of the Upper Class,* Susan Ostrander concludes that the upper-class women she interviewed did not merely feel superior to other women, they felt *morally* superior (26–27).

41. Interview conducted for G. William Domhoff by research assistant Deborah Samuels, May 1975.

42. Peter W. Cookson, Jr., and Caroline Hodges Persell, *Preparing for Power: America's Elite Boarding Schools* (New York: Basic Books, 1985), 124–145.

make it easier for them to treat other people as objects to be hired and fired at will and to ignore the suffering and misery at the bottom levels of society.[43]

This attitude of superiority is in direct contrast to the feelings of inadequacy and inferiority that develop in many members of the working class. In *The Hidden Injuries of Class*, Richard Sennett and Jonathan Cobb conclude, on the basis of in-depth interviews with ordinary working men in Boston, that most people come to believe it is their own fault that they were not more successful in school. Because they did not do well in school, they conclude that they have no right to help govern. Moreover, the working men believe that highly educated people have a "power to judge" average people "because they seem internally more developed human beings." Thus, in the eyes of both upper-class and working-class Americans, upper-class people have earned the credentials to rule as a result of their education. Middle Americans and members of the underclasses are not unequivocal about this state of affairs because they believe in principle that everyone should be treated equally: "Cultured people acquire . . . a certain right to act as judges of others, because society has put them in a position to develop their insides; on the other hand, it is outrageous for society to do this, because people ought to treat each other as equals."[44] It's not fair, but that's the way things are: the average American seems to have a radical critique and a conservative agenda, and the result is grumbling acceptance of the status quo.[45]

When everyday people conclude that they are unfit to govern and that they in some sense deserve their subordinate position in the power structure, in effect a hidden social-psychological dialectic operates between the dominant upper class and the subordinate underclasses. This social-

43. Bronfman, "The Experience of Inherited Wealth." Bronfman's work clearly elucidates the negative side of upper-class psychology and shows how these negative aspects help to maintain the class structure.

44. Richard Sennett and Jonathan Cobb, *The Hidden Injuries of Class* (New York: Vintage Books, 1972), 25 and 39. See also Gordon Fellman, *The Deceived Majority: Politics and Protest in Middle America* (New Brunswick, N.J.: Transaction Books, 1973), chap. 4–6, and Melvin H. Kohn, *Class and Conformity: A Study of Values* (Chicago: University of Chicago Press, 1977).

45. Since Sennett and Cobb presented their analysis, a number of different theories have been developed to account for the specific mechanisms through which the aspirations of working-class children are leveled and the working class is "reproduced." For a discussion of the various theories, and an evaluation of them on the basis of his field study of the black and white peer groups discussed briefly in note 35, see MacLeod, *Ain't No Makin' It*, chap. 2 and 8.

psychological relationship complements the economic relationship between the capitalist and working classes. This dialectic of superiority and inadequacy, whatever the exact mechanisms by which it is transmitted, thus supplements the more overt forms of governance—ownership, monopolization of expertise, placement in government positions, and access to public officials—that maintain the class structure.

ABC as an Initiation Process

When we consider how the educational system functions to bring upper-class children into an elevated state and to discourage the aspirations of other children, we can begin to understand what the ABC program did for its students beyond formal education, social contacts, and cultural skills. What it did, very simply, was to negate the usual social-psychological dialectic between the powerful and the powerless by initiating its black students into a new social and psychological identity that overcame the effects of stigmatization and any inclinations toward an oppositional identity.

We use the word *initiate* quite literally, as in the sense of an initiation into adulthood or a secret society in a small traditional or tribal society. We believe with the French cultural anthropologist Arnold Van Genneps that initiations have always played an essential role in providing the reassurance, confidence, and security that human beings all over the world seem to need as they move from one stage or state to another. These "transition rites" or "rites of passage" seem to be especially important for males as they leave puberty for adulthood or enter new adult roles. The isolation and suffering at the outset of most, if not all, male initiation ceremonies are as necessary a part of the process as the later bonding with those who already exist in the exalted state.[46] However, in class-stratified societies such as the United States, initiation ceremonies can also serve to help create deference in other classes as well as to solidify self-confidence and social cohesion in the dominant clique, in-group, or class.

46. Arnold Van Genneps, *The Rites of Passage* (1906; reprint, Chicago: University of Chicago Press, 1960); Geza Roheim, "Transition Rites," *Psychoanalytic Quarterly,* 1942, *11,* 336–374; Roheim, *The Eternal Ones of the Dream* (New York: International Universities Press, 1945). For the classic experiment demonstrating how an initiation process leads to an increase in one's appreciation for the group one is joining, see Elliot Aronson and Judson Mills, "The Effect of Severity of Initiation on Liking for a Group," *Journal of Abnormal and Social Psychology,* 1959, *59,* 177–181.

Several striking parallels exist between traditional male initiation ceremonies and the ABC process. Moreover, many traditional practices also
survive in the fraternities, clubs, and other secret societies into which
powerful people are inducted in American society.[47] First, just as the tribal
initiates are quickly and unexpectedly taken away from their mothers and
placed in isolation far from home, so too were ABC students removed
rather suddenly from their youthful place of origin and put into a summer
program distant from familiar turf. Second, just as tribal initiates suffer
loneliness and homesickness, so too did ABC students find themselves
missing their homes and friends. Third, tribal initiates are usually told
they must abandon their previous childish and foolish ways if they are to
be true grown-ups, and they are forced to learn new styles, words, gestures, and skills. So, too, for ABC students; they were being stripped of
their previous cultural identities, including any oppositional tendencies,
and they were being asked to accept a mixture of useful academic skills
and in-group cultural signals. Fourth, while enduring homesickness and
culture shock, both tribal initiates and ABC students are made to realize
that they have been singled out as worthy of intense adult attention; they
are somehow special—in comparison to females for tribal males, in comparison to lower-class people for ABC students. Fifth, tribal initiates and
ABC students go through their ordeal with other youngsters just like
themselves; they thus come to feel a very close bond with these others
because they endure suffering together and view each other as superior
owing to the special treatment they have received.

When this long and difficult process was completed, successful ABC
students had more than just a feeling of specialness. They experienced
little or no guilt or "What did I do to deserve this?" Instead, they felt that
they had earned something through their own suffering, perserverance,
and hard work, as indeed they had. They had developed a new social
identity—they had been prepped for power. Now they had the social,
cultural, and intellectual capital to deal with anyone. Subjectively, they
felt they were no longer a "nobody," and they had the objective degrees,
blazers, manners, and connections to bolster this feeling and demonstrate
their status to others.

Thus all the pomp and circumstance and ritual paraphernalia of upper-
class social institutions have their role in perpetuating the power structure. More than just mere froth or "status symbols," these rites and symbols play a role in making upper-class people feel superior and in creating

47. Thomas Gregor, *Anxious Pleasures* (Chicago: University of Chicago Press, 1985).

awe and deference within the rest of the population. ABC, from this vantage point, is only a single expression of a typical process. It has been made more visible and understandable because it is performing its function on an unusual (lower-class) and distinctive (black) group of people.

In making this analysis of ABC as a rite of passage, we are not trying to claim that it is unique among remedial educational programs. On the contrary, we believe that a number of different types of programs serve in part to initiate involuntary minority youth into new identities that help to overcome the discrimination and prejudice they face, thereby leading to improvement in their school performance. For example, there is evidence that Head Start helps to initiate disadvantaged children into the dominant culture by treating them as special at a crucial time in their childhood, just as ABC does at a crucial time in adolescence. They are taken on trips, exposed to many new experiences, and treated with love and respect by people from outside their minority group. Although studies of Head Start graduates are somewhat mixed in their findings owing to the variations in individual programs, the overall picture suggests some improvement in cognitive and social skills even from the little extra attention such a brief program provides.[48]

The "I Have a Dream" program, created on the spur of the moment by millionaire Eugene Lang, also plays a psychological role similar to ABC's. When Lang returned to his old elementary school in East Harlem in 1981 to give the usual perfunctory graduation address, he impulsively tossed aside his prepared remarks because he realized they would be boring, or worse, patronizing, to students and parents alike. Instead, he promised the sixty-one black, Hispanic, and Asian American sixth-grade graduates that he would pay for the college education of every child in the class who graduated from high school. Lang's challenge electrified his listeners, and it started a whole new program. A few other millionaires and some corporations began to adopt grade school or junior high school classes in various cities around the country. They pledged to visit with the youngsters from time to time during their school years and to arrange trips for them, in addition to paying their college expenses when the time came. As enthusiasm for the idea grew, Lang established the "I Have a Dream" Foundation. As of September 1988, the families of ten of the original stu-

48. Kathleen Hebberler, "An Old and New Question on the Effects of Early Education for Children from Low-income Families," *Educational Evaluation and Policy Analysis*, 1985, 7 (3), 207–216; and O. Jackson Cole and Valora Washington, "A Critical Analysis of the Assessment of the Effect of Head Start on Minority Children," *Journal of Negro Education*, 1986, 55 (1), 91–106.

dents had moved; of the remaining fifty-one, forty-six had graduated from high school and thirty-six had enrolled in college. These rates of graduation (75 percent) and college enrollment (59 percent) are high by any standards, and exceptionally high in East Harlem, where the dropout rate is between 50 and 75 percent.[49]

Head Start, "I Have a Dream," and similar programs are effective, we believe, because they treat low-income children as special and give them extra attention. As a result, the children realize they are valued even though everything else in the culture implies they are unimportant. "I Have a Dream," for example, demonstrates that somebody of high status cares by guaranteeing the money for college, a measure of value that everyone understands in our money-oriented society. But the program also conveys the message of caring to children through the time prestigious people take to meet with them and through visits to places of power and privilege.

A program like ABC is successful, then, not only because it helps overcome the obvious effects of white racism on blacks as an involuntary minority—meaning such things as poverty, poor local schools, lack of funds for college, and lack of future job opportunities. It also deals with the less obvious but no less important ways in which racism attacks the psychological integrity of its victims. Thus, the ABC program shows that any tendencies toward an oppositional identity are far from immutable. Even at its fanciest and most refined, "white culture" can be readily assimilated by low-income blacks who weren't immersed in it until age fifteen or sixteen. If "chemistry" and "culture" were the only barriers to blacks doing well in white society, then the star graduates of ABC should be making it to the top.

But a proper upper-class style and good personal chemistry are not suf-

49. Susan Lapinski, "Now, They Have a Dream," *Parade Magazine*, September 7, 1986, 8–9; "Boston Fund Guarantees Student Aid," *Greensboro News & Record*, September 10, 1986, A7; William Rasberry, "Changing a Few Lives," *Washington Post*, July 8, 1987, A19; "Ohio State to Aid Blacks in Schools," *New York Times*, October 11, 1987, 18; Julia Lawlor, "You Must Have a Dream," *USA Today*, December 24–27, 1987, 1; James Kaplan, "The Continuing Education of Eugene Lang," *Manhattan, Inc.*, February 1988, 92–98; Joseph Berger, "East Harlem Students Clutch a College Dream," *New York Times*, August 27, 1989, 1. The September 1988 figures we have cited were provided in a telephone interview with Tony Lopez of the "I Have a Dream" Foundation. See also Wilhelmenia I. Rembert, Sandra L. Calvert, and J. Allen Watson, "Effects of an Academic Summer Camp Experience on Black Students' High School Scholastic Performance and Subsequent College Attendance Decisions," *College Student Journal*, 1986, 20 (4), 374–384.

ficient to make it to the top levels of the corporate power structure. Unfortunately, the ABC graduates have come up against the barriers of personal, cultural, and institutional racism just as they are reaching a key point in their careers. They have come near the top, but they are blocked from the top itself, and the usual white excuses, lack of education or the proper cultural style, do not hold.

To focus too strongly on oppositional identity, therefore, would be to miss the point that racism is still the fundamental problem. It would get us back to blaming the victims of racism for racism, as the "culture of poverty" and "lack of skills" arguments tend to do even when they are well meant. We therefore have to return to the issue of the relative importance of race and class in America. We need to see whether race exerts a stronger influence than class on the futures of black Americans.

Race and Class

The American class system can be thought of as a social ladder with fine gradations of status and occupation, or as antagonistic economic classes locked in conflict on the basis of ownership or nonownership of income-producing property. These two models are usually seen as contradictory, and Max Weber did introduce the status-group model partly as an alternative to Karl Marx's class-conflict model. However, both models may capture an aspect of social reality, as most recently pointed out by Reeve Vanneman and Lynn Weber Cannon in *The American Perception of Class*. Indeed, Vanneman and Cannon present evidence that most Americans think in terms of both models.[50]

The first model is based on a continuum of social classes or status groups, with gradations of status and power based on education, occupation, and income. Although people may differ slightly on how many social groupings they identify, generally scholars and laypersons alike have been comfortable thinking in terms of an upper class of rich people and corporate executives, an upper-middle class of professionals and managers, a middle class of salaried white-collar workers, a working class of craft and industrial blue-collar workers, and a lower or "poor" class that is sometimes called the "underclass" or "the other America."

50. Reeve Vanneman and Lynn Weber Cannon, *The American Perception of Class* (Philadelphia: Temple University Press, 1987).

The second model is based on the idea of class as a relationship between capitalists and workers, a relationship that is necessarily antagonistic because of their differing interests. Capitalists want to make as large a profit as possible, workers want to make as large a wage as possible, and the result is ongoing conflict, sometimes overt, sometimes in less obvious or symbolic forms.

A national survey conducted in 1975 by Mary R. Jackman and Robert W. Jackman provides evidence for the ease and consistency with which most Americans respond to questions about class identification that include the categories upper class, upper-middle class, middle class, working class, and poor. Moreover, people's subjective class identifications accord well with the expectations of most sociologists on the basis of income data and the status of occupations. This agreement extends to the fact that there is considerable overlap between the middle- and working-class categories, meaning that some blue-collar workers call themselves middle class and that many nonmanagerial white-collar workers call themselves working class.[51] In other words, the so-called middle and working classes comprise one big "middle America" or "working class."

Although the status-group model had its origins in an analysis that deemphasized economic classes, Jackman and Jackman stress that such groups in the United States are in fact clearly rooted in economic realities. Moreover, they abandon the use of the term *status groups* in favor of the term *social classes,* which is the term preferred by most Americans to the degree that they are willing to talk about class without euphemisms: "We conclude that socioeconomic distinctions produce patterns of informal association that are aptly described as 'amorphous communities.' Because they have a clear socioeconomic foundation, one that is grounded in the person's own experience in the 'market situation,' these communities should be regarded as social classes. Social classes incorporate Weber's concepts of class and status groups: they are loosely organized social groupings that have a socioeconomic basis."[52]

Vanneman and Cannon accept the general analysis presented by Jackman and Jackman, but they go a step further by identifying a large divide between the upper-middle and working-class rungs of the social ladder. That is, they provide evidence to show that a large gap exists between

51. Mary R. Jackman and Robert W. Jackman, *Class Awareness in the United States* (Berkeley: University of California Press, 1983). See also Richard Hamilton, *Class and Politics in the United States* (New York: Wiley, 1972).
52. Jackman and Jackman, *Class Awareness in the United States,* 189.

those involved in managing, planning, and self-employment, on the one hand, and those with ordinary white-collar and blue-collar jobs, on the other. They suggest that this managing and planning group stands between the small capitalist class and the large working class, playing a subordinate role in relation to capitalists and a controlling role in relation to workers. The workers usually lose in any conflict with the capitalists and their managerial allies, but that is not because the workers lack class consciousness or are too divided by race and ethnicity to act. Rather, it is because the capitalist class is so powerful in the United States.

Whatever the differences among social scientists who theorize about social classes, the rough synthesis we have presented in the previous few paragraphs is sufficient for a discussion of the relative importance of race and class. It makes it possible to comment on changes in residential patterns, rate of intermarriage, and social identity as people move up the social ladder or change social classes.

As members of most ethnic and racial groups in the United States acquire greater education, income, or wealth, they rise in social class. If they obtain an advanced degree from a major university, they join what Vanneman and Cannon call the managerial-planning class and what we and the Jackmans call the upper-middle class. If they strike it rich in business or marry a millionaire, they become part of the capitalist (upper) class.

A rise in social class is reflected in a number of important areas in life. These include place of residence, marriage partner, and schooling for children. Styles of life also relate to social class, as everyone knows. So, too, does social identity, most readily understood in terms of the salience of the various reference groups people use as a means of self-definition. Although it is clear that most Americans are very class conscious in the sense that they know where they stand and who benefits the most from the social system, there is reason to believe that ethnic and religious identities may be more significant than class to people at the lower levels of the social structure. Working-class people tend to define themselves first of all as Italian, Eastern European, or Irish, for example, or as Catholic, Protestant, or Jewish, a fact that reflects itself in political attitudes, voting patterns, and marriage patterns.[53]

53. For a classic discussion of social identity, see Herbert Hyman, "The Psychology of Social Status," *Archives of Psychology*, 1942, *38*, 1–95. For our empirical application of Hyman's view, see Richard L. Zweigenhaft and G. William Domhoff, *Jews in the Protestant Establishment* (New York: Praeger, 1982), chap. 5, "Identity and Class in the Corporate Elite." For a discussion of social identity based on experimental studies,

On the other hand, those who qualify as upper-middle class on the basis of their advanced education and professional credentials are more likely to think of themselves foremost in terms of their occupational or professional standing—as doctors or lawyers, for example. Thus, it is only at the top of the social structure, within the upper class, we would argue, that class is taken on as the most important social identity. It is still spoken of in euphemisms, but it takes precedence over ethnicity, religion, or occupation. People at this level call themselves "the community leaders," "the fortunate people from responsible families," or "the upper crust."

We can see the changing salience of social identities best perhaps with Eastern European Jews, most of whom arrived here between 1880 and 1920 as members of the working class and are now distributed throughout the social structure. They make a good case study not only because of their relatively recent arrival and their general movement into the higher levels of the social structure but because they were initially looked upon with scorn, suspicion, fear, or hatred by a white population that was almost completely Christian. That is, they were sealed off in their own "status group," not even acceptable for many decades to some of the German Jews who had preceded them by fifty to seventy-five years.

Success in education and business, however, has allowed Eastern European Jews to rise to the upper-middle and upper classes. As a result, they live in the same neighborhoods as other whites of their social status or wealth, their children attend the same schools, and they frequently intermarry. Although most still think of themselves as Jewish, those who are professionals have many non-Jewish friends in the same profession and do not participate regularly in religious observances. Those who are wealthy businesspeople downplay their Jewish affiliations, join non-Jewish organizations, and sometimes report that being Jewish means little to them. Some have changed their names, and some have become Unitarians or Episcopalians.[54]

We do not want to overstate the assimilation of Eastern European Jews in terms of their social identity. Their emotional attachment to Israel and

see Henri Tajfel, *Human Groups and Social Categories* (New York: Cambridge University Press, 1981). For evidence on social identity and politics, see Hamilton, *Class and Politics in the United States.* See also Ruby Jo Reeves Kennedy, "Single or Triple Melting-Pot? Intermarriage Trends in New Haven, 1790–1940," *American Journal of Sociology,* 1944, *49* (4), 331–339; Kennedy, "Single or Triple Melting-Pot? Intermarriage in New Haven, 1870–1950," *American Journal of Sociology,* 1952, *58* (1), 56–59.
54. Zweigenhaft and Domhoff, *Jews in the Protestant Establishment.*

the difference in their religion from that of most Americans keeps their Jewishness salient for most of them. Many identify enough with other badly treated groups to involve themselves in liberal causes more often than Protestants, and some intermarry with other minorities. Still, it is our belief, based on our previous research, that most Jews within the upper class are upper class first and Jewish second. Put another way, the fact that even Jews have been so fully assimilated into the essentially gentile upper class shows just how powerful class identifications are at that level.

If, however, we compare the situation of blacks with that of Jews, or of Japanese Americans and Chinese Americans, who are like blacks in that they differ in race from most Americans, the findings differ strikingly. Even with two decades of fair housing legislation, for example, there has been painfully little breakdown in the segregation of blacks, no matter what their educational or income level. Other minorities with grade school educations are more likely than blacks with Ph.D.'s to live in integrated neighborhoods. "Most blacks," concludes one study of trends from 1970 to 1980, "continue to reside in predominantly black neighborhoods, even in cities with relatively large and affluent black middle classes, such as New York, Chicago, and Philadelphia."[55] This conclusion certainly holds true for the ABC graduates we interviewed, the large majority of whom live in exclusively or predominantly black neighborhoods. Thus, we agree with Pettigrew that "a strong case can be made that this residential separation of black from white Americans is the bedrock structural foundation of modern discrimination in the United States."[56]

Residential segregation is made even more ominous by the fact that it helps to insure school segregation. More black students attend predominantly minority schools today than in 1976. This means that middle-class

55. Douglas S. Massey and Nancy A. Denton, "Trends in the Residential Segregation of Blacks, Hispanics and Asians: 1970–1980," *American Sociological Review*, 1987, *52*, 823; see also Douglas S. Massey, Gretchen A. Condran, and Nancy A. Denton, "The Effect of Residential Segregation on Black Social and Economic Well-Being," *Social Forces*, 1987, *66* (1), 29–56; Douglas S. Massey and Nancy A. Denton, "Suburbanization and Segregation in U.S. Metropolitan Areas," *American Journal of Sociology*, 1988, *19* (3), 522–526; Douglas S. Massey and Nancy A. Denton, "Residential Segregation of Mexicans, Puerto Ricans, and Cubans in Selected U.S. Metropolitan Areas," *Sociology and Social Research*, 1989, *73* (2), 73–83.
56. Thomas F. Pettigrew, "Integration and Pluralism," in *Modern Racism: Profiles in Controversy*, ed. Phyliss A. Katz and Dalmas A. Taylor (New York: Plenum Press, 1988), 26.

blacks who cannot afford a private school have to send their children to schools where the majority of the students are hostile to academic achievement.[57] The oppositional identity that censors academic achievement as "acting white" thus serves as a magnet that pulls the black middle class back into the lower classes. This may be one reason for Landry's finding that as of 1976 only 58 percent of black males born into middle-class families retained their middle-class standing as compared to 82 percent of white males.[58] It is also congruent with the finding mentioned earlier that middle-class black students do less well in school than other minorities or whites at the same income levels.[59] Indeed, it has been known since the Coleman Report of the 1960s that the "social class" of a school is more important in predicting the academic achievement of black students than the social class of the students. As Pettigrew summarized back in 1969, "By the twelfth grade, lower-status Negro children attending higher-status schools perform as a group slightly better than higher-status Negro children in lower-status schools."[60]

Intermarriage is perhaps the most sensitive indicator that a minority group is being assimilated into the larger social-class system. But national longitudinal data on intermarriage show that interethnic marriage rates have climbed over the past few decades for all groups except blacks. Black-white intermarriage rates in the United States remain among the lowest in the Western world.[61] As we have seen, few black ABC graduates married whites. Unlike the successful Jews in the corporate world we wrote about in our previous book, who were more likely than other Jews to intermarry, there was no evidence of a similar pattern for the most successful black ABC graduates. In addition, though the likelihood of intermarriage increased even more for the children of the Jews we interviewed, housing and school segregation make it unlikely there will be such an increase in intermarriage for the children of the ABC graduates.

The importance of race is demonstrated not only in these patterns of

---

57. The number of blacks attending Catholic schools has recently increased. See, for example, Carol Ascher, "Black Students and Private Schooling," *Urban Review*, 1986, *18* (2), 137–145, and Portia H. Shields, "Holy Angels: Pocket of Excellence," *Journal of Negro Education*, 1989, *58* (2), 203–211.

58. Landry, *New Black Middle Class*, 108.

59. Ogbu, "Class Stratification, Racial Stratification, and Schooling."

60. Thomas F. Pettigrew, "The Negro and Education: Problems and Proposals," in *Race and the Social Sciences*, ed. Irwin Katz and Patricia Gurin (New York: Basic Books, 1969), 59.

61. Pettigrew, "Integration and Pluralism," 26.

continuing segregation but in more integrated settings where class might seem to be more important. Being one of just a few blacks at a prep school, for example, led many ABC students to think more about what it meant to be black in the United States than they had previously. Thus, even while they were learning upper-class styles, they were also becoming more race conscious. For example, Greg Pennington thought that his years at Western Reserve Academy made him "blacker:" "I think I got a lot clearer on my cultural identity. . . . When you're in a homogeneous community, you don't think about what it means to be black, so especially coming from this black school to this prep school environment, that pretty much forced me to spend a lot of time thinking about what it meant to me to be black, and especially what it meant to be in that kind of environment. I became much blacker having gone to Western Reserve."

Similarly, Cher Lewis noted that in her black community in Richmond she never experienced racism directly. Only at the Abbott Academy did she have to acknowledge that some people didn't like her because she was black. Although married to a white, she does not question the importance of race in her life—the title of the book she thinks about writing is "Black in a White Family." Jennifer Casey Pierre grew up in a black neighborhood in Baltimore, and she, too, became especially aware of her blackness when she went to the Baldwin School: "When I was growing up I did not realize that I was black. I knew the skin and that there was a difference, but in terms of understanding the history and all that, no knowledge. Television was a major influence in my life and most of the actors I saw on TV were white, so I used to have this vision of someday getting married and some white guy on this horse, you know, blond hair, would come by and get me. Well . . . when I went to Baldwin, I was a black militant. . . . Upon arriving at the school, the other ABC student from Richmond . . . and I mixed a solution of Tide and vinegar to get the chemical out of our hair so we could return to the natural hair form. And that was the start of the whole thing. I found that I was very militant."

Interactions within corporations also tended to heighten race consciousness because of the "triple jeopardy" blacks face there.[62] Not only do they encounter the usual negative stereotypes and the assumption by most whites that they are "tokens," hired only because of affirmative action, but they must also cope with their "solo" role—being the only

62. Pettigrew and Martin, "Shaping the Organizational Context for Black American Inclusion."

black employee in their company or at their level. Faced with this triple jeopardy, black employees become even more self- and race-conscious.

Nor do we see an attempt on the part of ABC graduates to leave the black community behind. Some are involved in careers that directly serve a black clientele. For example, Cecily Robbins directs the Big Sisters Program for Washington, D.C.—most of her work is with black adults and children. Similarly, LaPearl Winfrey's psychological practice, located in downtown Chicago, is with a group of black therapists, and most of her clients are black women. Others do volunteer work that reveals their ongoing commitment to those in the inner cities—Jennifer Casey Pierre, for example, has been a county court volunteer in Winston-Salem, an activity that has involved her with many black children who have found themselves in legal trouble. And Eric Coleman has a large minority constituency in his legislative district in Connecticut.

Participation in the ABC program certainly did not reduce the black consciousness of one of its later and most famous graduates, Tracy Chapman, the singer-songwriter sensation of the late 1980s, and the class-consciousness she communicates in her music is revolutionary. From a low-income family in Cleveland, Chapman won an ABC scholarship to Wooster School in Danbury, Connecticut, and spent three years there, graduating in 1982. She then went on to Tufts University, where she majored in anthropology and graduated in 1986. She played her guitar, wrote songs, and developed her unique style by herself during her prep school years. One of her best-known songs, "Talkin' 'bout a Revolution"—with inspirational phrases stating that "Poor people gonna rise up and take what's theirs" and "Finally the tables are starting to turn"—was written during her senior year at Wooster School.[63]

Whereas our previous research on successful Jewish businesspeople led us to conclude that the higher they moved in the corporate world, and the longer they were there, the fewer were their Jewish activities and the less salient was their Jewish identity, we did not draw the same conclusion about the successful black ABC graduates we interviewed. Though they were more middle-class than they had been in style and manner, they were not less black.

Our conclusions on the greater salience of race among middle-class blacks are in keeping with the findings from a national survey conducted

---

63. Roger Catlin, "Chapman: A Class of '82 Act in Danbury," *Hartford Courant*, November 13, 1988, G1.

in 1975. Middle-class blacks report feeling a far stronger bond with other blacks than with their class. The authors conclude, "This suggests that for these people, affective class bonds are distinctly secondary to their racial identity."[64]

Although we believe that race remains paramount in black interactions with the white community, we also believe that class has become even more important within the black community, as Wilson (and others before him) emphasize.[65] Once the ABC graduates acquired prep school and Ivy League tastes, for example, it was very hard for them to go home again, and it is noteworthy in this regard to recall that with only one exception, every marriage by an ABC graduate to someone from "back home" ended in failure. However, to say that the ABC graduates were no longer completely comfortable in a lower-class setting is not the same as saying they were uncomfortable with other blacks. Instead, they became part of the black middle class. Thus, we believe the major effect of the ABC program, whether this was intended or not, was to increase class stratification in the black community and strengthen the black middle class, at least temporarily.

In short, even though class has become more important for ABC graduates and the fact that they are educated professionals is central to their social identity, the importance of race has not diminished. The ongoing slights, the strong pressures to marry within one's own race, media accounts of physical attacks on black property, the ceiling so many have encountered in their careers, the residential segregation that continues to separate whites from blacks, and the ongoing worry that their children will fall prey to the oppositional culture are continuous reminders that white racism has not decreased on many important issues. Blacks therefore continue to share a sense of collective social identity centered in an opposition to racism that keeps race the most salient part of their personal and social identity. The unusual educational experience of ABC graduates, living and learning as they did with the children of the wealthiest families in America, allows them to interact comfortably, and

---

64. Jackman and Jackman, *Class Awareness in the United States*, 52. Working-class blacks also showed a similar pattern, but in less dramatic form; only among poor blacks were feelings of class equally strong.

65. For a brief discussion of those who preceded Wilson in noticing the increasing stratification within the black community, see "The Changing—Not Declining—Significance of Race," review of *The Declining Significance of Race*, by Thomas Pettigrew, as reprinted in Willie, *The Caste and Class Controversy*, 111–116.

perhaps with special insight, with white Americans, but they have not been assimilated into the white class structure except in a few rare instances of intermarriage.

We therefore agree with Pettigrew that the experience of blacks in the United States has been different from that of other minority groups and that race remains exceedingly important: "Many American groups have suffered discrimination in various forms. But . . . the phenomenon for blacks is different, made so by their being the only group to experience the confluence of race, slavery, and segregation. It is race, as socially defined by British tradition, that defines black Americans. Based on this distinction, black Americans endured two full centuries of chattel slavery and another century of legalized and enforced segregation. The United States is still struggling to this day to remove this legacy of the past. Direct vestiges of these systems remain deeply entrenched throughout American social structure."[66]

Moreover, it now appears that the racist vestiges referred to by Pettigrew may be even more deeply entrenched than the most cautious observers thought possible just a decade ago. The hopeful commentaries on the rise of a black middle class overlooked the great importance of governmental and community pressure in creating middle-class occupational opportunities for blacks. In an insightful and sobering article published in 1983, Sharon Collins amassed a wide range of information to argue more fully and convincingly than past commentators that direct intervention by the federal government stimulated and enforced black attainments, both within government and outside it. She first shows that four "policy vehicles" created the impetus for the growth of the black middle class in the 1960s and 1970s—the Equal Employment Opportunity Commission, the Office of Federal Contract Compliance Programs, federal contract set-aside programs, and federally funded social welfare services. For example, 879,000 blacks were employed by federal, state, and local governments in 1960—this constituted 13 percent of the total number of black people employed. By 1982, owing to the expansion of federally funded programs, the number of blacks employed by federal, state, and local governments had increased to 2,549,000—23 percent of the black total. Collins also examined the kinds of jobs blacks hold within the white and black private sectors and found that the growth there too has been in large part the result of government policy. In the white private sector, as we

66. Pettigrew, "Integration and Pluralism," 24–25.

noted in the previous chapter, a substantial portion of the black employees have been hired to fill positions in personnel, public relations, or in offices designed to address government hiring policies. Thus, Collins concluded, because so many jobs held by blacks—in both public and private spheres—depend on federal policy rather than on economic factors, the economic situation of middle-class blacks is precarious.[67]

The concerns expressed by Collins have proved to be well founded, for what a black social movement gained through action in the streets has been eroded by a white countermovement at the ballot box. The so-called Reagan-Bush Revolution has really been a white counterrevolution. Its attack on government spending has in part been an attack on the few good jobs held by minorities (and women). Reaganites ignored affirmative action laws and civil rights enforcement when they could not eliminate the laws, leading to black losses in the private sector and education as well. They cut back on student grants and loans for higher education, which differentially affected black students, while arguing for tax credits for parents who send their children to segregated private schools. They allowed the Equal Employment Opportunity Commission to languish. They overturned as "racist" a prointegration quota arrangement in a large New York apartment complex that had created one of the few integrated residential settings in the United States. The list is endless. The Reaganites, backed by more than 67 percent of white men and 62 percent of white women in 1984—figures that would be even higher if Jews were excluded—have fought a silent race war against black Americans.[68]

Contrary to the idea that class is now more important than race for some blacks, it may take a renewed civil rights movement even to retain the gains made in the 1960s. Clearly, race is still more influential than class in the United States.

But this does not mean all is lost. It only means that another battle must be fought. As more blacks gain economic and political power, and

67. Sharon M. Collins, "The Making of the Black Middle Class," *Social Problems*, 1983, *30* (4), 369–382. See also Kenneth B. Clark, "The Role of Race," *New York Times Magazine*, October 5, 1980, 30; Michael K. Brown and Stephen P. Erie, "Blacks and the Legacy of the Great Society: The Economic and Political Impact of Federal Social Policy," *Public Policy*, 1981, *29*, 299–330; and Robert G. Newby, "The Political Economy of the Black Middle Class: Trends from 1960 to 1980" (Paper presented at the annual meeting of the Society for the Study of Social Problems, Toronto, 1981).
68. "Portrait of the Electorate," *New York Times*, November 10, 1988, A16. By contrast, 12 percent of black men and 7 percent of black women voted for Reagan in 1984. In 1988, 63 percent of white men and 56 percent of white women voted for Bush.

as more black-white voting coalitions form in the Democratic party, the cultural myths underlying racism can be overcome. What power created, power can undo. Meanwhile, the inspirational journeys of ABC students like Vest Monroe, Cher Lewis, Eric Coleman, and Doris McMillon, who left the ghetto as young teenagers and ended up near the top just a few years later, remain as a constant reminder of what is possible when black Americans are given a real chance.

Appendix A: The Sample

We began with the hope of surveying a representative sample of ABC graduates and then interviewing a subset of that sample. Because it proved extremely difficult to obtain any names of ABC graduates from the organization, however, we ended up having to develop a snowball sample from the list of sixty names finally given to us after more than a year of effort.

We first wrote to the president of ABC describing our interest in the program and asking if we might meet with her to discuss conducting a study of the early ABC students. We did not hear from her. A month went by and we sent a follow-up letter, but we still got no response. When we tried to contact her by phone, she was not available to speak with us, but her assistant told us that our request was under consideration. A few months later, we were told that we would be sent a mailing list of early ABC graduates; when it didn't arrive, we phoned again, only to be told that one of the members of the ABC board had objected to our being given this information. We proposed what we thought would be an acceptable compromise: we would prepare fifty letters and send them, along with envelopes addressed to us, to the ABC office in Boston. ABC would send them out to the graduates with a cover letter indicating that if they were willing to participate in our research they could send the envelope back to us with a note indicating how we could contact them directly.

Although we were assured numerous times that the letters were to be mailed and at one point were told that they had been mailed, they never were. By the summer of 1985 we had essentially given up on obtaining the names and addresses of ABC graduates and, thus, on conducting the study. However, in October 1985, an informant provided us with the names and addresses of sixty early graduates of the program. Because we had emphasized our interest in examining how ABC graduates were doing in the corporate world, the list we were given included men and women who, according to ABC records, had worked in one of nineteen different occupational areas (these were coded into their computerized files under the following categories: advertising, brokerage business, business administration, commercial banking, contracting, design, editing, financial analysis, hotel-restaurant service, investment banking, investment counseling, management consulting, manufacturing, marketing, merchandising, newspaper publishing, public relations, publishing, radio-television broadcasting). We were warned that the ABC mailing list was woefully out-of-date and that ABC had received a grant specifically to update their knowledge of the whereabouts and activities of graduates.

Although some of the addresses were no longer current, we were happy to have a way into the larger network of ABC graduates, for we assumed that if we could make contact with some of the people on the list we would then be able to find additional graduates of the program. We abandoned our original plan to conduct a mailed survey simultaneously with an interview study (we had neither enough names and addresses nor the assurance that the addresses we had were current) and began to prepare solely for an interview study. We sent a letter to each of the sixty people explaining our general interest in the ABC program and, more particularly, in conducting face-to-face interviews. Twenty-three of the sixty responded, indicating a willingness to be interviewed. None wrote to say that he or she was not willing, and our subsequent attempts to contact those who did not respond lead us to believe that most of the nonrespondents were no longer living at the addresses on the ABC mailing list. Over the course of the next year, the first author traveled to the cities in which twelve of the twenty-three lived and interviewed them. In addition, a colleague put him in touch with an early ABC graduate living in a nearby city, and she was also interviewed.

For the interviews we used a semistructured set of questions that moved chronologically from the time they first heard about A Better Chance through their recollections of their participation in the summer orientation program, their prep school experiences, their years in college, their careers, and their personal relationships. (For the questions that guided these interviews, see appendix B.)

We increased the size of our sample by using the technique known as "snowball sampling." At the conclusion of each interview, we asked for the names and, if possible, addresses and phone numbers of other graduates. Many knew the general whereabouts of other ABC students whom they had met in the summer program, in prep school, in college, or in the cities in which they currently lived, though many had lost touch with friends they had made in the program fifteen to twenty years earlier. Some knew specifically how to contact ABC friends, and all but one were willing to provide names, addresses, and phone numbers. (The one who was unwilling said he would do so, but only after first obtaining his friends' permission.) After certain preliminaries (an introductory letter, then a follow-up phone call), these ABC graduates were interviewed, as were ABC alumni whom they, in turn, recommended. Using this snowball technique, between the fall of 1985 and the fall of 1987 we interviewed twelve more alumni of the ABC program.

Formally speaking, snowball sampling is a method of developing a research sample on the basis of referrals made by people who "know of others who possess some characteristics that are of research interest."[1] Some have even argued that it is an ideal method for some forms of sociological research "because it allows for the sampling of natural interactional units," the very stuff of which cliques, groups, classes, and other networks are constructed.[2] However, in practice, the method is usually used with difficult-to-reach populations or esoteric groups where the knowledge of insiders is necessary to locate members. ABC alumni are not an inherently esoteric group, of course, but they became so for us when we could not obtain a full list of the alumni.

Not all the problems of developing a snowball sample pertained to our work. For example, we had no trouble finding some respondents through the list our ABC informant provided to start the referral chains or in verifying the "eligibility" of those who were referred for inclusion in our study. It did make sense, however, to pursue as many new chains as we could to avoid becoming focused on one part of the overall ABC group. It also helped to ask explicitly for types of ABC participants who might not

1. Patrick Biernacki and Dan Waldorf, "Snowball Sampling: Problems and Techniques of Chain Referral Sampling," *Sociological Methods and Research*, 1981, *10* (2), 141–163.
2. James S. Coleman, "Relational Analysis: The Study of Social Organizations with Survey Methods," *Human Organization*, 1958, *17* (4), 28–36 (as summarized by Biernacki and Waldorf, "Snowball Sampling," 141).

naturally be thought of; for example, we asked about those who had failed, dropped out, or somehow "fouled up."[3] At the same time, we also sought some duplication of key types of interviewees, such as those who had become highly successful in large corporations, to see if the new interviews confirmed the analysis we were developing.

By October 1987 the chains we had developed were based almost entirely on interviews conducted in large cities along the East Coast. When we arranged a trip to Cleveland to interview another link in one of our chains, we were able to convince our ABC informant to provide us with ABC alumni lists for Cleveland and for Chicago. Using the same technique we had used previously—a letter followed by a phone call—we were able to schedule and conduct an additional two interviews in Cleveland and four in Chicago. Finally, a few months later, our ABC informant provided us with the ABC alumni list for the state of North Carolina. Again using the same procedure, we conducted another six interviews.

When we finished, we had conducted thirty-eight interviews: one with a person recommended by a colleague; thirteen with individuals on the first list our informant sent us; another twelve with people located through the "snowball technique"; and another twelve with people on the Cleveland, Chicago, and North Carolina lists our informant subsequently sent to us. The interviews, all but one of which was recorded, lasted between forty-five minutes and three hours. They took place in the offices and homes of ABC graduates, in indoor restaurants and outdoor cafes, and in hotel lobbies.

It is, of course, never clear how many interviews are "necessary" in a study like this. Glaser and Strauss suggest that there is no one right number. They believe interviews should stop when no new information is being uncovered. They use the term *saturation* to refer to the point at which "no additional data are being found whereby the sociologist can develop properties of the category."[4] Using this framework, Susan Ostrander found that interviews with thirty-six upper-class women in a large Midwestern city were enough to give her a very clear picture of the main concerns and routines in the lives of these women. The great emphasis they put on their careers as "volunteers" who run a wide range of social agencies, and the fact that they saw this work partly in terms of limiting government involvement in social welfare, permeated the interviews.

3. Biernacki and Waldorf, "Snowball Sampling," 155.
4. Barney G. Glaser and Anselm L. Strauss, *The Discovery of Grounded Theory: Strategies for Qualitative Research* (Chicago: Aldine, 1967), 61.

So did their deference to their husbands and their pride in being good homemakers.[5] Ostrander's findings were supported by subsequent interview and observational studies in cities on the East and West coasts.[6]

Similarly, by the time we had completed thirty interviews with wealthy Jewish businessmen for our previous book, the main patterns in their experiences had emerged, including the differences in their European origins and in the number of generations their families had been wealthy. Their assimilation into certain social and economic institutions had become clear, as had their exclusion from most social clubs.[7] More recent studies of Jews in the corporate elite report similar findings.[8]

Although we closely followed our interview schedule, in some cases our respondents gave long answers to early items that anticipated later questions; we therefore did not have to ask each and every question explicitly. Also, in some cases particular answers led us to ask a series of questions that were not on our list. When we spoke with a former president of his class at Andover, for example, we spent considerable time asking about student politics in 1969 because he had been one of three black class presidents elected at that school in that year (see chapter 3). And again guided by the work of Glaser and Strauss and of Ostrander, as we conducted more interviews we saw the need to place less emphasis on issues that we had come to understand and more emphasis on others that we were still seeking to understand. Thus we were in part working within the tradition of the interview as an inductive method of discovery.[9]

The thirty-eight people we interviewed may not be a perfectly repre-

5. Susan A. Ostrander, *Women of the Upper Class* (Philadelphia: Temple University Press, 1984), 11.

6. Margo MacLeod, "Influential Women Volunteers: Reexamining the Concept of Power" (Paper presented at the annual meeting of the American Sociological Association, San Antonio, 1984); MacLeod, "Quiet Power: Women Volunteer Leaders" (Ph.D. diss., Yale University, 1988); Arlene Kaplan Daniels, *Invisible Careers* (Chicago: University of Chicago Press, 1988); Teresa Odendahl, *Charity Begins at Home* (New York: Basic Books, 1990).

7. Richard L. Zweigenhaft and G. William Domhoff, *Jews in the Protestant Establishment* (New York: Praeger, 1982).

8. Richard L. Zweigenhaft, "Women and Minorities of the Corporation: Will They Make It to the Top?" in *Power Elites and Organizations*, ed. G. William Domhoff and Thomas R. Dye (Beverly Hills, Calif.: Sage, 1987), 37–62, and Abraham Korman, *The Outsiders: Jews and Corporate America* (Lexington, Mass.: Lexington, 1988).

9. Susan A. Ostrander, "Upper-Class Women: Class Consciousness as Conduct and Meaning," in *Power Structure Research*, ed. G. William Domhoff (Beverly Hills, Calif.: Sage, 1980), 74–76.

sentative sample of the hundreds of early black graduates of the ABC program, but they are similar in a number of respects to those who entered the program in the 1960s and early 1970s. Most of those we interviewed grew up in inner cities along the East Coast or in the Midwest; the hometowns represented included New York, New Haven, Boston, Chicago, Cleveland, Detroit, Philadelphia, Washington, D.C., Richmond, and Atlanta; some were from smaller towns in the Midwest (such as Steubenville, Ohio) and in the South (such as Henderson, North Carolina, and Clarksdale, Mississippi). A handful had parents or grandparents who had attended college, but most were the first in their family to obtain a college education. The parents of approximately a third of our interviewees never started high school, and many of the others had not graduated.

During the course of the interviews, we also asked about the experiences of other ABC students they had known (some of whom they were still in touch with, some of whom they were not). This provided us, in an indirect way, with a broader sample of ABC students.

In addition to the interviews with ABC graduates, we also interviewed, either in person or by phone, scores of individuals who had worked for or with ABC, including all of the former heads of the program, two of the three headmasters who had founded the program (the third died in 1971), people who had recruited ABC students in the early years, people who had worked in the summer orientation programs, and many administrators at independent schools and colleges.

Interviews, however, were not our only source of information. We were also able to draw on a number of studies of ABC students performed in the late 1960s and early 1970s. Some of these, especially those by Alden Wessman and George Perry, were carefully controlled research efforts that included the testing and retesting of ABC students, control groups of white students in the same prep schools, and control groups of black students in public schools.[10] In addition to their considerable value in and of themselves, these studies confirm our belief that our interview sample is a representative one.

There were additional sources of archival, journalistic, and anecdotal data from which to draw. This material included the annual reports published by the ABC program, local histories of prep schools, books about

10. Alden E. Wessman, "Evaluation of Project ABC (A Better Chance): An Evaluation of Dartmouth College—Independent Schools Scholarship Program for Disadvantaged High School Students" (Final report, Office of Education, Bureau of Research, April 1969, ERIC Document 031549), and Perry, "A Better Chance."

prep schools, books about the upper class that included discussions of prep school life, articles appearing in magazines as diverse as *Readers Digest*, the *Atlantic Monthly*, the *Independent Schools Bulletin*, the *Journal of Negro Education*, *Ebony*, and *Mother Jones*, and letters received from teachers and students who had participated in the ABC program. Finally, we drew on an interview conducted with an ABC student at Stanford University in 1974 by one of the second author's research assistants.

We made use of all of our interviews in our attempt to understand the ABC program and the lives of the graduates we interviewed. However, we have drawn our quotations from those interviewees whose experience and comments most clearly exemplified the patterns we found.

Appendix B: Questions Asked in

Interviews with ABC Graduates

1. How did you come to be in the ABC program?
2. How did you hear about it?
3. Did your parents encourage you to participate? Did others encourage you?
4. What was your family background? What did your parents do, and how much education had they received?
5. Think back to your first summer. Where did you go? What year was it? What was it like being there? What do you remember about the summer program? Are you still in touch with people you met that summer?
6. Where did you go to prep school? How many blacks were there at that school when you were there? How many of them were ABC? Did ABC blacks and non-ABC blacks have difficulty getting along?
7. What was your impression of the white students? What were they like? Where they accepting? Did white students invite you to their homes? Did you experience racism while there?
8. With whom did you room? How did that work out? Did you change roommates while there? Why?
9. Did you date while you were in prep school? What was social life like for you?
10. Do you think that you changed while you were there. How? What about your speech? Your dress? Your values? Your goals?

11. Was it difficult to go back home after you had been at prep school for a while?
12. How many people from your prep school have you been in touch with in the past two years? Are those you are in touch with black or white?
13. How do you think the prep school experience affected you?
14. Where did you go to college? Why did you decide to go there? How did you pay for college? What did you major in?
15. Whom did you hang out with? Prep school graduates? Blacks? Whites? Whom did you room with?
16. What was your social life like while in college?
17. What did you do after college? Graduate school or professional school? Where? What was that like?
18. Then, when you went to work, how did you decide on the job you took? What has been your experience in your job (or jobs)? Do you feel accepted? Do you think you have an equal shot at promotion in your company?
19. Do you ever worry that you've been moved along only because you're black?
20. What is your relationship with your family?
21. How would you describe your current friends?
22. Are you married?
23. Where did you meet your wife (husband)? What is her (his) background? Is she (he) black or white? Did you date whites?
24. Where do you live? How would you describe your neighborhood? What is the racial makeup of your neighborhood?
25. How would you describe your politics? Whom did you vote for in the 1980 and 1984 presidential elections?
26. Do you know of ABC "casualties," people who were adversely affected by the experience? What were the particular problems they couldn't overcome?
27. With whom do you feel the most comfortable? Prep school friends? People from the old neighborhood?

Index